Ancient Rome

Ancient Rome
An Introductory History

Paul A. Zoch

UNIVERSITY OF OKLAHOMA PRESS

NORMAN

Published with the assistance of the National Endowment for the Humanities, a federal agency which supports the study of such fields as history, philosophy, literature, and language.

Library of Congress Cataloging-in-Publication Data

Zoch, Paul A. (Paul Allen), 1962–
   Ancient Rome : an introductory history / Paul A. Zoch
     p.   cm.
   Includes bibliographical references and index.
   ISBN 978-0-8061-3287-7
   1. Rome—History.   I. Title.
   DG210.Z63   1998
   937—dc21   98-12881
                                     CIP

The paper in this book meets the guidelines for permanance and durability of the Committee on Production Guidelines for Book Longevity of the Council on Library Resources, Inc. ∞

5   6   7   8   9   10

Contents

Illustrations

Maps

Preface

In my first year of teaching high-school Latin, I gave my second-year students a bonus question on a translation test: "For three points, identify when the Roman Empire was at its height." I decided to accept any answer from 100 B.C. to A.D. 200. The answers were distressing: one senior, a good but not great student, answered 3000 B.C. Only three students out of the class of twenty-two received the three points. The students giggled at their own ignorance of basic history. I realized that if even second-year Latin students do not know such basic information, few other high-school students do—and I must confess that when I was in high school, I was not much better off. Such was the genesis of this book.

Ancient Rome: An Introductory History cannot hope to compete in the quality and depth of its scholarship with the excellent histories written by world-renowned scholars such as Cary, Scullard, Mommsen, and Grant, by all those involved in the massive *Cambridge Ancient History*, and by others. However, by the inclusion of stories, legends, and myths from original sources, it does offer high-school students and general readers greater accessibility to the factual history of ancient Rome, for it seeks to entertain at the same time as to inform. This book presents a traditional, chronological history of ancient Rome, illustrating the major and minor themes, events, and personalities through generous selections of Latin literature and other original sources in English translation. Readers will learn about Roman history from Aeneas through Marcus Aurelius, meeting along the way such characters and personalities as Tarquinius Superbus, Lucretia,

Brutus, Cincinnatus, Q. Fabius Maximus, Hannibal, Pompey, Nero, and many others.

The frequent quotations from original sources serve another purpose. Roman culture and values are usually best revealed to the novice not through scholarly discussions, but through the Romans' own literature and descriptions. The reader is thus more likely to understand the Romans as people and how their values and beliefs drove their actions. It is also as people, with their own values and beliefs—some similar to ours, some different—that the Romans are most likely to interest students and general readers and make the study of Roman history relevant. Here is the considered judgment of Diane Ravitch, a leading scholar of history in U.S. education:

Children might enjoy the study of history if they began in the early grades to listen to and read lively historical literature, such as myths, legends, hero stories, and true stories about great men and women in their community, state, nation, and world. Not only in the early grades but throughout the kindergarten to twelfth grade sequence, students should read lively narrative accounts of extraordinary events and remark-able people. Present practice seems calculated to persuade young people that social studies is a train of self-evident, unrelated facts, told in a dry manner. (Diane Ravitch, "The Plight of History in American Schools," in *Historical Literacy*, ed. Paul Gagnon and the Bradley Commission on History in the Schools, 63.)

My history provides the "lively narrative accounts" that Ravitch and others recommend. Yet the trained historian might object to a few quotations that are not in strict accordance with the attempt to know history *wie es eigentlich gewesen*. Two examples are the speech of Coriolanus's mother and Marius's speech lambasting the nobles. A scholarly discussion of such speeches would not only disrupt the narrative but would distract the student, who cannot be assumed to have the scholarly background necessary for under-standing the discussion. This book provides readers with that important background through lively readings.

A note about the translations: All the translations of original sources in this book are my own.

Acknowledgments

As a teacher, I understand how great a role teachers play in students' development, and I would like to acknowledge here a few of my own teachers for their influence on me. I am very grateful to Alan Fear and Allen Boxman, and more recently, Professor Carl Rubino (formerly of the University of Texas at Austin) and Professor Ian Thomson of Indiana University, Bloomington.

I also thank my family for all that they have done for me, and especially my wife, Denise, for her support and patience.

I am grateful to Dr. Sidney Feit for reading an early version of this history and encouraging me to continue developing it; and especially to my colleague in Houston, Dr. Chester Natunewicz, who also read an early version and made invaluable suggestions for its improvement.

Ancient Rome

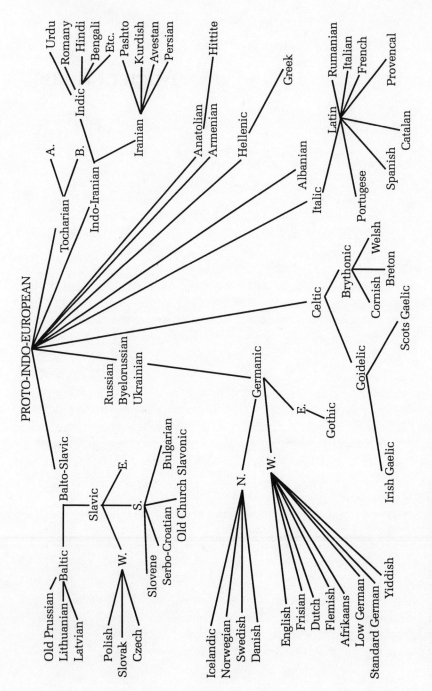

The family tree of Indo-European languages.

CHAPTER 1

A Linguistic Introduction

What do such languages as English, Latin, Greek (ancient and modern), German, Gaelic, Russian, Kurdish, Sanskrit, and Hindi have in common? Not much, it would seem. Yet, despite the thousands of miles and years separating them, those languages all have a common ancestry—that is, they are all descended from one prehistoric language and culture, which we call Indo-European.

The Indo-European people are believed to have lived around the Black and Caspian Seas. Around 3500–2500 B.C., they began migrating to parts of Europe and Asia, bringing with them their language and culture. All languages change as they are spoken, and as the speakers come into contact with speakers of other languages. Indo-European was no exception: It evolved, and from it arose the languages already mentioned, along with a host of others (see table). No written texts in Indo-European survive—not until 3000 B.C. did the Mesopotamians develop the world's first writing system. The earliest surviving written records of any Indo-European language are documents in Hittite that date back to 1300 B.C., and examples of Vedic Sanskrit, dating back to 1200 B.C. Parts of the work of the ancient Greek poet Homer might date back to 1000 B.C., and the oldest literary texts in Latin date back to approximately 250 B.C.. (See Arlotto, *Introduction to Historical Linguistics*, pp. 104–105.)

Despite the lack of texts in Indo-European, you can see the similarities among its different "descendant" languages by comparing their grammars and vocabularies. For example, the table shows some common words in several languages.

English	father	mother	brother	eat
Latin	pater	mater	frater	edo
Greek	pater	meter	phrater	edomai
Sanskrit	pitar	matar	bhratar	admi
German	Vater	Mutter	Bruder	essen
Indo-European	*pəter	*māter	bhrater	*ed

To take another example, the Indo-European root, *gno*, "to know," comes into English from Greek, Latin, and Anglo-Saxon (a Germanic language that became English). From Greek *gno* come words such as *agnostic* and *diagnosis*; from Latin *gnosco* come words such as *noble*, *ignorance*, *note*, *connotation*, and *denotation*; from the Anglo-Saxon *gno* we get the words *know* and *knowledge*.

Latin is the most important ancient representative of the Italic branch of the Indo-European family of languages. Like Indo-European, Latin also changed over time. When the Romans conquered western Europe and settled colonies of Italians and Romans in the conquered lands, the natives of those lands learned Latin from the settlers; over the centuries Latin fused with the native languages (in western Europe, various Celtic languages) to produce the Romance languages, which are the languages derived from Latin. They are Italian, French, Spanish, Portuguese, Romanian, Provençal, Rhaeto-Romance, and Catalan.

The similarities between Latin and the Romance languages are easy to see, and students of Latin will notice thousands more, if they learn a Romance language as well.

Latin	pater	homo	populus	filius
French	pere	homme	peuple	fils
Spanish	padre	hombre	pueblo	hijo
Italian	padre	uomo	popolo	figlio
Portuguese	pai	homem	povo	filho

English, a Germanic language, gained its largely Latinate vocabulary mostly in five major time periods.

1. Starting in 110 B.C., the Romans fought wars with the Germanic tribes and established colonies in Germany. They thus left a Latin influence on the Germanic languages. For example, the German word *Wein* comes from the Latin word *vinum*, "wine," and the city of Cologne owes its name to the Latin word *colonia*, "colony." Much later, in the fifth century A.D., some Germanic tribes, called Anglo-Saxons, invaded England and in so doing brought to the Celtic languages of England Latin words that they had learned from the Romans. The Latin words that were adopted at this time included *cheese*, from Latin *caseus* through German *Kaese*.

2. In 55 B.C. the Romans invaded England under the leadership of Julius Caesar; a century later, in A.D. 43, under Emperor Claudius, England became a Roman province. The language of the Roman government in England was, of course, Latin, and it influenced the Celtic languages spoken there. Among the Latin words that came in at this time was *castra*, "camp," which appears in English place-names as *caster* (Lancaster) or as *chester* (Rochester).

3. In A.D. 597 missionaries began traveling to England to convert the natives to Christianity. The language of the Catholic Church was Latin (the Bible was not translated into English until the late fourteenth century), and Latin words therefore became as much a part of people's lives as worship.

4. Under the leadership of William the Conqueror, the Normans, people of northern France (Normandy), won the Battle of Hastings in 1066 and subsequently occupied England during the eleventh, twelfth, and thirteenth centuries. The Norman dialect of French (a Romance language) was the language of the government during the occupation. This time period marked the greatest influx of Latinate words into English.

5. A further group of Latinate words came into English during the Renaissance. Scholars throughout Europe communicated in the one language, Latin, that was familiar to all educated people. They borrowed words from Latin to express ideas for which no word existed in their native languages. Thus, an ancient, "dead" language was used to describe new things, and more Latinate words enriched the English language and thought.

CHAPTER 2

Rome's Origins
according to the Ancients

The Romans did not know about the Indo-Europeans; what they believed to be their ancient history is more properly called mythology or legend. The history of Rome's first three centuries of existence is difficult to know for certain. The ancient historians who wrote about Rome's beginnings frequently themselves did not know what had happened, because the Romans did not start writing their history until centuries after Rome was founded. The historians also were not critical of their sources in the same way that historians today would be; frequently they were more concerned about the moral and patriotic value of history than about historical truth, and sometimes they cared more about writing well and praising their ancestors than about writing truthfully. Still another problem is the loss of much Latin literature: In the days before photocopiers and cheap paper, books had to be copied by hand (the English word *manuscript* means "handwritten" in Latin) onto expensive papyrus, which was made by pasting together reeds that grew in Egypt, or onto vellum (also known as parchment), which was made from the skin of cattle, sheep, and goats. Consequently few copies were made of most books. Many of these copies perished over the centuries, and in many cases no copies at all of a particular work survive. Such works are known today only by mentions or excerpts in other works. When our literary sources fail, we have recourse to other sources of information. From archaeology we learn much by studying the myriad objects that the ancients dropped, lost, abandoned, threw away, or forgot about; we can also study the monuments and buildings they erected in praise of the gods (or in praise of themselves) or in memory of key victories or important people. Despite these problems with sources, it is possible to piece together the early history of Rome in such a way as to show the development of Roman society and government and the beginnings of civilization in western Europe. We can also study the Romans as people: What values did they cherish? What did they want their past to be?

AENEAS

Ancient writers, both Greek and Roman, found a noble ancestry for the Latin people and for Rome's power in the figure of Aeneas, a Trojan prince. When Troy was sacked by the Greeks in 1200 B.C., Aeneas fled with his son Ascanius, his father Anchises, and friends to found a new Troy; Aeneas' wife Creusa did not live to accompany her husband on his journey.

Aeneas was not one of the outstanding heros in Homer's *Iliad*, which tells the tale of Troy; the few references to him, however, attest both to his *pietas* (a Latin word meaning "fulfillment of the obligations placed upon a person by family, community, and gods") and to his valor in war; he was respected equally with Hector, the great Trojan warrior whom only Achilles could conquer. The two ideas of *pietas* and valor in battle were very important to the Romans, and the poets writing about Rome's past found in Aeneas an ancestor who embodied these values: while fighting valiantly against Achilles, Aeneas is saved from certain death because he has worshipped the gods.

The Latin poet Vergil's epic poem *The Aeneid* (written from 26 to 19 B.C.) tells the story of Aeneas' wanderings. According to Vergil, Aeneas left Troy, knowing that it was his destiny to found a city from which a great empire would eventually arise. Because he did not know where to go to found his city, he traveled through the Mediterranean region in search of his destiny. During his travels he met Dido, queen of Carthage, a city in northern Africa.

Because the goddess Venus, Aeneas' mother, feared for her son's safety in Carthage, she caused Dido to fall passionately in love with him. Aeneas likewise fell in love with Dido and stayed in Carthage with her, until he was reminded by the god Mercury that his duty and destiny—to establish what would become the Roman empire—were more important than his love for Dido. Aeneas sadly left Africa, abandoning Dido and breaking her heart. Dido, who had thought that Aeneas was going to marry her, committed suicide as Aeneas and his allies sailed away, but first she cursed Aeneas and all his descendants, saying: "Carthaginians, hound his descendants and all his future race with your hatred! Give this gift to my ashes: no love, no treaties between our peoples. Arise, some avenger, from my bones to pursue the Trojan settlers with fire and the sword, now, later, whenever you have the power to do so. I beg our shores to be against theirs, our seas against theirs, swords against swords. Let our descendants and theirs fight it out!" (*Aeneid* IV.622–627).

In Vergil's poem, Dido's curse explains the savage wars, called the Punic Wars, that Rome and Carthage fought in the third and second centuries B.C.

Aeneas landed in Italy, where he visited the Underworld and heard his father (who died shortly after leaving Troy) prophesy of Rome's coming greatness: "My son, behold—with Mars' blessing—that renowned Rome will make an empire as great as the Earth, and a spirit that will rival Olympus, and will surround the seven hills within one wall: Rome, blessed with her generations of men" (*Aeneid* VI.781–784).

Later on during the visit, Anchises tells Aeneas of his and his descendants' mission: "Some people will be better at shaping bronze statues that seem to breathe; others will produce living faces from a marble block, while still others will deliver cleverer speeches or plot the movements of the heavens or explain the risings of the stars. You, Roman, remember to rule peoples with your power, for that is what you do best: accustom them to peace, spare the conquered, and war down the proud" (*Aeneid* VI.847–853).

Having now a clearer understanding of his purpose in life, and inspired by his father's words, Aeneas heroically fought wars with the hostile natives of Italy and founded the town Lavinium, naming it after his new, Italian wife, Lavinia. Aeneas' son Ascanius founded the town Alba Longa.

After his death Aeneas was deified and was later worshiped as Aeneas Indiges, "the native-born."

CHAPTER 3

Romulus and Remus
Found Rome

Long after Alba Longa was founded by the son of Aeneas, the king of the city, Numitor, was deposed by his brother Amulius and driven into exile. Fearing that the descendants of Numitor would rob him of the throne that he had just stolen, Amulius murdered Numitor's sons and made his only daughter, Rhea Silvia, a Vestal Virgin. For a Vestal Virgin to break her vows of chastity in service of the goddess Vesta (the goddess of the hearth) would earn her the punishment of being buried alive. In spite of her special status, Rhea Silvia became pregnant by the god Mars; she bore twin sons, Romulus and Remus.

Amulius learned of the twins' existence and ordered that they be put in a basket and thrown into the Tiber River, so they could not rob him of his throne. The Tiber happened to be unusually high, however, and the attendant was not able to put the basket into the river proper, as he could not reach it. Instead he left the basket floating in the shallow water near the shore. The water then magically receded and left the twins safe on land. A passing she-wolf heard the babies' cries and nursed them until Faustulus, the shepherd of the royal flock, found the boys under a fig tree (called *ficus Ruminalis*, "the fig tree of Rumina," a minor goddess, perhaps of nursing), and brought them home.

Romulus and Remus grew up and quickly distinguished themselves from other young men of their age with their bravery and daring. Other young men followed the two, and together they fearlessly hunted wild beasts and robbed robbers of their loot, distributing it among their fellow shepherds.

She-wolf from the Capitol, sixth–fifth century B.C. (Courtesy of the
Archer M. Huntington Art Gallery, University of Texas at Austin,
William J. Battle Collection of Plaster Casts)

The robbers, angry at losing their loot, ambushed the twins
during a festival; Romulus managed to escape, but Remus did not,
and the robbers took him to King Amulius, claiming that the
brothers had made raids on Numitor's lands. Numitor suspected
that the two were his grandsons, and was just about to acknowledge Remus as his grandchild (by this time Faustulus had already
told Romulus the truth about his origins). Before Amulius could
eliminate the brothers, Romulus and his fellow shepherds attacked
and killed him, rescued Remus, and restored Numitor to his rightful throne.

Romulus and Remus then decided to found a city on the banks
of the Tiber, where they had been abandoned, rescued, and raised.
Since they were the same age, it was not possible to tell who was
older, and thus who would rule the new city. They agreed to use
augury, the practice of looking for signs of approval or disapproval
from the gods, usually by birds, to decide who should rule. Remus

stood on the Aventine Hill, and Romulus on the Palatine, each watching for signs from the gods; Remus had no sooner seen six vultures than Romulus saw twelve, and the followers of each saluted their leader as king. During the argument that followed, Romulus killed Remus. Another version of the story has Remus mockingly jump over Romulus' half-built walls, to demonstrate that the walls were too low; Romulus then kills him, saying, "And the same goes for any other person who jumps over my walls!" Romulus became king and named the city after himself. The traditional date for the founding of Rome is April 21, 753 B.C.

The city on the Palatine Hill grew, and King Romulus established customs and laws that would unify the new citizens into a harmonious political body and imbue them with respect for the king's power. One custom was for the king to be accompanied by twelve *lictors* (attendants, more or less, who announced his coming and cleared all citizens but Vestal Virgins and matrons from his path) so the people would respect his power and authority; each lictor carried a *fascis* (a bundle of sticks wrapped around an axe, which symbolized the king's ability to punish citizens, either with a beating using the sticks or with decapitation using the axe). Romulus wore a toga with a purple border, purple being the color of royalty. He also created the Senate, a council of elders; the word *senatus* is derived from *senex*, which means "old." The one hundred members of the Senate were called *patres*, "fathers," since they were the fathers of the different clans, and their descendants were called *patricians*. The patricians were the leading citizens of Rome and constituted the nobility. The common people were the *plebs* (from which comes the English word *plebeian*, "common, vulgar").

To attract more people to the new city, Romulus established a sanctuary (*asylum*, "place where one cannot be seized") to which men fled from their troubles in their native cities. The city, however, lacked one essential element for population growth: women. Romulus sent envoys to the neighboring cities to solicit an alliance, with the privilege of intermarriage between the citizens of the two communities. The other cities wanted to curb the growth of the new rival, and accordingly rejected Romulus' offers, even telling the Romans that the only way they would be able to get

women was to have a sanctuary for women, too. The young
Romans were very bitter at that insult.

THE RAPE OF THE SABINE WOMEN

Romulus then invented another plan for bringing women into
the city. He prepared his city for games in honor of the god
Neptune and invited the inhabitants of the neighboring towns to
join the celebration. Many of them came to the games, bringing
their wives and children, and they admired the new city. Once the
time for the show had come, and when everybody was eagerly
anticipating the start, the signal was given: The young Romans
swarmed upon the crowd and carried off the single women.

The outraged parents called upon the gods to avenge the crime
they had suffered at the hands of the Romans. They charged the
Romans with breaking the laws of hospitality: They had left the
safety of their own homes and towns to honor Neptune in Rome,
but instead had become the victims of that most unholy deed. The
different towns prepared for war; the Romans quickly defeated the
smaller and less prepared towns, with Romulus earning great
honor. In one of those battles he killed the enemy commander in
single combat; to show his gratitude he built a temple for Jupiter
Feretrius and offered *spolia opima*, the spoils of an enemy commander killed by a Roman commander in single combat. The word
feretrius might be derived from the verb *ferio*, "to strike."

The tribes of the Sabines, however, led by their king, Titus
Tatius, gave stiffer opposition. The Sabines were a tough, hardy
people in the hills northeast of Rome, whom the Romans would
later compare to the Spartans for their bravery and simple morality. In making war upon them the Romans faced not only strong
opposition, but even a traitor within their own city. A Roman girl,
Tarpeia, the daughter of Spurius Tarpeius, the commander of the
citadel on the Capitol, one of the hills of Rome, was bribed by
offers of gold, and admitted armed Sabines into the citadel; the
Sabines, however, killed her instead of giving the promised gold.
The price she had demanded for admitting them into the citadel
was what they wore on their arms. She meant their gold bracelets;

they, however, hurled on her something else they wore on their arms—their shields—and crushed her to death, to show that agreements with traitors would not be kept. The Tarpeian Rock, which is a cliff on the southwest corner of the Capitol, was named after her; from the Tarpeian Rock murderers and traitors were hurled to their deaths.

The Sabines thus were able to occupy the citadel of Rome. During one of the battles the Romans fought to recapture the citadel, the Roman army started losing and began to flee. To stop their flight, Romulus prayed to the father of the gods, Jupiter, and promised to build him a temple if the Roman army were inspired to stay its ground and fight. After hearing that Jupiter Optimus Maximus (Jupiter the Best and Greatest) ordered them to stop and fight, the Romans stopped running and renewed their attack. To show his gratitude and fulfill his part of the bargain, Romulus later dedicated the temple to Jupiter Stator, "Jupiter the Stayer."

The Sabines and Romans were continuing the fierce battle when some of the Sabine women, including one named Hersilia, ran into the midst of the battle, through the flying missiles and arrows, beseeching the Romans not to kill their fathers and begging the Sabines not to kill their husbands—otherwise they would be left widows and orphans.

The soldiers, touched by the pitiful sight of the women and their babies, stopped fighting. The leaders agreed not only to a truce, but also to the union of two communities. The power would be based in Rome, and the Sabines would become Roman citizens. Roman citizens were henceforth called Quirites, supposedly after the Sabine town Cures. (Modern classicists reject that etymology, but the Romans believed it.) Romulus also divided all the citizens into thirty *curiae*, which he named after the Sabine women. Those *curiae* formed assemblies (*comitia curiata*) in which citizens would vote. To further honor the Sabine women, it was agreed that they were to be free from all common labor in the house except for spinning wool, and two holidays were celebrated in their honor, the Matronalia and the Carmentalia. Tradition says that the Sabine king, Titus Tatius, became joint king with Romulus but was later murdered in Lavinium by the relative of a man whom his relatives had murdered.

One day in 716 B.C. Romulus was reviewing his troops when suddenly a storm arose; thick clouds hid Romulus from the soldiers' view, and when the clouds dissipated, the soldiers saw that Romulus was no longer there. After recovering from their shock and sadness—they felt orphaned by his loss—they proclaimed that he had become a god. Not much later, one man named Proculus Julius claimed that Romulus had come down to him from the sky and had said, "Go now, and tell the Romans that the gods want my Rome to be the ruler of the world. Therefore, let them practice the art of war and make it a custom with their descendants that human powers cannot withstand Roman weapons!" (Livy I.16.7). Romulus then returned to heaven. A less flattering version of the story has the senators tearing Romulus to pieces for becoming a tyrant. Whatever Romulus' manner of death, later Romans worshiped him for establishing a new nation and leaving it strong and secure: "Do you see," wrote Cicero almost seven hundred years later, "that with his sagacity this one man did not just create a new nation, but even left it already full-grown and almost mature?" (*De republica* II.11.1).

CHAPTER 4

Kings after Romulus

After the death of Romulus, there was an *interregnum* (a period of time in which a senator would exercise royal power for five days, and then pass it to another). Then, in 715 B.C., Numa Pompilius, a Sabine with a great reputation for justice and piety, became the next king of Rome. Our major source of the time says that the common people chose him as Romulus' successor, the senators approved of the choice, and Jupiter sent a favorable sign during the inauguration. Romulus had been a warrior, waging war not only on the towns whose daughters the young Romans had seized, but also on the Etruscan cities Veii and Fidenae. Numa, in contrast, was peace-loving, and he tried to temper the Romans' desire for war.

To prevent the Romans from degenerating into idleness and dissipation, once they were freed from the demands and discipline of war, King Numa imbued them with a religious fervor. To accomplish this, he spread the rumor that he had secret meetings with the goddess Egeria, who gave him information on how to maintain the goodwill of the gods, which the Romans called *pax deorum* (peace of the gods). He built the Temple of Janus, whose gates, when open, indicated that Rome was at war and, when closed, showed that the city was at peace. He appointed priests (*flamines*), one for Jupiter alone (*flamen Dialis*), and others for Mars and Quirinus, both gods of war; Quirinus was of Sabine origin, and associated with the Quirinal Hill. He is credited with building the Regia, the seat of authority of the *pontifex maximus*, or high priest. He created the *salii*, minor priests in service of Mars. At the beginning and end of the season for war, they would dance (*salire*) through the city, beating their shields; they also protected a shield that was believed to have fallen from heaven.

King Numa created Rome's cult of the Vestal Virgins, who were greatly honored by the Romans for giving up the goals of marriage and a family to tend the eternal fire of Vesta. He is credited with dividing the Roman year into twelve lunar months and with appointing days when business could and could not be conducted: Days when business could be conducted were *fas* (literally, "speakable") and those when business could not be conducted were *nefas* ("not speakable," and thus unholy, which gave rise to the English word *nefarious*). He wrote complete directions for performing the rites of worship of all the gods: which animals were to be sacrificed, how much money was to be spent on the rites, which were the days of worship, and in which temple the rites were to be held. Some later Romans believed that Numa had acquired his learning from Pythagoras, who lived in southern Italy. Pythagoras, however, lived more than one hundred fifty years after Numa became king. Numa died after ruling for forty-three years.

TULLUS HOSTILIUS BECOMES KING

After another interregnum, Tullus Hostilius (673–642 B.C.) became king. He was even more warlike than Romulus had been. The citizens of Rome and Alba Longa, who had been making border raids on each other, now prepared for war—actually a civil war, since the two cities had a common origin. Alba Longa at that time may have been the head of the Latin League, a confederacy of cities and towns in Latium, an area south of Rome; one of the issues in this conflict was primacy in the Latin League. Before the final battle, Mettius Fufetius, the dictator of Alba Longa, called Hostilius to a conference and suggested that the two cities not fight the battle. He argued that the Etruscans, people who had a powerful confederacy of cities in northern and central Italy, would soon swoop down upon the tired and wounded victors, whether those of Rome or of Alba Longa, and thus take both cities. Still, they needed to decide who would be dominant, Rome or Alba Longa.

The Horatii

It happened that in each army were triplet brothers. Mettius and Tullus agreed that each city would be represented in battle by its triplets, and that the city whose triplets won would rule the losers' city. The Romans' triplets were the Horatii, and those of Alba Longa were the Curiatii. The fight began, with both armies watching and cheering their boys on.

The signal was given. Like an army, with their deadly weapons ready for battle, the triplets dashed forward against their enemy, bringing into battle all the courage of their great armies. Neither the Horatii nor the Curiatii thought about the danger; their only concern was whether the city would rule or be ruled, and what future they would create for their city.

Immediately upon the men's first clashing together, their weapons rang out, and their glittering swords flashed in the light. The spectators were seized by great dread, their voices and breaths halting in unfailing hopes of victory; as they watched the men dodging and thrusting with their weapons, and receiving wounds and bleeding, two Horatii fell dead, one on top of the other, and the Curiatii were wounded. As the two Romans fell, the Alban army cried out with joy; immediately the Roman army lost all hope, but now worried about the one surviving Roman, who was surrounded by the three Curiatii. It happened that he had not been wounded; alone, he was certainly no match against the three together, but against them one at a time, he was a dangerous foe.

Therefore, to take them on one at a time, he immediately dashed away, seeing that each of his enemies would follow as his wounded body allowed. Once he had fled some distance from where the battle had been fought, he looked back and saw them following with great distances between them; one was not far away at all. He turned back on him in a fierce attack; by the time the Alban army shouted to the other two Curiatii to help their brother, Horatius had already cut down his opponent and, victorious, was seeking the next fight. Then, with the kind of roar that usually arises after the unexpected happens, the Romans encourage their soldier; he hurries to finish off the battle. Before the one Curiatius, who was not far away, could reach his brother, Horatius had already dispatched him: now the two remained—one Horatius and one

Curiatius—and the battle was on equal terms, but the men were not equal in hope or strength. The one had not received any wounds and was charged up with his double victory; that made him a fierce opponent for the third duel. The other, however, was exhausted from his wounds and the chase, and was demoralized by the slaughter of his brothers before his very eyes; he dragged his weary body to meet his conquerer.

Theirs was not much of a battle. Proud and confident, Horatius cried, "I have given two men to the ghosts of my brothers; I will give the third to the reason for this war, so that Rome may rule Alba Longa!"

Horatius thrust his sword down into the neck of his opponent, who could barely hold up his weapons, and then took his weapons as spoils. Shouting triumphantly, the Romans received Horatius with congratulations, their joy as great as their fear had been. (Livy I.XXV.3)

Horatius, although a hero, soon found himself in trouble. As he was returning from the battle, bearing the spoils of those whom he had killed, he was met at the Capena Gate by his sister, who had been engaged to one of the Curiatii. She saw among the spoils a cloak that she had woven with her own hands, as a gift for her fiancé. She began mourning for her dead boyfriend and tearfully called his name. Enraged, her brother shouted, "Since you have forgotten your country and your brothers, both dead and alive, take your misplaced love and go to your fiancé. May all who mourn the foe do the same!" and stabbed her.

Horatius was seized and put on trial, and convicted of *perduellio* (a type of treason). King Tullus did not want the hero to receive the death sentence, however, and urged him to appeal his sentence to the people. Only his recent heroism and a tearful speech by his father—who by this time had lost two sons and a daughter—saved him from the punishment of death.

The Treachery of Mettius Fufetius

Mettius was now unpopular in Alba Longa because the city had lost its sovereignty. He sought to regain the city's independence through treachery. He secretly induced the Latin colony Fidenae to revolt against Rome and convinced the Etruscan city Veii to join him in a war against Rome.

Tullus summoned Mettius and his army so they could put down the revolt at Fidenae, and he placed Mettius and his troops across from the soldiers of Fidenae, near the mountains. Slowly and imperceptibly, Mettius and his troops drifted to the mountains, hoping to help whichever side was winning.

A messenger soon told Tullus that the Albans had deserted, but Tullus replied, in a very loud voice, that the Albans had gone to attack the unprotected rear of the Fidenates (the army of Fidenae). The Fidenates, who spoke Latin, heard and understood the message. They became alarmed and retreated; Tullus then routed the enemy.

Mettius soon came to congratulate Tullus for the victory. Tullus thanked him, and asked him and his soldiers to join him at dawn for a purification ceremony. At dawn the Albans came and were seated closest to Tullus. The Romans, armed, then came into the meeting-place and surrounded the Albans. Tullus addressed the Romans, saying that he had not ordered the Albans to depart; he had lied about their departure so that the Romans would not lose hope and thus lose the battle. He did not blame the Alban soldiers, who were only following the orders of their commander, but he did blame Mettius, who had given the orders. The Romans then surrounded Mettius, and Tullus addressed him:

"Mettius Fufetius, if you could learn trustworthiness and how to live up to your treaties, I would let you live to learn the lessons from me. Since your way of thinking is incurable, you must now with your punishment teach the human race to consider sacred the things that you have violated. Since a short time ago you had a mind torn in its loyalty to Fidenae or Rome, you will now offer your body to be torn in two."

After having two four-wheeled chariots brought forward, Tullus had Mettius stretched out and bound to the chariots. Then the horses, facing opposite directions, were lashed, carrying the mutilated corpse on each chariot, where his body parts were still attached to the chains. All turned their eyes from the hideous sight. That was the first and last time a punishment of a type so heedless of human laws occurred among us Romans; otherwise, we can say with pride that no other nation has been more content with gentle punishments. (Livy I.28)

The citizens of Alba Longa were brought to Rome, and Roman legions were sent to Alba Longa to destroy it. (A *legion* was a unit of the Roman army containing, at full strength, six thousand soldiers, but usually only three to four thousand.) Rome took over the leadership of the Latin League. The number of Roman citizens was doubled, and the Caelian Hill was added to the city.

Tullus, having become sick with a plague that was then afflicting Rome, undertook unfamiliar sacrifices and rites to Jupiter. Apparently he did not perform them correctly, for his palace was struck by lightning in 642 B.C., and he died in the fire.

ANCUS MARCIUS BECOMES KING

After an interregnum, the Romans then elected Ancus Marcius king. The Latins, thinking him a weak king, made raids on Roman territory and responded arrogantly to Ancus' demands for redress. Before declaring war on the Latins, Ancus decided to establish rites by which Rome could justly declare war, so it would not offend the gods.

In the ceremony for declaring war, the Roman envoy stood at the border of the hostile country and called upon the gods to witness that his demands were just; if his demands were unjust, he said, let him never be a citizen of his country. The envoy then crossed the border and repeated the speech to the first citizen he met, and then again in the marketplace. If the Romans voted for war, the *fetials* (priests whose duty was declaring and deciding upon the justice of a war) then went to the border and gave a formal speech detailing the wrongs of the enemy. They would then throw a bloody spear into the enemy's territory, as the formal declaration of war.

Ancus Marcius is given the credit for establishing the first Roman colony, where the Tiber meets the Tyrrhenian Sea. The settlement received the name Ostia (from *os*, "mouth, opening") and became the port of Rome as well as the source of salt, a valuable and essential commodity. He also built Rome's prison, the *carcer* (seen in the English word *incarceration*), on the Capitoline Hill; the steps leading to the *carcer* were called the Scalae Gemoniae, or Mourning Steps, because the bodies of executed criminals were thrown out on them. He seized and fortified the Janiculum, a ridge on the west bank of the Tiber, because of its great strategic importance in the defense of the city; to ease communication with the troops on the Janiculum, he built the Pons Sublicius, a wooden bridge across the Tiber.

During Ancus Marcius' reign an Etruscan man named Lucumo left Tarquinii, the city of his birth, and came to Rome. As he and his wife, Tanaquil, reached the gates of Rome, an eagle landed on Lucumo's head and then flew away with his hat. The eagle returned a minute later, and placed the hat back on Lucumo's head. Tanaquil, who was skilled in interpreting such signs, said it foretold her husband's future greatness.

Ambitious and wealthy, Lucumo soon became a friend to all. He was now known by the nickname Tarquinius, after his native city. He even became an adviser to King Ancus and a guardian of the king's children. When Ancus died in 617, Tarquinius sent the king's sons on a hunting expedition. During their absence, he solicited votes for his own campaign to become king. His popularity, his knowledge of the city and its customs, and his familiarity with Ancus won him the necessary votes, and he became king. To further protect his power, he packed the Senate with loyal followers.

KING TARQUIN

King Tarquin (616–579 B.C.; later called Tarquinius Priscus, or Tarquin the Elder, to distinguish him from another Tarquin) then captured the Latin town Apiolae and returned to Rome with a great amount of loot. He celebrated public games on a lavish scale never before seen in Rome. The games became a custom, called the Roman Games. In early Rome horse races and boxing matches supplied the entertainment in the *ludi* (games), while in later Rome wild beast hunts and gladiator combats were featured. Tarquin built the Circus Maximus, where chariot races were held. He also drained the low-lying areas between the hills, where rainwater collected; eventually the Forum (the public square of Rome) was built where once there had been a swamp. He may have started construction of the Temple of Jupiter on the Capitol.

The Sabines soon attacked Rome, disrupting Tarquin's plan to encircle the whole city with a stone wall. During the battles with the Sabines, Tarquin saw a weakness in the formation of the Roman cavalry and went about solving the problem. The augurs, however, had not given him their approval for reforming the cavalry, and an augur came to the king and told him that he needed to get the sanction of the augurs before proceeding with his plans.

Tarquin, in a contemptuous voice, said, "Come now, my devout fellow, take the auspices, and tell whether or not what I am thinking can be done."

The augur was not daunted by Tarquin's dare. He took the auspices and said that what the king had been thinking could indeed be done.

"But," said Tarquin, "I was thinking that you could split a sharpening-stone with a razor blade. Take these things," he said, handing him a razor and sharpening-stone, "and do what those birds of yours predicted could happen."

The augur did not hesitate. He took the razor and cut the sharpening-stone in half. Tarquin never again doubted the validity of the augurs; instead of reforming the cavalry as he had originally planned, he simply doubled the number of knights (Livy I.36.4).

One day a woman came to Tarquin and offered to sell him nine books filled with oracles from the Sibyl, a woman who had prophetic powers. Tarquin, however, did not understand how valuable the knowledge of the future was, and thought the price too high; the woman left and burned three of the books. Later she returned and offered to sell him the six remaining books at the same price she had asked for all nine. Tarquin, thinking that the price now was even worse, still refused to buy them. So the woman left and burned three more of the books. Later, she came back to Tarquin and offered to sell him the last three at the same price she had once asked for all nine. In amazement Tarquin summoned the augurs and asked them what to do. Recognizing that the books contained prophecies, they advised him to buy the books at the price she was asking. He did so, and appointed men to guard the Sibylline books. During times of crisis, when the Senate was perplexed, it would order that the Sibylline books be consulted to find divine advice on how to solve or address the problem; the priests then searched through the Sibyl's mystical, enigmatic sayings to find advice that fit the particular problem they were facing. When the original books were destroyed in 83 B.C., a new collection was made.

During Tarquin's reign there occurred a very odd thing. A boy named Servius Tullius, the son of a female slave in the king's household, was sleeping when his head burst into flames. The noise caused by the excitement of those nearby brought Tarquin and Tanaquil to the child's bed. Just as a servant was about to throw water onto the child's head, the queen stopped him, saying that the child had to sleep until he awoke on his own. A few minutes later the child woke up, and the fire on his head died out, leaving him unharmed.

Tanaquil said to the king, "Do you see this child here, whom we are bringing up in such lowly conditions? You can be sure that someday he'll be a light of safety upon our troubled affairs and a guardian of our palace in its distress. From now on, let's nurture him with all our love and care, since he will later be the source of great honor in public and private." From then on the child Servius received the education and upbringing of a king's son. He became a man impressive in all ways, and Tarquin even gave him his daughter in marriage. Soon Servius became one of the most distinguished men in the state (Livy I.39).

The Assassination of Tarquin

In the thirty-eighth year of Tarquin's reign, the sons of Ancus Marcius, his predecessor, began to cause trouble. They began to badmouth Tarquin for being a foreigner and for adopting the son of a slave as his heir. They hired two men to murder the king.

The two assassins presented themselves at the palace and started fighting with each other. When the king's attendants appeared, the two kept shouting at each other and demanded to see the king, so he could arbitrate their dispute. They were taken to the king, and as one began to explain his case, the other killed Tarquin.

Tanaquil kept a clear head. She ordered the palace to be closed and made preparations for nursing the king as if there was hope of his recovery. Then she summoned Servius and said, "Servius, if you're a man, the kingdom belongs to you, not those whose hired men committed that horrible crime. Stand tall and follow the gods as your leaders, for they showed long ago with that divine fire on your head that your life would be brilliant. Now let that heaven-sent fire inspire you, now get going!" (Livy I.41.3).

She then told the people that the king had been merely stunned by a blow, and that they should give their obedience to Servius until Tarquin had fully recovered. Servius made appearances on behalf of Tarquin and acted as king, all the time strengthening his position; soon he was acknowledged as king. Since Servius' position was so strong, Ancus' sons went into voluntary exile. To prevent Tarquin's sons, Lucius and Arruns, from being bitter about their loss of the throne as the sons of Ancus Marcius had been, Servius gave them his daughters (both named Tullia) in marriage. Nothing, however, could assuage their bitterness and jealousy.

SERVIUS, KING OF ROME

Servius' main accomplishment was the division of the Roman *plebs* (common people) into classes and his institution of the census. There were several classes, with the knights (*equites*), who formed the cavalry, at the head of them all. During the republic and empire the knights, or equestrians, were conspicuous because of the gold ring that they were allowed to wear.

First Class   Men who had capital valued at 100,000 *asses* (the *as* was the basic unit of Roman currency) or more. They were required to equip themselves with helmet, round shield, greaves, breastplate, sword, and spear. Two centuries of engineers also belonged to this class.

Second Class   Men whose property was valued between 100,000 and 75,000 *asses*. They had to equip themselves with the same equipment as the men of the first class, except for the breastplate, and they were allowed a long shield instead of a round one.

Third Class   Men whose property was valued at 50,000 *asses*. They had to supply the same equipment as those in the second class, except for the greaves.

Fourth Class   Men whose property was valued at 25,000 *asses*. They had to supply only the spear and javelin.

Fifth Class   Men whose property was valued at 11,000 *asses*. They supplied slings and stones. Buglers and trumpeters also belonged to this class.

Proletarii   Those whose property was valued below 11,000 *asses*. They were formed into a single century and were exempt from military service. They were called proletarii because the only thing they could contribute to Rome was their children (proles).

Each class was further divided into groups of one hundred (*centum*), forming a *centuria*, which was the smallest unit of the Roman army. Those *centuriae*—eighteen of cavalry and one hundred seventy of foot soldiers—also were the basis of an assembly (the Comitia Centuriata, or Meetings by Hundreds) at which the soldiers voted. Whenever a vote was needed on, say, whether or not to go to war, the soldiers voted in order of class; thus, while the rich were expected to do more for the state, they also received political prerogatives for their added burdens. The richer always voted before the poorer, and rarely did a vote go even to the Second Class, for the classes above the Second Class had already decided the matter.

Servius also divided the city into four tribes, where citizens would register for the census. The census was the basis by which people were grouped into classes. He enacted a law that punished with death all who failed to register with the census. At the first census, eighty thousand men capable of bearing arms registered. After conducting the census, Servius also performed a *lustrum* (purification ceremony), whose purpose was to ward off evil; since the census and *lustrum* occurred every five years, *lustrum* came also to mean a period of five years.

Since the population of Rome was growing quickly and needed more space, Servius added the Quirinal, Viminal, and Esquiline Hills to the city. Rome now had its seven hills, the other four being the Palatine, Capitoline, Caelian, and the Aventine. Some Romans believed that Servius also built a wall around the city; parts of the "Wall of Servius" remain today, although modern scholars believe that the wall in question was actually built later, in 378 B.C. It was

4.5 meters thick and 8.5 meters high. On either side of the wall was a strip of land called the *pomerium*, originally a line made by a plow drawn by a bull and a cow to demarcate the religious boundaries of the city. An army could not cross the *pomerium* into the city except in triumph; consequently Roman soldiers mustered outside the city, on the Campus Martius, or Field of Mars.

CHAPTER 5

Tarquin's Coup d'État
and the End of the Monarchy

Lucius Tarquin, son of the first Tarquin, Tarquinius Priscus, wanted to be king himself, and not just King Servius' son-in-law. He began spreading malicious rumors about Servius, no doubt concerning Servius' lowly birth. Tullia, the king's daughter who had married Tarquin's brother Arruns, was as ambitious as her brother-in-law Tarquin; she thought her own husband, Arruns, was a wimp. To facilitate their evil plans, Tarquin killed his wife (Tullia's sister), and Tullia killed her husband Arruns. Tarquin and Tullia then got married and were able to plot against the king in secrecy.

After securing the support of the leading families by offering bribes, Tarquin made his move. He sat down in the king's chair in the Senate House and ordered the senators to come to King Tarquin. They dared not stay away, fearing reprisals. Upon their arrival, Tarquin vilified the king and his rise to the throne. When Servius heard what was happening, he hurried to the Senate House.

"Tarquin," he cried, "what is this? What recklessness has caused you to dare to summon the senators and sit in my chair while I, the king, am still alive?" (Livy I.47).

Tarquin then defiantly responded that he was simply keeping his father's chair, and that it was much better for a king's son, rather than a slave, to inherit the kingdom; the time had come for an end to Servius' boundless mockery and insults to his masters.

With some people in the crowd shouting support for Tarquin, others for Servius, Tarquin seized the aged Servius and threw him down the steps into the street. Tarquin's assassins then killed the king. Tullia, Tarquin's wife and Servius' daughter, later drove up in a carriage and was the first to salute her husband as king; while driving away, she ran over her father's bloody, mutilated body, which was lying in the street. Servius Tullius had been king for forty-four years.

TARQUIN THE PROUD

In this way Tarquinius Superbus (as he soon came to be called, for *superbus* means "proud, arrogant") began his rule, which left the Romans with a bitter hatred for monarchy. Breaking with tradition, he sought neither election to the throne by the people nor the Senate's approval of his power. He refused a burial for his father-in-law, and even made a joke of it, saying that Romulus had not been buried either. He executed the senators who had supported Servius and did not fill the vacant seats, thinking that the senators would be intimidated by their dwindling numbers. He did not consult the Senate, as previous kings had done, but ruled instead by his own power and authority, making whatever decisions he thought best. He employed a bodyguard, fearing that someone else might follow the precedent that he himself had set. He even seized the property of wealthy citizens.

Tarquin made great efforts to win the support of the Latins, Rome's neighbors to the south and southwest, in the event he should ever need outside help against his Roman subjects. Yet he treated some Latins as arrogantly as he treated the Romans. For example, Turnus, a Latin noble, recognized that Tarquin was aiming to take over Latium and told his Latin friends of Tarquin's plans. When Tarquin learned that Turnus was not well disposed toward him, he bribed Turnus' slaves to hide a large supply of weapons in Turnus' house; summoning the Latin nobles, Tarquin told them of Turnus' plot to assassinate him and to make himself king over them all. The king and the nobles entered Turnus' house and, of course, found there a large supply of weapons, which was "proof" of Turnus' plot. Turnus was then executed.

Tarquin did do a few good things for Rome. He may have built the Temple of Jupiter on the Capitol, although the credit may be due his father. He also built Rome's main sewer, the *cloaca maxima*.

One day a snake was seen slithering down a wooden pillar in the palace. Tarquin was so alarmed about this that he sent his sons to Delphi, to consult the oracle of Apollo (usually the Romans sought oracles from the Etruscans). Accompanying Tarquin's sons to Delphi was Brutus, the son of the king's sister.

Brutus had seen the king's ruthlessness, and he understood the danger of his own situation. He had concluded that he could survive only by appearing to pose no threat to the king; he therefore pretended to be stupid (his name means "dull") and made no protest when Tarquin seized his property or executed leading citizens. He was sent to Delphi with the king's sons to serve as the butt of their jokes. Brutus brought his own offering to Apollo, a gift resembling the giver: a rod of gold hidden inside a tube of wood.

At Delphi, the oracle of Apollo answered the questions asked by Tarquin's sons, as well as one they asked on their own behalf: who would be the next king of Rome? The oracle responded that the first among them to kiss his mother would have supreme authority in Rome. Tarquin's sons therefore drew lots to decide who would first kiss their mother when they arrived at Rome. As they were leaving the temple, however, Brutus pretended to trip and, while lying on the ground, kissed the Earth, the mother of all living things.

THE RAPE OF LUCRETIA

Immediately upon returning to Rome, the three young men had to hurry to Ardea, a town to which the Romans had laid siege. Soon the action in the war slowed down, and many officers were allowed to spend their time in leisure.

One night a party was held, and among those attending were Sextus Tarquinius (one of the king's sons) and a man named Collatinus. The topic of the conversation turned to their wives; each man praised his own, and they began to argue over whose wife was the most faithful. Finally, Collatinus proposed that they all return to Rome to see just what their wives were doing—that way they could decide whose wife was the most faithful. All agreed.

To one house after another they went, seeing their wives throwing parties with many guests and sumptuous food. The last wife they visited was Lucretia, the wife of Collatinus. When they came to Collatinus' house, they found Lucretia spinning wool, by lamplight, with her maidservants at her side. Without a doubt, Lucretia had won the "most faithful wife" contest. She invited the men inside for supper, and in the course of the evening Sextus Tarquinius fell madly in love with her. The men then returned to the war in Ardea.

A few days later, Sextus Tarquinius rode back to Rome (without Collatinus' knowledge) and appeared before Lucretia. She treated him as the honored guest that he was, and gave him the guest chamber to sleep in. During the night, when all was quiet, he stole into Lucretia's room.

"Lucretia," he said, "be quiet! I am Sextus Tarquinius. There is a sword in my hand. If you say anything at all, you will die." He then told her of his love, begging, pleading, and even threatening her, so she would submit to his desire. She refused. Seeing that she would not relent and that her fidelity was greater even than her fear of death, he threatened to kill her and then to cut the throat of a slave and lay his naked body next to hers, so that people would say that Lucretia had been justly killed after being caught in the most disgraceful adultery. Fearing for her good reputation, she submitted to his desires. After using her, he rode away.

Lucretia then wrote to her father and to her husband, urging them to return to Rome immediately, each with a trustworthy friend, for a terrible thing had happened. They came, bringing Publius Valerius and Brutus.

They found Lucretia sitting in her room, very sad. When they entered, she began to cry. Her husband asked, "Is everything all right?" She answered, "No. How can anything be all right for a woman who has lost her honor? Collatinus, another man has been in your bed; otherwise only my body has been violated, for my mind is innocent. My death will be my proof. But give your right hands in an oath that the adulterer will be avenged. Sextus Tarquinius is the one who last night, as an enemy armed for violence, but disguised as a guest, got his pleasure from me, but if you are real men, you will make him pay for that pleasure. You will see to it that he receives what he deserves. I recognize that although I am not guilty of wrongdoing, I am not free from punishment; no woman will ever live unchastely with Lucretia as her guide."

With a knife, which she had hidden under her dress, Lucretia then stabbed herself in the chest, and fell forward, dead. (Livy I.58.7–12)

Lucretia's father and husband were overwhelmed with grief. While they stood weeping helplessly, Brutus drew the bloody knife from Lucretia's body and holding it before him cried: "I swear by this blood—most chaste until the prince's crime—and gods, I call upon you as witness that I, with as much force as I can muster, will drive Lucius Tarquinius the Proud, with his wicked wife and the whole stock of his children, out of Rome, and I will not allow them or any other man to be king in Rome!" (Livy I.59.1–2).

Lucretia's father and husband, shocked by Brutus' sudden transformation into a man of action, swore the same oath and carried Lucretia's body into the Forum. The public's anger, stirred by the grief of the father and husband weeping before their eyes, the sight of the bloody and dead Lucretia, and Brutus' words reminding them of Tarquin's usurpation of power and tyrannical rule, inspired them to take up arms against the king and to drive monarchy from Rome. Tarquin, who was still besieging Ardea, found Rome's gates closed to him when he returned to the city. Tarquin had ruled for twenty-five years. Monarchy in Rome ended in 509 B.C., and the *res publica*, the Roman republic, was born.

CHAPTER 6

The *Res Publica*
"Senatus Populusque Romanus"

To understand the history of republican, and then imperial, Rome, you must first understand the structure of the government: the parts of government, their powers, and their relations to each other. The description given here covers government offices that developed gradually over centuries, and did not exist in this form as early as the sixth century B.C. What is described here is the government of the Roman republic in its fully developed form, in the first and second centuries B.C.

The Romans called their city a *res publica*, "property of the people" (Cicero, *De republica* I.25). Despite the term *res publica* (which gives us the English word *republic*), Rome was not a democracy. The government had three parts: the magistrates (government officials), the Senate, and the people (hence the phrase "senatus populusque Romanus," or "SPQR," meaning "the senate and the people of Rome"). Rome was governed mostly by the Senate and the magistrates, who were drawn largely from the Senate; Roman government thus was largely aristocratic. The Senate and its magistrates for most of Rome's history were dominated by the patricians, the ruling families of Rome, who could trace their ancestry back to the original senators chosen by Romulus. The common people's role in the government was the election of the magistrates.

THE MAGISTRATES
The Consuls

Being a *consul* was the dream of ambitious Romans, for the two consuls chosen every year were the chief magistrates of Rome and commanders-in-chief of the armies; the position conferred great glory (through military exploits) and even nobility upon the consul and his family forever. The two consuls assumed the king's position and authority: The broad purple stripe on their togas denoted their quasi-royal status. The Romans no doubt created the two consuls out of their fear and hatred of monarchy, for if one consul became too ambitious, the other consul could oppose him (in fact, all Roman magistrates except for the dictator had at least one colleague, to prevent abuses of power). The twelve lictors, each carrying a fascis while walking before the consuls, showed the consuls' *imperium*. The consuls could lead an army and administer justice, and they sat in a *sella curulis*, an ivory chair, also a symbol of *imperium*.

While leading an army, the consuls (who wore scarlet military cloaks called *paludamenta*) had the power to punish soldiers— including executing them—without a trial. They could propose laws and issue edicts. They could convene the Senate and popular assemblies. The consuls received foreign embassies and conducted state business. They negotiated treaties and surrenders, subject to ratification by the people. The consuls were further honored by having the year named after them; the Romans dated their years by the two consuls of the year. Thus, we read at the beginning of the fifth book of Caesar's *Gallic Wars*, "L. Domitio Ap. Claudio consulibus"—that is, "during the consulship of Lucius Domitius and Appius Claudius," which was 54 B.C.

The consuls were limited in their power by the term of office (one year), and by the veto both of the other consul at the time and of the tribunes (see below). The consuls depended upon the Senate for advice, for there were many ex-consuls in the Senate, and consuls who ignored the Senate found their administration hampered by its interference. Consuls were immune to prosecution while in office, and upon leaving office had to swear that they had done the state no harm. The minimum age for a consul was forty-two.

The Dictator

The *dictator* was appointed only during times of national crisis, when an enemy threatened Rome or its allies and the situation

demanded prompt, unanimous, and decisive leadership of the
Romans, or when the consuls were disabled or otherwise unable to
perform their duties. The dictator's power was not subject to
appeal or veto until after 300 B.C., when a citizen gained the right
to appeal a dictator's capital sentence. The supreme power held by
the dictator was symbolized by his having twenty-four lictors (in
contrast to the twelve lictors of each consul). The only check on
his power was the duration of his rule—six months at the most. It
was customary for the dictator to step down at the end of the
crisis, before the six months had elapsed. The Senate recommended that a dictator be appointed, but the consuls actually
nominated him; a law passed by the Comitia Centuriata installed
the dictator in office. Because of the dictator's nearly unlimited
power, the Romans did not entrust the dictatorship to any but the
most highly respected among them. The dictator had an assistant,
called the master of the horse (*magister equitum*), who commanded
the cavalry; his *imperium* was shown by his twelve lictors.

The Censors

The two *censors* had no *imperium*, but their position was
nonetheless a powerful one. They were in charge of the census,
which was conducted every five years. The census involved not
only counting the number of citizens but also assessing each man's
wealth. The censors assigned each man to one of the classes and
decided whether or not a senator had the amount of wealth
necessary for that post. The censors also performed the *lustrum* at
the end of the census.

Another duty of the censors was revision of the Senate lists. A
senator who had lapsed in his morals could be struck from the list
by the censors; for example, Cato, as censor in 184 B.C., is said to
have expelled one senator from the Senate because he had
embraced his wife by daylight in the presence of their daughter.
The censors supervised public morals and occasionally passed
sumptuary laws (laws designed to curb the love of luxury). One
such law, the Lex Orchia, limited the number of guests one could
have at a party; another, passed by Julius Caesar, prevented
Romans from eating foods deemed too decadent. The censors also

awarded government contracts for, say, collecting taxes in the provinces or building bridges and roads. For example, Appius Claudius Caecus, censor in 312 B.C., has been honored for thousands of years now with the fame of the road he built, the Via Appia (Appian Way), ancient Rome's main road to southern Italy. He also built Rome's first aqueduct, the Aqua Appia. The censors' term lasted eighteen months.

The Praetor

The *praetor* was mostly in charge of the courts (in fact, the body of Roman law consists mostly of praetorian edicts), but often commanded small armies. His *imperium* was less than that of the consuls; the praetors were seen as junior colleagues of the consuls. The praetor's *imperium* was symbolized by his six lictors. The praetor, like the consul, was allowed to sit in a *sella curulis*. Being elected praetor by the Comitia Centuriata often made one a senator. The number of praetors varied; most of the time there were eight. There were two types of praetors: the *praetor urbanus*, who was responsible for the administration of justice in Rome, and the *praetor peregrinus*, who dealt with lawsuits in which one or both of the parties were foreigners. Praetors could convene and lead the Senate when the consuls were unable or out of Rome. The minimum age for the praetorship was thirty-nine.

The Quaestor

The *quaestor* (seeker) was a "go-fer" in Roman government. Quaestors were in charge of the treasury (*aerarium*, "room for bronze," which was also part of the Temple of Saturn) and public records, which were also stored in the *aerarium*. Quaestors also had a military function: A quaestor would be assigned to a consul or praetor during a war, and had the duty of paying the troops and procuring supplies for the general. During the battle itself, the quaestor might command a wing of the cavalry. After 80 B.C. being elected to a quaestorship made one a senator. During Caesar's time there were twenty quaestors; the minimum age for a quaestor was thirty.

The Aediles

Aediles, originally subordinates to the tribunes (see below), were in charge of the infrastructure of Rome. They were responsible for maintenance of the roads, bridges, and buildings; supervision of weights and measures in the market, with power to fine merchants who had broken the law; and oversight of traffic regulations. One of their most important duties was cura annonae (ensuring that the city had an adequate supply of grain).

The aediles were also expected to supply games and amusements for the people. Although the government did allot some money for hosting the games, politically ambitious aediles would supplement that amount out of their own pockets, for the aedileship was an opportunity to advertise oneself for future political offices. For example, while serving as aedile in 67 B.C., Julius Caesar incurred great debts by giving lavish games (with 320 pairs of gladiators), theatrical performances, and public banquets. He thus kept his name on people's lips and in their minds until he ran for the praetorship a few years later. He more than recovered the cost of his aedileship with loot won during his praetorship in Spain in 62 B.C., when he conquered many towns and tribes.

The Tribunes

The ten *tribuni plebis*, "tribunes of the people," technically were not magistrates. Their function was to protect the common people from the abuses of power of the magistrates and the Senate, both of which were usually patrician; by law, the tribunes had to be plebeian—that is, of the common people. The tribunes had great power: They could stop anything the government was doing simply by vetoing its actions (this was called *intercessio*). The tribunes were supposed to be sacrosanct: They were not to be harmed by anybody, even by holders of *imperium*. The tribunes were elected annually by the Concilium Plebis (the assembly of the common people, or Popular Assembly). After 149 B.C. tribunes were automatically enrolled in the Senate.

THE SENATE

Since the magistrates changed every year, the Senate was the stable political body in Rome and represented the community's collected political wisdom. It met in the *curia*, or Senate House. Made up of former consuls, censors, praetors, tribunes, aediles, and even quaestors, the Senate had experience in all matters relating to the state—military, legal, political, foreign, domestic, and religious—and advised the various magistrates, who were expected to carry out the Senate's recommendations. Magistrates who ignored the Senate's advice found that the Senate had its ways of getting revenge. Technically, the Senate had no power: It could not pass laws, it could only advise and recommend. Its decisions were called *consulta* or *decreta*. The Senate's prestige (*auctoritas*), however, invested it with great influence. For a while the Senate could veto laws made by the popular assemblies (the Comitia Centuriata and Concilium Plebis), but eventually that power lapsed. The Senate also determined Rome's expenditures and revenues, the rate of tribute of allies, and taxes of subject communities. Disputes between Italian communities, different provinces, and client states came before the Senate for arbitration.

Senators were not elected and had no constituents; once in the Senate, they remained senators for life, unless they made enemies of the censors or failed to maintain the requisite property. Depending upon the time period, one became a senator after becoming a praetor; after being recommended by the consul or a dictator; or after becoming a quaestor. Senators were not paid for their services, and most did not need the money. They came from the landed class of Rome and also had to fulfill a substantial property requirement to become senators. Senators by law were barred from engaging in business and owning large ships, so as to avoid any conflicts of interest. If a senator became consul and was awarded a military command, he could make money from the loot gained from the people he had conquered. Once Rome gained its great empire and needed governors of the various provinces, ex-consuls and ex-praetors could make a lot of money as governors.

Meetings of the Senate were chaired by each consul in alternate months. The consul conducting the meeting would announce the agenda and lead the discussion, calling upon senators to give their opinions. During the discussions of business, there was a definite hierarchy among the participants. First, the consuls, *princeps senatus* ("chief of the Senate," the senior senator), and ex-consuls would be asked to give their opinions; then the praetors would speak; and so on through the ranks. Once called upon to give his opinion, a senator could speak for as long as he wished; Cato the Younger (95–46 B.C.) frustrated a few meetings of the Senate with filibusters.

Depending upon the time, there were three hundred senators, or six hundred, or—for a time when Julius Caesar was dictator—nine hundred (his successor Augustus reduced the number to six hundred). Senators enjoyed reserved seats at religious ceremonies and public entertainments. They wore special shoes and the *latus clavus*, a wide purple stripe, on their togas.

THE CURSUS HONORUM

The well-born Roman boy who wanted to earn great *gloria* would start on what the Romans called the *cursus honorum*, the "course of honors," or the ladder of offices leading to the top, the consulship. He would start out as a quaestor; then usually, but not always, become an aedile. As aedile, he would give fabulous games and parties, to win the gratitude—and the votes—of the people for his next office, the praetorship. By law, he would have to wait three years between the praetorship and the consulship. After serving as consul, he might become a censor.

THE ASSEMBLIES OF THE PEOPLE

The Roman people met in a several *comitia* (assemblies). Although there were three types of *comitia* (*centuriata*, *tributa*, and *curiata*), we will discuss only the most important, the Comitia Centuriata.

The Comitia Centuriata was a timocratic assembly (one in which the richer voted before the poorer) of Roman men of military age.

(See the description of the classes in chapter 4.) It elected the magistrates, approved laws recommended by the Senate, declared war, and heard appeals of citizens condemned for capital crimes. It met on the Field of Mars outside the city, since armies were not allowed past the *pomerium* into the city.

The Concilium Plebis, or Popular Assembly, was an assembly of the common people that elected the tribunes. Eventually this assembly could pass laws, at first with the approval of the Senate, and later without Senate approval. A law passed by the Popular Assembly was called a *plebiscitum* (English *plebiscite*, "a vote by the people").

THE PRIESTS

Rome had a state religion. Under the monarchy the king was in charge of religion; during the early republic religious duties were overseen by the *rex sacrorum* (king for the sacred rites). Eventually this official was superseded by the college of priests, the *pontifices*. Chief among them was the pontifex maximus, who lived in a state-owned house called the Regia. The *pontifices* were advisory to the consuls and Senate; they had no formal power, but the magistrates were expected to heed their advice. The *pontifices* had power over the Vestal Virgins, the augurs, the *haruspices* (who examined the vital organs of animals to foretell the future), and the *flamines*, who were priests serving one god in particular.

CHAPTER 7

Traitors and Heroes
of the Early Republic

Once Tarquin the Proud had been expelled, in 509 B.C., Brutus and Collatinus assumed the leadership of the infant republic, as Rome's first consuls. Brutus promptly added three hundred members of the equestrian class to the Senate, whose numbers had been depleted by Tarquin's political murders. These senators were called conscripts (in Latin, *patres conscripti*) to distinguish them from the original senatorial families.

Collatinus served only a part of his term. His name, *Tarquinius Collatinus*, so frightened the citizens with their newly acquired liberty that they asked him to resign; although stunned by the request, Collatinus complied and went into voluntary exile.

Publius Valerius replaced Collatinus, but he too came under suspicion of aiming for monarchy. First, he began building a house set high on a hill, which could be made into a fortress and used for looking down upon the citizens. Second, when his colleague Brutus died (see below), he did not seek a replacement for him. To reassure the common people, Valerius had his house torn down and rebuilt on the lowest part of the hill, so they could all look down upon him, and he also started the custom of having the *fasces* lowered in the presence of the people, to show that the power and greatness of the people were greater than that of the consul. Later Romans also believed (contrary to modern scholarship) that Valerius passed a law guaranteeing that a citizen convicted of a capital offense could appeal the sentence to the citizens. For the respect and love that Valerius showed the common people, he earned the nickname Poplicola (Lover of the People).

BRUTUS EXECUTES HIS SONS

During his consulship Brutus faced an attempt by some Romans to recall Tarquin, the exiled former king. Tarquin had sent a mission to Rome ostensibly to recover his property, but in reality to stir up unrest among the nobles, who (according to the members of the mission) would suffer the most under the rule of law of the republic: Under the rule of a friendly king, the nobles could be forgiven for petty violations of the law, but blind justice in a community ruled by law was incapable of showing favor. The conspiracy succeeded in drawing Brutus' sons, Titus and Tiberius, into the conspiracy. The members of the conspiracy signed letters pledging their support for Tarquin. A loyal slave, however, overheard their plans and reported the conspiracy to the consuls, to whom the signed letters gave absolute proof of the members' involvement in the conspiracy.

The consuls took immediate action, arresting and imprisoning the conspirators. The punishment for conspiring to bring back the kings was death, and since one of the duties of the consuls was to administer justice, Brutus was required to pass judgment on his own sons. The prisoners—including Titus and Tiberius—were stripped, flogged, and beheaded. The slave who had reported the conspiracy was rewarded with freedom and Roman citizenship.

Brutus did not need his consular powers to execute his sons: As *paterfamilias*, or "father of the family," he had the father's absolute power of life and death, called *patria potestas*, over his children.

Tarquin, frustrated in that attempt to regain supreme power in Rome, now persuaded the Etruscans to help him. Rome won the battle that followed, but lost its liberator, Brutus. Tarquin's son Arruns had seen Brutus on the battlefield and furiously charged toward him for a duel; Brutus took up the challenge, and in the duel they killed each other. Tarquin next sought help from Lars Porsenna, the king of the Etruscan city Clusium. Porsenna and his city at that time were very powerful, and the citizens of Rome thus became very worried about the approaching war with him.

HORATIUS AT THE BRIDGE

Horatius Cocles (One-eyed Horatius) stands out as a hero in the battle that soon followed. Horatius and other Roman soldiers were guarding Rome's one vulnerable point, the Pons Sublicius, when the Etruscans suddenly attacked. The Romans, caught by surprise, lost their customary discipline and fled, but Horatius stayed at his post. Having stopped as many of the fleeing Romans as he could, he convinced them to destroy the bridge behind him, to prevent the Etruscans from having a clear path to the city, while he held back the Etruscan army.

He strides to the first part of the bridge, easily distinguished from those Romans with their backs turned in flight from the fighting. In his hands, his weapons, ready for engaging in hand-to-hand combat; the enemy was stunned, marveling at his recklessness. Fear of disgrace convinced two men, Spurius Larcius and Titus Herminius, both famous by birth and deeds, to stay with him. With them he survived the first storm of danger and the most chaotic part of the battle. Then, since only a little part of the bridge remained, he forced them too to seek safety with those who were destroying the bridge.

Casting his fiery eyes threateningly upon the Etruscan nobles, Horatius now challenged them one by one to combat, or he thundered at them all that they, simply a pack of slaves of overbearing kings, were coming to assail the freedom of others, since they no longer knew what freedom was. They hesitated for a moment, each waiting for the others to start the battle. At last shame made them advance, and raising a shout on all sides, they all cast their javelins at their solitary enemy. When the javelins stuck on Horatius' raised shield, he no less stubbornly controlled the bridge with his formidable presence; then, when they were about to try to thrust him aside with an attack, they were filled with sudden fear at the sound of the bridge crashing down and the Romans' joyful shouting, and held up their attack.

Then Horatius says, "I beg you, sacred Father Tiber, to receive these weapons and this soldier into your gentle flow." Thus, he jumped, weapons and all, into the Tiber and, despite the many missiles falling from above, swam safely to his friends. (Livy II.10.5–11)

A statue of Horatius was placed in the Comitium, and he was granted as much land as he could drive a plow around in a day.

GAIUS MUCIUS SCAEVOLA (LEFTY)

Porsenna, frustrated at his failure to take Rome by storm, next tried to conquer it by besieging the city. Food soon became scarce in Rome, and the Romans' hope was dimming when Gaius Mucius, a young Roman aristocrat, presented himself to the Senate with his plan to assassinate Porsenna. The Senate consented.

When Mucius arrived at the Etruscans' camp, he stood in a densely packed crowd next to the king's tribunal. It happened to be payday for the soldiers, and the king's secretary, sitting next to the king and wearing almost the same type of clothes, worked busily as the common soldiers came up to him. Mucius feared asking which one was Porsenna, since his ignorance would betray him; as luck would have it, he stabbed the secretary instead of the king.

As he was making his escape through the frightened crowd, with his bloody sword opening a path for him, the king's bodyguards seized him and dragged him back, where a crowd had gathered because of the shouting. He was put before the king's tribunal. Even then, in such great danger to his life, he was one more to be feared than to feel fear. "I am a Roman citizen," he said. "People call me Gaius Mucius. I, your enemy, intended to kill you, my enemy; nor do I have less courage to die than I had to kill. It is the Roman way to do and suffer brave deeds. Nor am I the only one that has such hatred for you: behind me there is a long line of men seeking the same honor. From now on, be prepared for this struggle, so that you may fight for your life, hour by hour, so you may always have an armed enemy in your courtyard. We, the Roman youth, declare this war on you. You will fear no army and no battle. It will be a matter for you, alone, with men one by one."

The king, both outraged and terrified by the danger, threatened to have Mucius burned alive unless he immediately exposed the plot to which he had referred. "Look," said Mucius, "so you may understand how meaningless the body is for those who have their eyes set on glory!" And he thrust his right hand into a fire that had been lit for a sacrifice.

When Mucius had burned his hand, as if he had no feeling, the king, astonished by the unbelievable sight, jumped from his chair and ordered the young man to be moved from the altar. "You may leave," he said, "since you have dared to hurt yourself more than me. I would applaud you for your courage, if your courage were benefiting my country. I release you from my captor's power over you; free, unharmed, and untouched, you may go."

Then Mucius, as if returning the favor, said, "Since there is honor for courage here too, and since you have gotten from me as a kindness what you were unable to get by threats, I'll tell you this: we, three hundred noble youth of Rome, have sworn an oath to take this same path against you. I drew the first lot; other leading young men will come, as the lot dictates, until your luck finally deserts you." (Livy II.12.6)

Porsenna was so shaken by Mucius' disclosure of the plot that he sent envoys to Rome to propose peace. Peace was made, and Porsenna withdrew his troops from Rome's territory. Mucius was rewarded with a plot of land west of the Tiber, which came to be called the Mucian Meadows. Mucius also received a nickname, Scaevola (from *scaevus,-a,-um* "left"), which means "lefty."

That is the story from the Roman historian Livy (59 B.C.–A.D. 17). Porsenna probably did take over Rome for a while; at one point the Romans had to agree to hand over hostages so Porsenna would withdraw his troops from Roman territory. One of the hostages was a clever and courageous girl named Cloelia.

Cloelia

Since the Etruscans had pitched their camp not far at all from the banks of the Tiber, Cloelia, one of the female hostages, fooled her guards and, leading the troop of girls, swam across the Tiber, among the enemy's falling missiles; then she returned all the girls safely to their families in Rome. When this was reported to Porsenna, he was at first outraged and sent ambassadors to Rome to demand Cloelia's return. The other girls did not matter much, he said. Then his anger turned to admiration; he said that her deed was far beyond even that of a Horatius Cocles or a Gaius Mucius; but he was of the opinion that if

Cloelia leading the children across the Tiber. (Drawing by Christina Marent Westmoreland)

she were not returned as a hostage, the treaty would be considered broken. If she were returned, however, he would give her back safe, untouched, and chaste to her relatives.

Good faith was kept on both sides, and the Romans restored their guarantee of peace, in accordance with the treaty; courage was not only safe in the king's court, it was even held in honor. After praising the girl, he said that he was giving her back with some of the hostages, and she could choose whatever fellow hostages she wanted. When all the young people had been brought forward, Cloelia is said to have chosen those who were in puberty. "After all," Cloelia said, "it is seemly for unmarried girls, and proper in the opinion of all the hostages, that the age that is most vulnerable to being molested is most deserving of being free from the enemies' clutches." When peace had been restored, the Romans honored the courage unfamiliar in a woman with a new type of honor, an equestrian statue of a girl sitting on a horse; the statue was placed at the top of the Sacred Way. (Livy II.13.6–11)

ROME'S NEIGHBORS

The Etruscans (in Latin, Tusci or Tyrrheni, seen in the names Tuscany and Tyrrhenian Sea) to the north of Rome, who were trying to regain their power in Rome, were not the only enemies the Romans faced. The Gauls in the far north of the peninsula posed a constant threat to Rome and its neighbors, but the Etruscans were still powerful enough to keep them in northern Italy, away from Rome. Rome's enemies to the east were the relentless Aequi and the Sabines, and to the southeast, the Samnites. With the Latins to the south Rome had an alliance, but this did not always prevent hostilities between the Romans and Latins. To the south of the sometimes friendly Latins were the Volsci, a constant threat to the Latins and to the Romans. In the far south of the Italian peninsula were Greeks, who were not yet a large concern of the Romans. As Rome expanded its power, it naturally came into conflict with those peoples.

By virtue of their common language, institutions, and religion, Rome and the towns of Latium had developed a mostly religious, but sometimes political, alliance called the Latin League. During the monarchy Rome was the dominant partner in the alliance, but after the expulsion of the kings the city lost its superiority over the Latins. Rome attempted to reassert its superiority over the Latins at the Battle of Lake Regillus in 496 B.C.

Rome won the battle, but barely. Three years later, in 493, Rome and Latium reached an agreement, called the Foedus Cassianum, which formed a common army of defense; each party pledged to contribute an equal contingent. The side that had summoned the help of the others would take command.

The battle was important for other reasons, too. When the outcome was still in doubt, the dictator Aulus Postumius vowed a temple to the gods known as the Dioscuri—the twins Castor and Pollux, the Gemini of the Zodiac—if they fought on the Romans' side. Suddenly the gods appeared on horseback, helping the Romans to victory. Roman legend also says that after the battle had been fought, but before news of the outcome arrived in Rome, two handsome young men, who were hot and sweaty, as if from fighting in a battle, were seen in the Forum, watering their horses; the two young men announced the Romans' victory. The next day, a letter from the dictator arrived in Rome, telling of the victory; try as they might, the citizens could not find the two young men, and concluded that they must have been Castor and Pollux themselves. In gratitude, the Romans built a temple of Castor and Pollux where the two had been seen in the Forum. Roman tradition also says that before the news of the battle had come to Rome, the two gods told one Roman man, who had no knowledge of the outcome, to go report the victory at Rome; to prove that they were gods, they stroked his beard, turning it a reddish color. After that his family was known as Ahenobarbus, or Bronze Beard. One famous descendant of the Ahenobarbus family was the emperor Nero, 550 years later.

The Three Hundred and Six Fabii

The Romans were facing wars with the Aequi, the Volsci, and the Etruscans, but did not have adequate forces to engage all three enemies at the same time. The clan of the Fabii decided to take a stand for Rome. The spokesman for the clan happened to be consul, and he proposed to the Senate that the Fabii take up the war against the Etruscan city Veii; then the Romans could concentrate their forces against the Aequi and the Volsci. The Senate agreed. The next morning, all the Fabii of military age—three hundred and seven of them—appeared at the consul's house, ready to go to war.

While patrolling the border between Rome and Etruria, the Fabii beat the Veientes in many small battles, and kept them from pillaging Roman territory. The Veientes become angry and insulted, since their large forces were being held back from their pillaging and looting by the small army of the Fabii. The Veientes then formed a plan to rid themselves of the Fabii.

These three columns are what remains of the Temple of Castor and Pollux. (Author photograph)

The Veientes let loose some cattle in a plain. The Fabii saw the cattle and carelessly went to round them up, having no fear of the Veientes after beating them in the small battles. The Fabii were rounding up the cattle when the concealed Veientes suddenly burst forth from their hiding places: the Fabii were surrounded. After a long and hard-fought battle, all the Fabii but one were killed.

CHAPTER 8

Class Conflict in Rome

When the Romans expelled the Tarquins from the city in 509 B.C., the uprising—mostly of nobles, and led by a nobleman, Brutus—was a response to tyrannical practices that mostly affected only the nobility. In the following decades and even centuries Roman government, now aristocratic, often came under fire, but from plebeians protesting the tyranny of the aristocracy. Early in the fifth century, as the Romans were fighting the Aequi, Volsci, and Veientes, the plebeians became increasingly unhappy with the aristocratic government, for common people held no political offices and had little representation in the government. Moreover, as small-scale farmers, they lacked the financial resources to alleviate their lot. The farmer's life is difficult enough, but Roman farmers were also subject to periods of service in the Roman army, and Roman soldiers at that time did not receive pay for their military service. Many Romans, under the double burden of farming and soldiering, fell into debt and became vulnerable to the debt laws, which allowed the debtor in default of his loan to be sold into slavery or even killed by his creditor. Since the lenders were the wealthy aristocrats, the debtors and common people received little aid from the government.

The only help that the common people received had a social, not a legal, basis and actually served to strengthen the power of the aristocracy. This was the patron-client relationship. A poor, powerless person in need could seek the help and protection of a rich, powerful person—generally a noble—who, as the patron, would give the poor person—now his client—the legal and financial help he needed, but in turn would expect help and support from the client when his own time of need arose. This relationship had almost religious overtones, and was passed down from generation to generation. While many patrons no doubt helped many plebeians avoid starvation, eviction from their houses, or prosecution in courts of law, the relationship still strengthened the power of the nobles. It shows how powerless the common people were in relation to the nobles, for patrons helped clients at their own pleasure and to meet their own goals. Further, many nobles amassed great numbers of clients because doing so increased their political power. The plebeians felt that with the expulsion of the monarchy, they had exchanged one king for a host of kings.

The citizens were grumbling that while they were fighting wars abroad for empire and freedom, at home they were enslaved and oppressed by other citizens; the freedom of the common people was safer in war than in peace and among the enemy than among fellow citizens. The outstanding calamity of one man further inflamed the common people's bitterness, already burning hot on its own.

A certain man of advanced age rushed into the forum, bearing the signs of all his misfortunes. His clothing was covered with filth, but fouler still was the condition of his body, pale and racked by disease. What's more, a long unkempt beard and hair made his face look like an animal's. He was nonetheless recognized, despite the change from what he had once been, and the people said that he had once been a centurion [in charge of 100 soldiers and roughly equivalent to a sergeant in the U.S. army]. Pitying him, they talked about his other awards for valor. He himself showed his proof of honorable battles—the wounds on his chest, a wound for each battle. To their asking why he had deteriorated so, he responded (now a great crowd had congregated, as if an assembly had been called) that while fighting in the Sabine war, he had not only lost his year's crop after the destruction of his farm, but also his cottage had been burned down, all his possessions stolen, and his flocks driven off; on top of that, taxes were levied during those hard times, forcing him to borrow money.

After interest was added to other losses, he finally lost the farm that his ancestors had worked, and then he lost everything else. After that, destruction came to his body like a disease; he was taken by his creditors not to slavery but to a workhouse and to the executioner. Then he showed his back, scarred with recent lashes of the whip. (Livy II.23.2–7)

The plebeians began to clamor for a change, but the senators and consuls could not agree how to alleviate their distress. During the deliberations, news came that the Volsci were marching on Rome— news that is said to have caused the common people to cheer and to encourage each other not to fight. They preferred that the city should perish rather than that the patricians should continue ruling them. The consul Servilius then issued an edict making it illegal to put a Roman citizen into chains or into prison for debt, thus keeping him from serving in the army; to seize or sell the property of any soldier on active service; or to interfere with his children or grandchildren. The Romans then conquered the Volsci.

The problem was still not solved. Servilius could accomplish very little against the opposition not only of the Senate—many of whom were allied to the creditors—but also of the other consul, Appius Claudius, who allowed creditors to put debtors in chains and in prison. Groups of citizens ganged up to protect fellow citizens who were about to be arrested, and beat back the lictors sent to make the arrest.

THE PLEBEIANS SECEDE; *TRIBUNI PLEBIS* CREATED

Finally, the common people decided to secede from Rome. With their weapons and provisions they encamped on the Sacred Mount, outside the city. Rome was surrounded by enemies, who were constantly looking to attack, so the city was vulnerable with most of its soldiers settling on the Sacred Mount. The Senate then sent Menenius Agrippa to speak with them, for they did not hate him as much as they hated the other senators. He gave this speech:

"Once upon a time, the parts of the body did not have one mind, as they now do, but each part had its own mind and its own voice. The parts of the body were indignant that by their work, slavery, and diligence, every-thing was sought for the stomach. The stomach, at rest in the middle, did nothing but enjoy the pleasures given it by the others. So they swore an oath that the hands would not carry food to the mouth, that the mouth would not receive the food that was given, and that the teeth would not chew the food that they had received. While they wanted to subdue the stomach by hunger, the members themselves and the whole body all at

the same time wasted away to nothing, all on acccount of their destructive anger. Consequently it became clear that it was not simply slavery to
the stomach, and that the stomach was no more being fed than it was
feeding, giving back to all the parts of the body the blood, equally
divided between the veins, that it had made from the digested food; and
that blood gives us existence and good health." (Livy II.32.8–11)

Menenius then compared that story to the political problems in
Rome, and the common people's anger cooled. The two sides
negotiated and reached this decision: The plebeians were to have
their own officers, called *tribunes*, who would represent them and
protect them from the magistrates' abuses of power. The tribunes
would be sacrosanct (immune to the power of those holding
imperium), and no man from the patrician class could be a tribune.
Eventually the tribunes gained the power to veto any action of the
magistrates; armed with this *intercessio*, one tribune could put a
halt to what the Senate and consuls were doing (see chapter 6).

THE TWELVE TABLES

The patricians still kept great power over the common people,
because the tribunes were the plebeians' sole representatives in the
government. All the magistrates were patricians, and the patricians
alone knew the laws, which were not recorded, but were passed
down orally through the generations. Undoubtedly the patricians
changed the laws as they thought necessary and expedient. This
imbalance of knowledge led to abuses of power and to civil strife.
Finally, the two sides agreed to appoint a panel of ten men (called
decemviri) to write down the laws for all to see, read, and learn.
While this was taking place, normal government was suspended,
and the ten ruled Rome, with their decisions immune to veto or
appeal.

Roman tradition says that three Romans were sent to Athens to
study the laws of Solon, one of the Seven Wise Men of Greece,
who had created reforms to save Athens from civil war in 594 B.C.
After returning to Rome, in 451 B.C. the *decemviri* produced ten
tables of laws, which were written on bronze or wooden tablets
(Latin *tabulae*). More were needed, however, so the ten then

produced two more tables. The Twelve Tables, as they were called, became the foundation of Roman law. Once they had completed their work, the *decemviri* soon began to abuse their power and became hated by all; the usual government was then restored.

Although Roman schoolboys are said to have learned the Twelve Tables by heart, only fragments of the Twelve Tables survive, and their meaning is not always clear. Yet we can see in them both the Romans' concern for creating a civil, orderly society and also their respect for individual rights and property. Some of the laws, for example, established standards for legal procedure: how one citizen might call another to court, and what to do if he refused to come or ran away. Another such law stipulated that a judge who accepted a bribe should suffer capital punishment, and that a person who lied under oath must be hurled from the Tarpeian Rock.

Other laws detailed certain civil rights. For example, a citizen was guaranteed a trial before execution. A man in default of a debt was allowed a grace period of thirty days before being liable to arrest and being summoned to court; after the grace period, he could be put in chains and imprisoned, if the creditor wished, yet if the creditor decided to imprison the debtor, he had to feed him. One law prohibited marriage between plebeians and patricians; another guaranteed that a measure approved by the people had the force of law.

The Romans' concern for property rights is seen in other laws. If a man willfully destroyed another's building or heap of grain, he was to be flogged and burned at the stake, but if the destruction occurred because of his negligence or by accident, he had to repair the damage; if he was very poor, he would receive a lighter punishment. Another law concerning property probably gave Roman women some protection from abusive husbands and their families. With the exception of the Vestal Virgins, Roman women, by law (because of their supposed "lightness of mind," *levitas animi*), were not allowed to be independent; they had to have a male guardian, whether a father, husband, or other male family member, who exercised legal rights for them. A married woman and her father's family retained legal power over her and her property if once a year she spent three continuous nights (*trinoctium*) away from her husband's house; otherwise, she and her property—

including her dowry, which could be a substantial sum of money—would fall under the legal control of her husband and his family. Because of the *trinoctium*, a Roman woman could seek not just moral and emotional support from her own family, but even legal support, for she was not totally dependent upon her husband and his family. Another measure to protect the powerless held that if a patron defrauded his client, he was to be considered cursed.

The Twelve Tables formed the basis of *ius civile*, "civil law"—that is, law that concerns the rights of citizens. As the Roman empire expanded, Roman law naturally became the law of the entire empire. In the Middle Ages, scholars rediscovered Roman law and used it as the basis for the law codes of European countries. Roman law thus became one of the most important elements in the development of Western civiliation (Wolff, *Roman Law*, p. 4).

CONTINUING CLASS CONFLICT

Although their legal position was stronger under the law of the Twelve Tables, the plebeians in Rome still faced many difficulties. The patricians controlled the government, the army, and the courts, and plebeians were excluded from positions of power and authority not only by tradition and precedent, but also by religion and law. For example, until 445 the plebeians were barred even from intermarriage with the patricians. That same year the tribunes agitated for a law to allow the plebeians to run for the consulship, although they still had not gained even the quaestorship. The patricians fiercely contested the bill, arguing that because the plebeians were not allowed to take the auspices (that is, to interpret the will of the gods from observations of natural phenomena), which was one of the consular duties, they could not be consuls. The plebeians were outraged.

The tribunes, making use of their veto, were obstructing everything the magistrates and Senate tried to accomplish, including the enlistment of soldiers to face Rome's enemies, who were using Rome's internal discord as an opportunity to invade. The patricians therefore suspended the consulship and allowed the creation of a new type of magistrate, the "military tribune with consular power." This new office was open to the plebeians, although they

were still barred from the consulship. At first there were three
military tribunes; later the number was increased to five. However,
no plebeian was elected military tribune until 400 B.C., ten years
after the election of the first plebeian quaestor.

During those turbulent times, the Senate in 406 finally approved
payment for soldiers. That the republic, governed by the nobles,
had been waging wars for more than a century but had never yet
paid the common soldiers for their time away from their farms
reveals the depth of the problems between the classes: The patricians could afford to go off on long campaigns, while the common
soldiers suffered greatly from such absences—the story of the
impoverished centurion was probably not uncommon. If victorious, the soldiers could gain loot from the conquered, but the
commanding officer decided whether or not to allow the soldiers
to loot the defeated side, and he and his staff decided who
received what.

It was not until the passage of the Leges Liciniae Sextiae in 367
B.C. that plebeians were allowed to run for the consulship and join
the board in charge of performing the sacred rites. The next year,
in 366, the tribune G. Licinius Stolo, one of the authors of the
Leges Liciniae Sextiae, became the first plebeian to be elected
consul. Gradually it became a tradition that one of the two consuls
should be a plebeian. (It is worth noting that Lucius Genucius,
who in 362 became the first plebeian consul to lead the army
against a serious enemy, was disastrously defeated and killed, thus
allowing the patricians to claim that the gods were angry that the
plebeians had polluted the consulship.) Also in 366 the praetorship was created, and plebeians were allowed to run for this
office. G. Marcius Rutilus was the first plebeian elected dictator
(356) and censor (351).

To the ordinary plebeians, it probably meant little that men of
their class held positions of high authority and power. The
ordinary plebeians would still be plagued by the persistent problems of debt and land hunger. Later, when Rome had captured
huge numbers of slaves in overseas wars, the plebeians suffered
from unemployment and underemployment, for cheap and abun-
dant slavery made it unnecessary for the wealthy to hire workers.
The plebeians in the government, being rich and well connected,

did not share the concerns of the ordinary plebeians; although grouped in the same class with ordinary plebeians, the high-status plebeians were themselves nobles and had much more in common with the patricians, with whom they had social dealings, marriage alliances, political deals, and business interests. They had little connection with the poor and distant *vulgus* ("masses," hence the English word *vulgar*) clamoring for land, jobs, and grain. As late as 287 B.C. the plebeians seceded once again, this time to the Janiculum, because of debt laws and usury; their secession forced the passage of the Lex Hortensia, which allowed bills passed by the Popular Assembly to become law. The class problems remained unsolved, and caused more civil turmoil in the late second and first centuries B.C.

CHAPTER 9

Coriolanus, Cincinnatus, and Camillus

In the fifth century B.C. the Romans and their allies waged war on the Sabines, Aequi, Volsci, and Veientes. They managed by wise diplomacy to avert constant war with the Sabines: They gave a large piece of land to a Sabine chieftain, Attius Clausus, who settled there with all his dependents. His family is better known as the Claudius family, or Claudii. The Aequi gave the Romans more persistent problems, but the Romans eventually wore them out.

CORIOLANUS

One of the outstanding figures of Rome during the early fifth century was not a young, powerful warrior but rather Veturia, an elderly noblewoman, the mother of a son named Coriolanus. In 491 Rome was suffering from famine, and the Romans had to import grain from Sicily. When the Senate was debating what price the common people should pay for the grain, Coriolanus, who hated the tribunate and was bitter about the power the plebeians were gaining, advised his colleagues in the Senate to hold the grain hostage and thus force the plebeians to give up the tribunate. The common people were outraged, and the members of the Senate thought it politically expedient to sacrifice Coriolanus to their wrath. A date was set for him to go on trial for tyrannical behavior, but on the day of his trial Coriolanus went into exile among Rome's enemies, the Volsci. Soon the Volsci, led by Coriolanus, started attacking Rome's allies. After many victories over Rome's allies and subjects, Coriolanus and his Volscian army pitched camp 8 kilometers from Rome and devastated the countryside, though

Coriolanus made sure that his soldiers did not destroy the property of any patricians. Rome was in trouble. Envoys from Rome
went to Coriolanus' camp to ask him to withdraw, but he refused.
Again, envoys were sent, and again he declined to move. Next the
priests, wearing their sacred garments, went to beg him to withdraw, but they too failed in their mission. While the Romans
hurriedly gathered together their army, Coriolanus' mother Veturia,
his wife Volumnia and their children, and other women of Rome,
weeping, marched out of the city to meet Coriolanus in his camp.

"If my eyes aren't fooling me," one of Coriolanus' officers said to him,
"your mother, wife, and children are here."

Coriolanus, almost crazy and in a panic, got up from his seat to hug
his mother. She changed from begging to anger. "Before you hug me,"
she said, "let me know whether I have come to my son or to my enemy,
and whether I am your prisoner or your mother in your camp. Have my
long life and unhappy old age brought me to this, that I should see you
first an exile and then an enemy of Rome? Could you destroy this land
that produced and nourished you? Although you came here with dangerous intentions and threats, didn't your anger die down as soon as you
entered the borders? Once Rome came into view, didn't the thought enter
your mind, 'Inside those walls are my house, my household gods, my
mother, my wife, and my children'?

"I can only conclude that if I hadn't given birth, Rome wouldn't be
under attack; if I had no son, I would have died free, in a free country.
But I can allow nothing more wretched for me and more disgraceful for
you, since I am the most wretched, and will be for a long, long time. And
your children? You will decide whether it is a premature death or a long
slavery that awaits them."

His wife and children hugged each other; the weeping of the whole
crowd of women as they bewailed their and their country's fate finally
broke the man. After embracing his family, he sent them away and
moved his camp away from the city. (Livy II.40.4–10)

CINCINNATUS (CURLY)

A hero of Rome during this time was L. Quinctius, called
Cincinnatus, or Curly, because of his curly hair. After losing a minor

Venturia scolding Coriolanus. (Drawing by Christina Marent Westmoreland)

battle with the Aequi in 458 B.C., the consul Minucius decided to keep his army within the fortifications of his camp so as not to risk any more losses. The Aequi interpreted his actions as fear and consequently built barriers to trap Minucius and his army within their camp. Five Roman soldiers escaped before being trapped and told the Romans about the danger to the army. The Romans decided to bypass the other consul and elect a dictator instead.

The only hope of the Roman empire, L. Quinctius, was then living across the Tiber on a farm three acres in size. . . . Greeted there by the messengers from the Senate, as he was perhaps working hard on a ditch with his shovel, or plowing—it is certain only that he was busy with some type of farm work—he returned their greeting, and he was asked to put on a toga [a man's formal attire] so he could hear the Senate's commands, with their hopes that it might benefit both him and the republic. Surprised, he asked, "Is everything all right?" and told his wife Racilia to quickly bring him a toga from their cottage. After he had wiped off the dust and sweat, and put on his toga, he went to the messengers, who congratulated him and greeted him as dictator, and summoned him to the city; then they informed him of the terror in the army. A state ship was ready for him; his three sons, walking on the road, received him, and then other relatives and friends, and then the greater part of the senators. (Livy III.26.7–11)

Cincinnatus ordered all men of military age to assemble before dawn in the Campus Martius; the army marched that day to Algidus, where Minucius and his men had been trapped by the enemy. That night the Roman soldiers silently surrounded the enemies' camp; the Romans won the ensuing battle, and Cincinnatus rescued Minucius and his army.

Back at Rome, the grateful Senate ordered the victorious Cincinnatus to enter the city with the same retinue that had accompanied him upon his arrival as dictator. "The enemy generals were led before his chariot, then came the army's standards, followed by the army, loaded down with loot. Tables of food are said to have been set before the houses of all the citizens, and the soldiers eating from the tables followed the chariot with a triumphal song and jokes, like a body of partygoers" (Livy III.29.4).

Cincinnatus' entry into Rome was an example of the Roman *triumph*, a sort of parade for victorious generals and their armies. First came men showing the gold, silver, weapons, and loot captured in the war. They also carried placards bearing drawings or names of the cities and generals that had been captured, indicating the rivers or mountains crossed, and depicting the major battles fought. Then came the white oxen that would be sacrificed to Jupiter, and the hostages and prisoners in chains. The general himself, in a four-horse chariot adorned with gold, ivory, and jewels, then approached with his entourage, which might include his children as well as his lictors, the Senate, and his assistants. He wore the *vestis triumphalis* (clothing of triumph): a *tunica palmata* (a tunic embroidered with palm branches, the symbol of victory) and a *toga picta* (painted toga) of purple or gold. He wore a crown of laurel, either for purposes of purification or for protection from evil spirits, while a slave standing behind him held a golden crown over his head. The general's face was painted red. In his left hand he held a golden scepter, and in the other a staff of laurel. For a day he was allowed to look like Jupiter. Lest the general become too puffed up with pride by being compared to Jupiter, the slave holding the golden crown above his head constantly whispered in his ear, "Remember: you are only mortal," while his soldiers, who came next in the procession, sang dirty songs to embarrass him. To further ward off evil, the general wore a *bulla* (amulet) and an iron ring. The triumph would end up at the Temple of Capitoline Jupiter, because the triumph was originally a religious procession, probably to honor Jupiter for giving the Romans the victory. During their triumphs, Julius Caesar and Emperor Claudius climbed the steps of the temple on their knees, probably to further humble themselves.

There was also a lesser type of triumph, called an *ovatio*. The general in the *ovatio* entered on horseback or on foot, wore a toga with a purple border and a crown of myrtle, and carried no scepter. This was a much less spectacular event, and something of a consolation prize for those whose victories were not great enough to warrant a triumph.

After his triumph, just fifteen days after he had assumed the position of dictator, Cincinnatus resigned his position of almost unlimited power, which he could have held for six months. Having done his job, he returned to his plow.

THE DEFEAT OF VEII

During the eighth, seventh, and sixth centuries B.C. the Etruscans dominated central Italy, ruling Rome through the Etruscan kings and extending their power into Latium. At the same time the Romans expelled their kings, the Latins too drove the Etruscans out of Latium. Although weakened by internal dissension, the Etruscans were by no means finished as a power. About 405 B.C. the Romans dedicated themselves to the conquest of Veii, the powerful and wealthy Etruscan city less than 15 kilometers north of Rome. The Roman soldiers besieging Veii swore not to return to Rome until they had conquered. Veii was about the same size as Rome, and its position on a mountain, surrounded on three sides by a moat, made it extremely difficult to besiege; the Veientes were also helped by some members of the Etruscan alliance, one of which was the powerful Etruscan city Tarquinii.

In Roman legend the siege of Veii lasted ten years (precisely as long as the Greeks' siege of Troy). The siege of Veii was the most ambitious conquest the Romans had yet undertaken, and the most difficult struggle the city had ever faced. As the siege dragged on, the Romans appointed M. Furius Camillus dictator. In 396, led by Camillus, the Romans took Veii by tunneling into the city. The acquisition of Veii's land doubled the size of Rome. In addition, the Roman soldiers carried off a great deal of loot. When seeing the huge amount of treasure, which was greater than anybody had hoped or dreamed, Camillus prayed that the gods, if jealous of Rome's good fortune, might allow him to somehow appease their jealousy with the smallest suffering of himself or the city. While saying the prayer, Camillus turned around and tripped, a terrible omen.

The siege of Veii affords an excellent example of what the Romans called *evocatio*. When the Romans took over a city, they feared the wrath of the gods dwelling there, so they asked those gods to leave that city and come to Rome. Once they had brought the god to Rome, they worshipped him along with the usual

Roman gods. Accordingly, Camillus as he marched on Veii addressed the gods of Rome and Veii: "Led by you and your divine power, Pythian Apollo, I am proceeding to destroy the city Veii, and I vow to you one-tenth of the spoils. Queen Juno, you who now live in Veii, I beseech you to accompany us, once we have won this war, into our city and to let it be your city too in the future, where a temple worthy of your majesty will receive you" (Livy V.21.2–4).

Young soldiers were specially chosen to remove the statue of Juno and the temple's treasures; before they entered the temple they bathed and dressed in white. One soldier, in awe of the temple and the goddess, asked Juno whether or not she wanted to go to Rome; his companions swore that the statue nodded its head in reply.

CAMILLUS AND ROMAN HONOR

While besieging Veii, the Romans were attacked by Veii's allies, the Etruscan city Falerii. In revenge, the Romans then attacked Falerii. During the siege of their city, the Falerians learned that one trusted and respected member of their society was not above abusing his position for profit; they also learned about Roman honor and morals.

It was the custom in Falerii that teachers taught as well as supervised their pupils, and many boys were entrusted to the care of one man. . . . The teacher who excelled in knowledge taught the children of the leading citizens. During peacetime one teacher had established the routine of leading the boys out before the city for play and exercise; during the war, that routine was in no way interrupted. Taking the boys from the city gates for sometimes shorter and sometimes longer distances, with the play and talk varied, one day when he could he led the boys farther than usual, straight through the enemy outposts and from there into the Romans' camp, directly into the headquarters of Camillus, the general.

There he added to his despicable deed words even more loathsome, that he had handed the city Falerii into the Romans' hands, since he had given the Romans power over the sons of Falerii's chief citizens. When

Camillus heard this, he said, "Wicked man, you have brought your despicable offer to a people and general who are not like you. There is no alliance between Rome and Falerii, as happens by agreement between humans. But there are laws of war just as there are laws of peace, and we have learned to fight wars no less justly than bravely. We have brought our arms not against the age of life which is spared even when cities are captured, but against armed men and against those who, without provocation and wrongdoing from us, attacked our camp during the siege of Veii. With your new crime, as much as it was in your power, you have conquered your countrymen; I, however, will conquer them with Roman skill, courage, work, and weapons."

The teacher was stripped, and his hands were tied behind his back; then Camillus handed him over to the boys to be led back to Falerii, and gave them switches to whip him as they drove the traitor back to the city. When the people in the city saw the boys bringing the teacher back, at first they gathered in great numbers, and then the senate was convened. So great was their change of heart that those who only recently had been so wild with anger and hatred that they would have preferred being destroyed like Veii to having a disgraceful peace like Capena's [which had surrendered to Rome] now unanimously sought peace.

In the marketplace and Senate House, the Falerians talked of nothing but Roman trustworthiness and Camillus' sense of justice. By agreement of all, legates went to Camillus in his camp and, after gaining his permission, they went to the Roman Senate, to surrender Falerii to Rome.

Once they were led into the Senate, they said this: "Gentlemen of the Senate, we have been conquered by you and your general; may no man or god begrudge you that victory. We surrender, seeing that we will live better lives under your rule than under our own. Two healthy examples have come out of this war for the benefit of mankind: You preferred honor in war to an immediate victory. Won over by your trustworthiness, we voluntarily acknowledge your victory." (Livy V.27.1–14)

CHAPTER 10

The Gauls Sack Rome

In 390 B.C. arrived one of early Rome's darkest hours. The Gauls, a Celtic people who were migrating westward from central Europe, swept down upon Italy; one of their victims was Rome. Supposedly they had recently drunk wine for the first time and liked it so much that they wanted the country that produced it. Another story says that the Gauls attacked Rome in revenge after a Roman envoy killed a Gallic envoy because of his arrogant words. The Romans had been warned of the Gauls' coming: A plebeian had heard one night a divine voice ordering him to let the magistrates know of the impending danger, but those whom he told simply laughed at him.

The Gallic and Roman armies met at the juncture of the Allia and Tiber Rivers. The Roman army fell apart, because of bad leadership (the generals had not constructed any defenses, chosen an area for a camp, or checked the auspices) and fear of the Gauls' superior numbers. The Gauls' victory was so devastating that the Romans afterward cursed the day of the battle, July 18, so that no business could ever be conducted on dies alliensis, "the day of the Allia." The Gauls massacred the fleeing Romans and descended upon Rome. No Roman army hindered them, and their entry into Rome was so easy that they thought the Romans were laying a trap for them.

The Romans had evacuated the city, some fleeing into the countryside and others taking refuge in the citadel, the Capitol. It was a pitiful sight to see the Vestal Virgins carrying the images of the gods out of the city to safety in friendly cities; the Etruscan city

Caere received the Romans' gods and sacred objects, and the Romans were grateful for Caere's help.

THE SIEGE OF THE CAPITOL

After a few days, the Gauls laid siege to the Capitol, which had been fortified and provisioned. To lure the Romans out of the Capitol, which remained the last free part of the city and the bastion of Roman civilization, the Gauls started destroying the buildings and houses, until half the city was in ruins. The original Twelve Tables are said to have perished in the destruction.

Meanwhile at Rome the siege was bogged down and not much was happening on either side, which was the Gauls' intention, to keep any Romans from breaking through the posts [and communicating with other Romans who had fled]. Suddenly a Roman youth turned the attention of both Romans and Gauls onto himself. It was the custom of the Fabian clan to perform a sacrifice on the Quirinal Hill. When Fabius descended from the Capitol to go perform the sacrifice, wearing his clothes in cere-monial fashion and carrying the holy objects, he walked right through the middle of the Gauls' posts to the Quirinal, paying no attention at all to the threats and shouts. After solemnly performing all the sacred rites, he returned the same way that he had come, with an unwavering step and calm face, expecting that the gods would be kind to those who have not been kept from worship even by their fear of death. Thus he returned to his family on the Capitol, leaving the Gauls either astonished by his audacity or moved by his piety; after all, they themselves are hardly negligent of religious matters. (Livy V.46.1–3)

Camillus, the hero in the Romans' defeat of Veii and Falerii a few years earlier, had gone into exile at Ardea after being accused of mishandling spoils taken from Veii. The man whom Rome most needed was in exile, and rather bitter about his city's treatment of him. Despite his anger, Camillus now made preparations to rescue his city from its present danger. He was appointed dictator in absentia, and he approached neighboring cities with pleas for help against the Gauls.

The Sacred Geese of Juno

Meanwhile the citadel of Rome and the Capitol were in great danger. The
Gauls had either noticed human tracks where the messenger had come
from Veii [where some Romans had fled for safety and were now waiting
for an opportunity to save Rome], or on their own had noticed, next to
the Temple of Carmentis, a rock suitable for climbing. At any rate, one
night they first sent one unarmed man to try the way; then, by passing
their weapons along where the going was rough, leaning on one another,
and lifting others in turn and pulling them up, as the lay of the land
demanded, they arrived at the summit in such silence that they not only
fooled the guards, but did not awaken even the dogs, animals attentive to
sounds in the night. They did not fool the sacred geese of Juno, however;
even in the middle of a great shortage of food, the Romans had kept their
hands off the sacred geese. This saved Rome: Their honking and flapping
of wings awoke M. Manlius, distinguished in war and consul three years
before. He snatched up his weapons and, at the same time that he urged
others to get their weapons, while the others were in a panic, with his
shield he hit one Gaul (who by now was standing at the top) and sent
him down the hill. Falling, that Gaul knocked down those closest to him,
and Manlius killed other frightened Gauls who had dropped their
weapons to hold onto the rocks. By now other Romans had joined
Manlius and, with javelins and missiles, sent the enemies falling down
the rocks. As they fell, they knocked other Gauls down the hill, head
first. (Livy V.47)

Because of this display of heroism, M. Manlius received a
nickname, Capitolinus (Of the Capitol), which he passed down to
his descendants. The soldier whose negligence had allowed the
Gauls to come that close to seizing the citadel was thrown from the
Capitol to his death.

"Ferro, Non Auro"

The siege was wearing out both the besiegers and the besieged.
After occupying Rome for seven months, the Gauls were suffering
from hunger and disease, while the Romans in the Capitol were

The Dying Gaul, from Pergamum, third century B.C. (Courtesy of the Archer M. Huntington Art Gallery, University of Texas at Austin, William J. Battle Collection of Plaster Casts)

running low on provisions. The Romans are nonetheless said to have thrown loaves of bread from the walls of the citadel to the Gauls below, to prove that they were not short of food. In these dire circumstances the Romans agreed to pay, and the Gauls agreed to accept, a ransom of a thousand pounds of gold so the Gauls would leave. Since the treasury did not have enough gold, the women of Rome voluntarily contributed their jewelry to the ransom. When the Roman commander objected to the heavier weight standard being used by the Gauls, the Gallic chieftain Brennus is said to have thrown his sword on the scale while saying the words hateful to Roman ears, "Vae victis!" (Woe to the vanquished!).

During the weighing of the gold, Camillus appeared. He said that the agreement was invalid because it had been made contrary to his orders as dictator. Instead, he ordered his soldiers to recover their city "ferro, non auro" (with iron, not gold). He warned the Gauls to prepare to fight. The Romans won the battles that followed, even capturing the Gauls' camp and annihilating that particular tribe of Gauls, the Senones.

"HIC MANEBIMUS OPTIME"

When the Romans saw the ruins of their city, the tribunes began urging the common people to vote not to rebuild Rome and instead to move to the site of Veii, which had not been destroyed and would be more easily defended in the future. Undoubtedly the tribunes also hoped that in the new location there would be a fairer distribution of land between the plebeians and patricians. Although Camillus' stirring and impassioned speech convinced many to stay, many others remained undecided. What convinced them was a sign from the gods: As the Senate was debating whether or not to move, some soldiers were passing through the Forum after guard duty; the senators overheard the centurion give his soldiers the orders to halt, saying, "Hic manebimus optime" (Here will be the best place for us to stay). That was their sign to stay.

The Romans learned from their military mistakes and reformed the army so that they would never again experience another Allia.

To make the army more flexible, each legion was divided into thirty *maniples* (literally, "handfuls"), each of which contained one hundred twenty to two hundred men. The strength of the reformed army was soon tested, for many of Rome's enemies, encouraged by the Gauls' initial victory, chose that moment to renew war with Rome. The Latins and Hernici revolted from their alliance, and the Volscians and Etruscans were armed and ready to attack. The Romans named as dictator the man who had rescued them from the previous peril, Camillus. He conquered the Volscians so thoroughly that they surrendered, after seventy years of warfare. He then turned to the Aequi and captured their army camp and their main city, Bolae. He next took on the Etruscans, who were marching on Sutrium, a city allied to Rome. The Etruscans took Sutrium, but on the same day Camillus recaptured it and gave it back to its inhabitants: All in one day Sutrium had been free, captured by the enemy, and then recaptured and restored to its citizens. Camillus then returned to Rome and celebrated a well-deserved triumph.

Shortly afterward, in 386, Etruria once again prepared for war. His dictatorship having lapsed, Camillus was now only a military tribune, one of several equal in authority; nonetheless, the other military tribunes volunteered to subordinate themselves and their power to him. Once the Roman soldiers had seen the size of the enemy army, they became afraid and reluctant to fight, despite Camillus' order to attack. He harangued the soldiers, again gave the signal to attack, and, despite his age (he was so old and frail that he had to be lifted onto his horse), led the attack. He even threw the standards (*signum*, a bronze or gold eagle on a pole, which preceded the soldiers into battle, like a flag) into the midst of the enemy ranks. By this act he forced his soldiers to fight, for losing the standards was the sign of utter defeat and a great dishonor to soldiers. The Romans won that battle, led by the aged Camillus.

In 382 B.C. the Volscians joined with the people of Praeneste and attacked a Roman colony. Again the Romans turned to Camillus, with one Lucius Furius to assist him. Seeing the enemy army, the soldiers and Lucius Furius were eager to fight, but Camillus would not permit it. Lucius Furius argued with Camillus, who told his assistant that he could not hold him back, but that he would pray that no harm would come to the Romans because of the younger man's decision.

Lucius Furius led the Romans against the enemy; the Romans started losing and began to flee. Camillus then harangued the soldiers for cowardice, and ran to the front line to lead them once again into battle. The soldiers followed the old man and eventually won the battle. Later, when Camillus was again appointed dictator, he named as his master of the horse the same Lucius Furius whose failure to follow his advice had endangered the army. Because of his heroism, Camillus was later called "the second founder of Rome."

TITUS MANLIUS TORQUATUS

Some time later there lived one Lucius Manlius, who had once been dictator but was very unpopular in Rome—so much so that after his dictatorship expired, a tribune, with the support of the common people, attacked him legally and sought to prosecute him. There were two reasons for his unpopularity: First, he was a harsh general and abusive to those whom he enlisted; his harshness had gained him the nickname Imperiosus. Second, he did not allow his son Titus to live the life one would expect a young nobleman to live. Titus was not allowed to live in the city, to consort with other young noblemen, or to achieve public recognition; instead, his father forced him to work in the country like a slave. Why? Because Titus stuttered. The tribune inflamed the people's anger against Lucius Manlius Imperiosus. Titus himself, however, was sad and angry that he was another source of his father's unpopularity. He formed a plan.

Secretly he armed himself with a knife one morning and, arriving at the gates of the city, went straight to the house of M. Pomponius the tribune. He told the doorman to tell his master that it was Titus Manlius, the son of Lucius, and that he needed to meet with him. The tribune had him brought in immediately, hoping that the son was very angry at his father or was bringing some new charge against his father, or had some advice for conducting the case. After giving and receiving greetings, Manlius told the tribune that there were some things that he wanted to discuss

with him, but without any witnesses present. Once those present had
been told to leave, he drew his knife and, standing above the tribune's
couch and pointing his knife blade at him, he threatened to stab him
unless he swore, on words that he had already written, that he would
never call an assembly for the sake of prosecuting his father. The tribune,
shaking with fear, swore the oath, as he was forced to do; how could he
not do so, seeing the blade flashing before his eyes, himself unarmed, the
young man very strong, fierce, and—which was more frightening—not
too smart? He swore the oath and later let it be known that he had
stopped his prosecution after being forced by the threat of violence.

As much as the common people would have preferred to be given the
opportunity to convict so cruel and arrogant a master, nonetheless they
did not think it bad that the son had done the bold deed for his father. It
was all the more praiseworthy because the father's harshness had not
turned his son's mind from his duty to his father. (Livy VII.5.3–8)

Soon afterward the Gauls again threatened Rome; they pitched
their camp about 5 kilometers from the city. A bridge over the river
Anio separated the two armies, and the two sides had frequent
skirmishes for possession of the bridge. Finally, an enormous Gaul
advanced to the bridge and said, "I call upon the the bravest man
that Rome has to come forward to a duel, so the outcome of our
duel may show which of our peoples is superior in war!" The Gaul
was huge, and no Roman made a move to fight him in single combat until Titus Manlius asked the dictator if he could leave his
position to go fight the Gaul, who now was sticking out his tongue
at the Romans. The dictator agreed.

Manlius did no taunting, no prancing about, no pointless display of his
agility with a sword; he just had a heart full of courage and quiet rage, for
he was bringing all his ferocity to decide the contest. When they stood
between the two armies, with the hearts of so many people full of hope
and fear, the Gaul, towering over Manlius like a mountain, held his
shield in front on his left arm, and slashed his sword down onto the
shield of his advancing enemy; his sword made a great noise, but caused
no wound. The Roman lifted up his sword and, with his shield, lifted up
the bottom part of his opponent's shield; then he slipped his whole body
between his opponent's body and weapons, making himself free from the

danger of wounds. He made two quick slashes with his sword, opening up his opponent's abdomen. His opponent's body lay stretched out over a vast area. Manlius left the body of the dead Gaul free from any abuse, and took for spoils only one blood-splattered necklace [*torquis* in Latin], which he put around his own neck. (Livy VII.10.8–12)

Titus Manlius received a nickname for his bravery and victory: Torquatus (Wearing a Necklace). His family likewise was honored with the nickname.

CHAPTER 11

The Wars with the Samnites

The Samnites were a loose confederation of peoples living in the Apennine Mountains southeast of Rome. Their soldiers were tough, for their life in the mountains demanded courage and afforded little of civilization's amenities. In 343 B.C. the Samnites attacked a group of people called the Sidicini, who then sought the help of their powerful neighbors in Campania, a wealthy and fertile region south of Latium; Campania's largest city was Capua, a city regarded by the Romans as wealthy, luxurious, decadent, and effeminate. Capua and Campania joined the Sidicini in an alliance against the Samnites, but their combined forces were not enough to withstand the enemy; Capua itself and Campania were soon attacked by the Samnites and in great danger of being taken over.

The citizens of Capua then asked the Romans for help against the Samnites. The Romans, doubting the sincerity of this emergency appeal, and citing the treaty and alliance that Rome already had with the Samnites, told the Campanians that they could do little against the Samnites, who were their friends. Nonetheless, the Romans said, they would send envoys to the Samnites and ask them to leave Capua and Campania alone.

The envoys of the Capuans and Campanians were distraught. To save their city, the envoys simply gave Capua and Campania to the Romans, reasoning that thus the Romans would have to protect their own property. The Romans now had a substantial excuse for not allowing the Samnites to take Campania. They already had a reason: They did not want the powerful nation of the Samnites to have the additional resources of the fertile fields of Campania and the wealth of Capua. Accordingly the Romans sent envoys to the

Samnites to ask them not to continue the attack; otherwise the Romans would have to defend their subjects, the Campanians.

The Samnite ambassadors refused Rome's request. To further anger the Romans, the Samnite ambassadors even made a point of immediately shouting out the orders to attack Campania, so that the Roman ambassadors could hear. Both sides prepared for war. The Romans won the first battle, at Mount Gaurus, although with great difficulty; they had never encountered so tough and stubborn an enemy. The Romans also defeated the Samnites at Suessula and, in another battle, even stormed the Samnites' camp. They were unable to follow up their victories, however, because of a mutiny in the Roman army. The Samnites asked the Romans for peace, and the Romans, distracted by their own problems, granted them a treaty in 341 B.C.

THE GREAT LATIN WAR

In 358 B.C. the Latins had agreed to a treaty that recognized Rome's supremacy over them. Nevertheless, the Latins began to flex their muscles by waging war on their enemies without Rome's consent or troops. In 341 the Latins attacked the Samnites, with whom the Romans had recently made a treaty of alliance. The Samnites complained to the Romans about the Latins' attack on their territory. The Romans could do little to restrain the Latins at the moment, so they summoned the Latin leaders to a conference. Considering how much they had done to help Rome achieve its powerful position, the Latins demanded that one consul and half of the Senate be drawn from the Latins. The Romans were outraged at the Latins' demand for strict equality in government and declared war on them. Helping the Romans in their battles against their former allies the Latins were the Romans' new allies and former enemies, the Samnites. Helping the Latins against the Romans were the Campanians, who hated the Samnites.

The Roman consuls were nervous about the conflict, which was something of a civil war. The political ramifications were serious, for a victorious Latium could shatter Rome's power. The Latins not only spoke the same language as the Romans, but also used similar military equipment, formations, and strategies. The Latin soldiers were formidable opponents. Doubtless too the consuls were nervous about their new allies, the Samnites, with whom they had been at war only a few years earlier. This battle was too important for sloppiness; the consuls therefore issued the order that no soldier was to leave his post to fight the enemy.

Titus Manlius Torquatus, the son of the Torquatus who had killed the huge Gaul (see chapter 10), was on reconnaissance when he happened to meet a Latin soldier whom he knew. The Latin baited Titus Manlius into engaging in a duel with him to show whether the Latin or the Roman cavalry was better; Titus Manlius, fearing he would appear a coward if he refused, accepted the challenge, knowing that in doing so he would be breaking the rules set by the consuls. The two men had their duel, and Titus Manlius won. He stripped the Latin of his armor and proudly rode back to his father, the consul.

"Father," he said, "so that everybody may say that I am my father's son, I bring back these cavalry spoils, taken from the knight whom I killed, after being challenged to a duel."

When the consul heard that, he immediately turned away from his son and ordered that the trumpet be sounded to summon the soldiers to an assembly. When the great crowd had assembled, he spoke:

"You, Titus Manlius, showed no respect either for the consul's power or for your father's authority when you, against our direct orders, deserted your post to fight the enemy, and when you, as much as was in your power, undermined the army discipline that, up to now, has made Rome strong. You have forced me to disregard the needs of either the country or myself. It will be better if we receive the punishment for our error than if the country is punished for our wrong; we will provide a sad, but beneficial, lesson to the youth of the future. I am moved by a father's natural love for his children, as well as by your show of courage, misguided though it was, by a false conception of glory. The consul's power must either be reestablished as inviolable with your death, or destroyed forever by your going unpunished; I therefore think that you (if there is any of my blood in you) will not object to restoring the military discipline which has fallen because of your mistake. Lictor, go and tie him to the stake." (Livy VIII.7.13–20)

Titus Manlius was then beheaded, as punishment for leaving his post.

Although the Romans won that hard-fought battle close to Mount Vesuvius, the Latins were not yet finished. The survivors regrouped, and more Latin soldiers joined them. They fought another battle against the Romans, this one at Trifanum. Again, the Romans won. The consuls then proceeded through all Latium and Campania, stamping out signs of revolt; Latium and Campania both surrendered. The Romans, however, were wisely gracious in their victory: They granted full Roman citizenship to many Latin and Campanian towns, making citizens of the recently conquered.

One of the cities Rome conquered during this time was Antium. The penalty that Antium paid to the Romans was the loss of its fleet. The prows (*rostra, rostrum* originally meant "beak, snout") were taken from the ships and used as decoration on a speaker's platform in the Forum. So the Latin word that originally meant "beak" and had changed to mean "the prow of a ship" came to mean, first in Latin and later in English, "a speaker's platform."

THE SECOND WAR WITH THE SAMNITES

The Romans' second war with the Samnites began with Palaepolis (Old City), a Greek city in Campania that lay close to Neapolis (New City) and may have been part of Neapolis. The Palaepolitans had attacked Rome's allies and had refused to pay reparations. The Palaepolitans no doubt were encouraged in their hostilities by the six thousand foreign soldiers (four thousand of whom were Samnites) who garrisoned their city.

As the Roman army arrived to attack the city, the citizens simultaneously surrendered to the Romans and tricked the Samnites into leaving. The Romans still had the Samnites to contend with, and defeated them in a battle. The rest of the war did not go so well.

DISASTER AT THE CAUDINE FORKS

In 321 B.C. the Roman army invaded Samnium. While the soldiers were raiding Samnite territory, shepherds grazing their flocks in the vicinity reported to them that the Samnite army had left Samnium and was besieging the town of Luceria, which lay in the territory of Apulia, and was allied to the Romans. Two roads could lead the Romans to the relief of the Lucerians: one was long, with open plains to its sides; the other was short, but with mountains rising to either side. The Romans went by the short path, through an area called Caudium. They had proceeded some distance when they noticed that trees had been chopped down and boulders had been piled up to bar their progress. They turned around, only to find that the way by which they had entered the gorge was blocked, not only by trees that had been chopped down, but also by Samnite soldiers. The Romans had been led into a trap; the shepherds had been planted there by the Samnite commander, Gavius Pontius.

Pontius had not expected that his plan would go so well. He was unsure what to do and wrote a letter to his father, an experienced general, asking him for advice. His father's first reply was to let the Roman soldiers go, unharmed, as soon as possible. The son did not like that advice, so he wrote his father another letter; this time, his father advised him to put all the Roman soldiers to death.

Now the son was even more confused and thought that old age must have blunted his father's acumen. Still, he sent a wagon to bring his father to him so they could discuss the course of action. The father came and explained his advice: By the first plan, which he considered the better of the two, the Samnites would, by a magnanimous gesture, secure unending peace with that very powerful people; by the other plan, the Samnites would merely postpone war for many generations, since Rome would find it difficult to replace the two armies that had been lost. There was no third alternative.

The son rejected both solutions. He told his father of his solution: to release the Romans, but to force them to give up their weapons and possessions, and to pass under the yoke—a symbol of slavery and a great source of shame to soldiers. He would also require that the Romans withdraw their colonies and forces from Samnite territory, and that six hundred Roman *equites* be handed over to the Samnites as hostages.

The father, after listening to his son, said, "That plan of yours is one that doesn't make friends or remove enemies. Just watch out for those whom you have enraged with public humiliation! Those men there are of the Roman race, which doesn't know how to give in, even when it has been conquered. The memory of whatever they are forced to do now will always remain branded in their hearts, and it will not allow them to rest until you have paid the penalty many times over" (Livy IX.3.12).

The father was right, but his son did not know it, and he proceeded with his plans for sending the Roman soldiers under the yoke.

First, they were ordered to lay down their weapons, and then to go outside the camp's walls, with only one article of clothing; then the first hostages were handed over and led away to their guards. Then the lictors were ordered to leave the consuls, and the consuls' military cloaks were torn off. This caused such great pity among the soldiers that those who only shortly before had been cursing the consuls and thinking that they should be handed over to the enemy for torture, now forgot their individual situations and turned their eyes away from the degradation of such great majesty, as if from something too abominable to be seen. The consuls, almost nude, were the first to be sent under the yoke. Then, as each was next in rank, so was he subjected to debasement and humiliation; then the legions passed, one by one, under the yoke. The armed Samnites stood around, calling them cowards and insulting them. They also threatened many with their swords, even wounding and killing those whose faces showed their bitterness at suffering such indignities and thereby offended their conquerors. (Livy IX.5.12–IX.6.2)

The second war with the Samnites had ended, in 321 B.C. One source says that the Romans reneged on their humiliating treaty and continued fighting from 316 to 314, but most historians believe that they abided by the terms.

In the following years, the Romans did not fight the Samnites again, but they did not remain inactive. They made alliances with the Samnites' neighbors, the most important being the region called Apulia. The Samnites were now surrounded by Rome's allies or subjects. The Romans were waiting for the opportunity to avenge the humiliating peace of the Caudine Forks.

THE THIRD SAMNITE WAR

The Samnites themselves offered Rome the opportunity to break
the treaty between them, by attacking Rome's allies the Lucanians,
who naturally asked Rome for help against the Samnites. Roman
fetials, the priests whose duties included deciding upon the justice
or injustice of a war, were sent to the Samnites to demand reparations for the injuries to the Lucanians, but were told by the
Samnites' messengers that if they met any Samnite council they
would not leave uninjured. The Romans then declared war on the
Samnites, in 298 B.C.

The Romans experienced many successes in the early stages of
the war. The consul Gnaeus Fulvius captured one of the Samnites'
main towns, Bovianum; Roman armies took other towns, such as
Romulea, Murgantia, and Ferentinum, and destroyed much of the
Samnites' territory. The Samnites nonetheless did not give up;
instead they instigated a general revolt of the Etruscans, Umbrians,
Gauls, and other peoples Rome had subdued in Italy. Rome was
facing a serious war not only with the Samnites, but also with the
Etruscans, and with their combined forces.

One of the great battles in the war was fought at Sentinum. The
Gauls, Umbrians, Etruscans, and Samnites had joined forces
against the Romans. In charge of the Romans' four legions were Q.
Fabius and P. Decius. Neither side was winning, when Decius
ordered his cavalry to attack; they drove far into the enemy forces,
but suddenly became alarmed by the enemy bearing down upon
them in war chariots. The Romans had never encountered those
war chariots before, and their horses bolted; the Roman cavalry
fled. Failing to restrain their flight, P. Decius decided to make the
ultimate sacrifice for the good of Rome. The Romans believed that
a general could sacrifice himself and the enemy army (in Latin,
devovere is the verb, *devotio* the noun) to the gods of the Underworld and to Mother Earth; Decius' father had sacrificed himself at
the Battle of Veseris. Here is how the younger Decius did it:

He ordered the priest M. Livius to dictate the words for sacrificing himself and the enemy's army on behalf of the army of Rome. He then
offered himself while saying the same prayers and wearing his toga in

ceremonial fashion, as his father had when he offered himself in the Latin War, at Veseris. Saying the solemn prayers, he had claimed that he was driving before himself terror, flight, slaughter, and bloodshed—all the wrath of the gods of the Underworld—and that he would pollute the standards, arms, and missiles of the enemy with awful destruction, and the place of his destruction would be the place of the destruction of the Gallic and Samnite armies. After bringing this curse on himself and the enemy, he turned his horse to where he saw the Gauls were the thickest, lashed his horse, and galloped into their midst, where he was killed by their deadly weapons. (Livy X.28.14–18)

Decius' death, according to the Romans, sealed the pact with the gods of the Underworld; the enemy army was therefore doomed. The Roman cavalry stopped its flight, and the Romans, hearing the priest say that the Gauls and Samnites now belonged to Mother Earth and the gods of the Underworld, renewed their attack. Helped by the Campanians who attacked the Gauls in the rear, the Roman and allied armies won the battle, killing the Samnite general and taking the Samnite camp.

The Samnites did not give up. They raised more armies and kept trying to spur those people subject to Rome to revolt. But they became desperate, for they were losing most of the battles and Samnium was being destroyed. As a last resort to defend their land and liberties, they created the Linen Legion:

There, almost in the middle of the camp, a place was closed off by wicker walls and covered by a linen roof, stretching out two hundred feet [61 meters] in all directions. Then, in accordance with an ancient book written on linen, a sacrifice was performed, with the priest being a certain Ovius Paccius, a man of great ancestry; he confirmed that he was performing this sacred rite in accordance with the most venerable religion of the Samnites, which their ancestors had used when they made their secret plans for taking Capua from the Etruscans.

Once the sacrifice had been completed, the commander sent out a messenger to order all those most noted for birth and accomplishments to appear before him; they were brought in one at a time. There was sacred paraphernalia lying around, to overwhelm one's mind with the presence of the sacred, and in the middle of the enclosed area were altars, and around them were slaughtered victims and centurions with their swords drawn. More like a sacrificial victim than a participant in a sacred rite, each man was moved to the altar and there he was forced to swear that he would tell no one what he had seen and heard there. They also forced him to swear some terrible oath that called for a curse on his head, his family, and all his kin if he either fled from battle or did not immediately kill anyone he saw fleeing from battle. At first, some men refused to take that oath; they were instantly slain around the altar and, lying there dead among the various sacrificial victims, served as a warning to the others not to refuse to take the oath. Once the foremost Samnites had been bound by this oath, ten of them were named by the commander, and each of them was ordered to pick a man until their number amounted to sixteen thousand. They were called the Linen Legion after the covering of the enclosure where the nobles had taken their oaths. Special weapons and crested helmets were given to them, so that they would stand out from the others. (Livy X.38.5–13)

That was merely a part of the Samnite army that the Romans were facing at the Battle at Aquilonia. The battle started badly for the Romans, for the keepers of the sacred chickens (birds that showed the goodwill of the gods by eating their grain and the displeasure of the gods by not eating) had lied about the auspices; the general, hearing that the keepers had falsely reported good auspices, simply noted that the liars brought the gods' retribution on their own heads, and placed them in the front lines. Before the battle started, the keeper who had lied was killed by a randomly thrown javelin. "The gods are here in the battle," cried the general on hearing this news, "and the guilty one has his punishment!" (Livy X.40.13).

The battle was hard, and although the Romans were winning, they were facing a formidable enemy. The consul Papirius had told the other consul, who was besieging a town miles away, to send cavalry to help him; when the Romans were winning, their cavalry came to take the Samnites in the rear. The cavalry also fooled the Samnites, for riding with the cavalry were servants on donkeys, trailing leafy branches along the ground, to raise the kind of dust storm that a huge body of cavalry would raise; terrified at the thought of being taken in the rear by a huge cavalry, the Samnites lost the battle.

The Romans did not stop with taking the Samnites' camp. They destroyed the Samnites' towns of Aquilonia and Cominium, and continued ravaging Samnite territory. The Samnites held out for three more years, finally seeking peace from the Romans in 290 B.C.

After establishing Roman supremacy in Samnium, the Romans changed the name of one of the Samnites' main cities, Malventum. This Oscan name in Latin sounds like "bad arrival," a terrible omen, so the Romans changed it to a more positive-sounding name, Beneventum, meaning "welcome."

The Romans continued their operations in Etruria for some time, mopping up the last remaining areas of rebellion, and beating back the Gauls. The other subject allies remained quiet for the time.

CHAPTER 12

King Pyrrhus' Pyrrhic Victories

Tarentum, a Greek city in the instep of Italy, had been founded in 706 B.C. and still had close ties to cities in mainland Greece. As the Romans extended their influence into southern Italy in the fourth century, they signed a treaty with Tarentum. In 282 B.C., however, when some Roman ships passed through Tarentine waters, the Tarentines, thinking that the Romans had broken the treaty, attacked the ships; the ships were seized, their sailors taken captive, and their commander killed in battle. The Romans at that time were still fighting against the Etruscans and Gauls, and did not want another war on their hands. So they sent ambassadors to propose that the Tarentines simply release the captives and the ships, and pay restitution. The Tarentines refused. The Romans next sent the consul Aemilius Barbula with his army; his orders, however, were only to negotiate a peace with the Tarentines. The negotiations were unsuccessful.

The Tarentines, worried about facing a war with the increasingly powerful Rome, called upon the assistance of Pyrrhus, king of Epirus, a kingdom in northwest Greece; he had a reputation as an excellent general. The Tarentines promised to provide him with an army of Tarentines, Lucanians, Samnites, and Messapians, all enemies of Rome, to augment the army that he would bring from Epirus.

Pyrrhus crossed over to Tarentum with twenty-five thousand soldiers and twenty elephants in 280 B.C. He immediately closed Tarentum's parks and *palaestrae* (places for exercise), and prohibited parties and festivals, maintaining that the Tarentines were not capable of saving themselves or of being saved: Apparently they needed discipline. The Tarentines were not pleased, but Pyrrhus now controlled their city.

Pyrrhus and the Romans fought their first battle that same year at Heraclea. There the Romans encountered elephants for the first time, when Pyrrhus used them to smash the lines of the Roman legions. Reportedly the Romans lost seven thousand soldiers, while Pyrrhus lost four thousand of his best men. Pyrrhus won the battle, but at a great cost.

The Romans sent ambassadors to Pyrrhus to discuss the ransom for the Roman and Italian prisoners he was holding. One of the ambassadors was Fabricius, who was famous among his country-men for his great poverty and his honesty. Meeting with the ambassadors, Pyrrhus was surprised to find that they were not seeking peace; after all, hadn't the Romans just been defeated? He offered to make peace and to release the prisoners, and he also offered "gifts"—bribes, in other words—to speed the negotiations along. Fabricius responded to Pyrrhus' offer:

"Pyrrhus, I applaud you for desiring peace, and I will bring it about, if it will help us. Since I am, as you say, an honorable man, you won't think it right for me to do anything against my country. Nor could I take any of those things which you are offering. I ask you, then, whether or not you really consider me an honorable man. After all, if I am not an honorable man, why do you think me worthy of gifts? If I am honorable, why do you urge me to take the gifts? Let me assure you that I have many things and that I do not need more. What I have now is enough, and I do not want anything that belongs to somebody else. Even though you consider your-self so rich, you are really very poor, for you would not have left Epirus and your possessions to come over here if you were satisfied with them and weren't trying for more. The man who lives in such a way and puts no end to his desire for more is the poorest of the poor." (Zonaras 8.4)

Pyrrhus then sent his officer Cineas to Rome with gifts to dis-tribute to other Roman senators and their wives, figuring that the women would pressure their husbands into making peace with Pyrrhus. Influenced by the gifts, many Romans adopted a kinder attitude toward Pyrrhus, and the Senate met to discuss making peace. During the discussion of the terms, by which Pyrrhus would pledge his support to Rome against the Gauls in exchange for Rome's grant of security and autonomy to Tarentum, the aged Appius Claudius Caecus (*caecus* means "blind") stood up and gave a stinging speech, which began with these words: "Romans, before this, I have been afflicted with bad luck as far as my eyes go, but now I am pained that, in addition to being blind, I am not deaf too, since I am hearing your disgraceful discussions and opinions which are destroying Rome's reputation." He concluded by saying, "Don't think that once you have made Pyrrhus your friend you'll get rid of him. Instead, you'll bring on yourself all those who have no respect for you, thinking that you're easy to beat, if Pyrrhus leaves without suffering the consequences for the wrongs that he has committed against you. He has even received pay, since the Tarentines and Samnites have come to sneer at the Romans" (Plutarch, *Pyrrhus* XIX.3).

Moved by this speech, the senators sent the reply to Pyrrhus that they would not negotiate peace with him until he had left Italy. While in Rome Cineas observed the Roman Senate, and on his return remarked to Pyrrhus that the Senate seemed like an assembly of kings, so great was the dignity and bearing of its members.

The next year, when Fabricius was consul, Pyrrhus' own doctor wrote to Fabricius offering to poison the king for the right price. Fabricius then wrote to Pyrrhus informing him of the doctor's offer to betray him: "You are waging war against just and honorable men, while you put your trust in evil and unjust men" (Plutarch, *Pyrrhus* XXI.2). Pyrrhus, in gratitude, released his Roman prisoners without ransom. The Romans, not wishing to receive any favors from him, released an equal number of prisoners whom they were holding.

Pyrrhus then proceeded north, where he and the Romans fought another battle in 279 B.C., at Asculum. Again Pyrrhus won, but again at a heavy cost, for the Romans could, without great difficulty, replace the six thousand soldiers whom they lost in the battle, while Pyrrhus would be hard pressed to replace the thirty-five hundred men he had lost. Thus the term *Pyrrhic victory* came into English: Pyrrhus won the battles, but his heavy losses turned his victories into defeats, for he could not recover from his victories. Cineas had already warned Pyrrhus that he was fighting with the Lernaean Hydra, the many-headed creature that grows two heads in the place of the one just cut off. When a friend congratulated Pyrrhus on his victory at Ausculum, Pyrrhus exclaimed, "If we beat the Romans in still another battle, we'll be completely destroyed."

Pyrrhus, disappointed in the progress of the war with Rome, and finding that the Italians subject to the Romans were not deserting them as he had thought they would, left for Sicily, where the Greek cities sought his help against Carthage. Pyrrhus won some battles in Sicily, but angered many with his despotic behavior, and returned to Tarentum in 276.

He faced the Roman armies again at the Battle of Beneventum, in 275. This time his elephants hurt him, by stampeding his own army. The Romans won the battle, and Pyrrhus speedily left Italy for Epirus, even leaving part of his army and one of his generals in Tarentum. That general and the Romans soon reached an understanding: He and his soldiers could leave unharmed if they gave Rome power over Tarentum. The general left, and the Romans made treaties with Tarentum and the other cities that had allied themselves with Pyrrhus.

Rome continued its battles against the other Italians who resisted Roman power. Within a few years, by 264 B.C., Rome was ruler of peninsular Italy.

HOW ROME MANAGED ITALY

Italy was by no means a unified country; the modern idea of a nation does not describe Italy in the third century B.C. In northern Italy were the Celtic-speaking tribes of Gauls, whose social organization (the only Gauls with political power were the priests and the knights) made them even more warlike than the Romans; their unsettled way of life was changing as they came increasingly under Roman domination. South of them, but north of Rome, were the Etruscans, a civilization that had long before declined; they spoke a non–Indo-European language and were completely alien to the Romans, although the Romans had learned a great deal from them. East of Rome, in the Apennine Mountains, were the Sabines and Aequi; to the southeast were the Samnites; close to Latium were the Volsci; and farther south were the Campanians. With the

Roman Italy. (Drawn by John Cotter)

exception of the Latins, Rome's non-Etruscan neighbors spoke Oscan and other languages distantly related to Latin. In southern Italy were the Greeks. The only people the Romans had much in common with were the Latins.

How did Rome manage to rule these diverse peoples? The situation was complicated, since various groups had different legal status with regard to the Roman government.

Civitas Romana (Roman citizenship). Roman citizens could vote, were expected to serve in the military, could marry other Roman citizens, had the right of engaging in commerce, and, after 167 B.C., did not have to pay direct taxes. Among the cherished rights enjoyed by Roman citizens was the *ius provocationis*, the right to appeal a capital sentence to the Comitia Centuriata. *Civitas Romana* extended to those Romans who were living in Roman colonies. After the Great Latin War, the Romans granted full Roman citizenship to some Latin towns, to bind them more closely to Rome.

Latinum nomen ("Latin rights," defined as *civitas sine suffragio*, "citizenship without the vote"). Holders of *Latinum nomen* enjoyed all the rights of Roman citizens except for the right to vote. Until 187 B.C. holders of Latin rights could obtain full Roman citizenship by moving to Rome; then the Latin towns asked the Romans to abolish that policy, as too many Latins were deserting their towns for that purpose. Citizenship without the vote was granted to many Latin towns after the Great Latin War, and also to the inhabitants of Latin colonies. Those holding *Latinum nomen* in a way enjoyed dual citizenship, for they had civil rights in Rome and in their home cities, which were largely autonomous; one important restriction on their city's government was foreign policy.

Civitas sine suffragio. To bind the special non-Latin Italian towns and cities closer to Rome, and to reward them for good and faithful service, the Romans started granting the inhabitants *civitas sine suffragio*. Towns and cities that received that grant were called *municipia*. To further ensure that the *municipia*, which were largely autonomous, would pursue policies advantageous to Rome, the Romans granted full Roman citizenship to the elected officials of the *municipia*.

Socii italici (Italian allies). The treatment of other cities, towns, and villages depended upon the provisions of the treaty that Rome made with them. The people inhabiting these places were called *socii italici* and included many peoples who either were persistently hostile to Rome, like the Gauls, Samnites, and Etruscans, or showed little inclination to adopt Roman ways, such as the Greeks. Being free noncitizens, they had no civil rights in Rome, such as the *ius provocationis*, although they enjoyed some basic rights through *ius gentium* (the law of nations), a type of international law. They could not marry Romans or Latins, or conduct business with Romans or Latins. They were liable to provide military service when the Romans called upon them for assistance, but they could not vote for or against their leader in war, or whether or not to go to war. Their towns were largely self-governing, with the important exception of foreign policy. They paid taxes to Rome.

Slaves and freedmen. Slaves were *res mancipi*, the property of their owner, and had no civil rights at all. They did enjoy a temporary respite from their servitude on the Saturnalia (a festival of Saturn, held on December 17), when they were allowed to speak their minds with impunity and to do as they liked. Inhabitants of Rome who were noncitizens, and who had never been slaves, were simply *liberi*, "free men." Ex-slaves were called *liberti*, "freedmen." Like slaves, they enjoyed no civil rights.

THE COLONIES

To keep subject peoples loyal, Rome and Latium established colonies throughout Italy. There were two types of colonies, Roman and Latin. The Roman colonies started out with two or three hundred families of Roman citizens; the Roman government sent out a dozen such groups to locations in Italy. Far more important are the Latin colonies. The Romans and Latins together sent out thirty of these, and they were much larger, containing eight to twenty thousand colonists. The colonies were established in areas that were hostile to Rome or slow to adopt Roman and Latin ways, such as Etruria, Gaul, and Samnium. The purpose was both to spread Latin and Roman civilization and, by a constant military presence, to keep the hostile peoples under control.

Roman citizens joining a Latin colony forfeited their Roman citizenship, but the sacrifice may have been worthwhile in view of the plentiful, fertile land they could farm in the colony. The joint Roman-Latin colonies were a huge success. The Latin language and civilization spread, and the military presence of the loyal colonists prevented rebellions among the subject peoples.

The Romans built excellent roads throughout the peninsula. The most important of these was the via Appia, the contract for which was awarded in 312 by then censor Appius Claudius Caecus. The roads facilitated communication with Rome, military transport, and also trade and social relations between the different peoples.

What Rome established in Italy was by no means a nation in the modern sense, for many Italians did not speak Latin or follow Latin and Roman customs; many could not vote for the leaders they would follow in war; many had no rights in Rome at all. Eventually all free-born Italians did gain full citizenship, but they had to become Latinized first, and then fight for some rights. Despite the appearance of tyranny in Rome's domination of the non-Latin Italians, Rome brought many good things to them, the greatest being peace. The centralized government of Rome eliminated the incessant warfare among the different peoples of Italy.

CHAPTER 13

The First Punic War

If in 270 B.C. a Roman had predicted that the city-state that had not yet even subdued all peninsular Italy would, a century later, rule not only peninsular Italy, but also the western Mediterranean, much of Spain, part of southern Gaul, parts of northern Africa, and part of Greece, he likely would have been thought crazy. The events of the next century catapulted Rome from a position of importance only in Italy to a position of world power. The wars with Carthage were the catalyst.

Carthage was a Phoenician (in Latin, the adjective is Punica) city, roughly in what is Tunis today. It was founded by people from Tyre (in Syria) in the eighth century B.C. as a trading post; according to myth the founder of Carthage was Dido, whose dying curse called upon her descendants to avenge the wrong done her by Aeneas (see chapter 2). Carthage grew and became the leading naval power and the chief trading center of the western Mediterranean. In the sixth century Carthage occupied Corsica and Sardinia, and after centuries of war with the Greeks of Sicily, it came to control the western half of that island, while the Greeks maintained control of the eastern half with its rich and powerful city of Syracuse. Rome and Carthage had signed treaties in 508 and 348, and were not on hostile terms with each other until 264 B.C.

The problems began in Sicily. Some mercenaries from Campania, who had been employed by the ruler of Syracuse, upon his death in 289 took control of the Sicilian town Messana, which lay not far from Syracuse and just across the straits from the toe of Italy. The mercenaries, who called themselves Mamertines (after Mamers, the Oscan form of the name Mars), killed many of Messana's citizens and stole their property. Hiero, the general of the Syracusan army, then defeated the renegade mercenaries in battle, for which victory he was named king of Syracuse; the mercenaries then sent embassies to Carthage and Rome, to ask for help. While the Romans debated the pros and cons of sending help, Carthage sent a garrison into the city.

The Romans were weary after the war with Pyrrhus, but feared that the Carthaginians, who already controlled much of Spain, Corsica, and Sardinia, would use Sicily as a base for attacking Italy: Messana was separated from the Italian mainland by the Strait of Messina, which is only a few miles wide. The renegade mercenaries hardly deserved help: Years earlier a Roman garrison had taken over Rhegium, the town that it was supposed to guard, and had stolen citizens' property; the Romans conquered their own garrison and executed the guilty soldiers (fellow Romans and Latins) to restore Rome's good reputation. But Rome's fear of Carthage prevailed. The Romans sent the consul Appius Claudius Caudex to help the Mamertines keep the Carthaginians out of Messana.

When Claudius arrived in Sicily he found that the situation had changed. The Mamertines had managed to trick the Carthaginian garrison into leaving the city (intolerant of failure, the Carthaginians later crucified the commander for cowardice), and Messana was now besieged by both King Hiero and the Carthaginians, who had made a treaty to drive the Mamertines out of Sicily. Claudius quickly conquered the army of Syracuse, prompting Hiero to withdraw from the conflict; he soon became a steadfast ally of Rome. Then Claudius defeated the Carthaginian army. The Carthaginians responded by sending an army of fifty thousand to Agrigentum in southwest Sicily, which they planned to establish as a base for subduing all of Sicily. Claudius sped across Sicily and defeated the Carthaginians at Agrigentum; then the Romans got the idea of conquering all Sicily. To achieve that end, however, they had to build a navy.

The Romans had no experience in building warships; they had had to depend upon seafaring Italians even to convey their troops from Italy to Sicily. While transporting their troops across the straits, the Romans encountered a bit of luck: One of the Carthaginian ships, in its eagerness to overtake the Roman transports, ran aground, and the Romans quickly captured the ship and its crew. The Romans then used this ship as a model for building their first navy, which consisted of a hundred quinqueremes and twenty triremes (scholars dispute whether the numbers *quinque,* "five," and *tri,* "three," referred to the number of men per oar or the number of banks of oars). The Romans then had to train their rowers to row with the call of the *keleustes,* the "order giver."

THE RAVEN

After one disastrous naval battle, in which they lost not only seventeen ships but also the ships' commander, the Romans quickly recognized their problems at sea. In ancient naval battles the goal was to ram and sink the enemy ship; the Roman ships, however, were clumsy and heavy in comparison to the light and quick Carthaginian vessels, and the Roman crews and commanders were inexperienced. It would be a very long time before the Roman navy would be able to win a traditional naval battle, especially against Carthage and its powerful navy.

Consequently, the Romans changed the rules of combat. On the prow of their ships they built something they called a raven. The raven consisted of three parts: a pole over 7 meters high, secured to the prow of the ship, with a pulley at the top; a long gangway, more than 1 meter wide and projecting from the base of the pole more than 7 meters off the prow; and a rope, connecting the gangway to the pulley. When an enemy vessel tried to ram a Roman ship, the sailors would pull the gangway up by means of the pulley and swing it to project over the enemy ship; then they would let it drop. A heavy spike on the end of the gangway would secure it to the deck of the enemy ship, allowing heavily armed Roman soldiers to board and defeat the enemy sailors, who certainly were not expecting hand-to-hand combat on board. Armed with the raven, the Romans would be a match for the excellent Carthaginian navy.

The Romans had their first opportunity to use the navy in 260 B.C. One of the consuls that year, Gaius Duilius, sailed to Mylae on the northeastern tip of Sicily, after hearing that the Carthaginian navy was burning and pillaging the area. The Carthaginians, seeing the Roman fleet, had nothing but contempt for the upstart Romans, and immediately attacked without even getting into battle formation. They were taken by surprise when the Romans' ships latched onto theirs and the sea battle turned into hand-to-hand combat on board their ships. Unprepared for that type of battle, the Carthaginians lost fifty ships and almost lost their commander as well.

While the Romans, receiving aid from Hiero, fought to drive the Carthaginians from Sicily, the consul M. Atilius Regulus and his army sailed to Africa, to invade Carthaginian territory. At the Battle of Ecnomus, off the African coast, in 256, the Carthaginian navy failed to prevent Regulus and his army from landing on African soil. The Romans then began to overrun the African countryside. After various losses, Carthage asked Regulus for peace, but considering his terms too harsh, they resumed fighting.

Desperate, the Carthaginians called in a Spartan mercenary, Xanthippus, to help them against the Romans. He took control of the army, revived the soldiers' morale and confidence, and then crushed the Roman army in Africa, even capturing the consul Regulus. The Carthaginians again sought peace from the Romans, and sent Regulus to Rome to persuade the Romans to accept their peace proposal; they made him swear to return to Carthage if he failed to secure either peace or an exchange of prisoners.

While the Senate was deliberating the Carthaginians' proposal for peace, Regulus remained quiet, until the Carthaginians who had escorted him to Rome granted him permission to speak. "Senators," he said, "I am one of you, even if I should be captured ten thousand times. My body belongs to the Carthaginians, but my spirit belongs to you. . . . I am of the opinion that making peace will not help you in any way at all."

He then explained to the Senate why he thought it in Rome's best interests to reject the proposal, and added, "I am well aware of the destruction that plainly lies before me, since they will certainly learn what advice I have given. Yet I put that which is beneficial to the state before my own safety" (Zonaras VIII.15).

The Senate tried to make peace simply to protect Regulus, since they knew that upon his return to Carthage he would be tortured and killed for convincing them to reject the peace proposals.

Regulus then falsely claimed that he had taken poison and would die soon; consequently, the Senate rejected the proposal and made no trade of prisoners. But Regulus, true to his oath, returned to Carthage, where he was tortured and killed.

The war continued, with the Romans suffering staggering losses in their navy through the inexperience of the commanders. For example, the Romans had just launched a new fleet of 200 ships, which promptly defeated the Carthaginian fleet at Hermaeum; the Roman fleet could not conquer the weather, however, and while returning to its base in Sicily encountered a storm that destroyed as many as 130 of those new ships. So the Romans built 220 more ships. Another storm destroyed 150 more Roman ships. The Carthaginian commanders knew how to avoid such storms. The Romans also lost 93 ships at Drepana when the commander, P. Claudius Pulcher, ignored the bad omen given by the sacred chickens' refusal to eat their food. In frustration, he flung the birds into the harbor, saying, "Since they don't want to eat, let 'em drink!" and attacked the Carthaginian fleet. Of course, he lost the battle. After many such losses, the Romans gave up on their navy—at least temporarily—and concentrated on the land war in Sicily.

On land the Romans were far superior to the Carthaginian forces. They had driven the Carthaginians from all Sicily except for Lilybaeum and Drepana, on the western side of the island. The Romans realized that they needed a navy once again, for the Carthaginians were sending reinforcements and supplies by sea to their soldiers in those two cities, who were trying to take another town. But the Roman treasury was empty; building another fleet seemed impossible until the Roman citizens voluntarily contributed money for a new fleet of two hundred ships. They appointed Gaius Lutatius Catulus commander of the new navy. Everyday he drilled his crews in preparation for the naval battle that the Romans simply had to win to bring the war to an end.

The new fleet surprised the Carthaginians, who did not expect the Romans to try the sea again. At the Aegates Islands, off the western coast of Sicily, the new Roman fleet defeated the Carthaginian fleet, which was trying to bring supplies to its soldiers in Sicily. The consuls then moved to besiege Lilybaeum; Carthage was broken, and sued for peace. A settlement was reached in 241 B.C.

The terms of the treaty had Carthage abandon Sicily and pay a war indemnity. The Romans later went one step further and took Corsica and Sardinia, a betrayal of trust that enraged the Carthaginians, leaving them bitter and hateful of the Romans. That hatred and bitterness erupted in another terrible war with Carthage twenty years later.

Whatever peace Rome saw did not last long. First, pirates from Illyricum were causing problems for Italian merchants in the Adriatic Sea. The Romans sent ambassadors to ask Teuta, the Illyrian queen, to stop the piracy, but she gave a noncommittal response. Unfortunately, one ambassador answered her rather bluntly, which prompted her to have him murdered. After the murder, the previous piracy, and the problems that the Illyrians were causing for the Italian merchants and nearby Greek cities and islands, the Romans sent an army against the pirates in 229 B.C. and seized control of the pirate islands. Rome's power in the Adriatic Sea now included the islands of Pharos and Corcyra, and the cities of Apollonia and Dyrrhachium. (The Greek name for Dyrrhachium was Epidamnus, a name the Romans avoided using, as it was a bad omen: *epi* in Greek means "to, toward" and *damn-* in Latin means "destruction.")

Second, the Gauls in northern Italy, south of the Alps, were a constant source of trouble for the Romans. After losing one battle with the Gauls, the Romans defeated them at Telamon, in Etruria, in 225 B.C. To prevent the Gauls from troubling Italy again, the Romans decided to conquer northern Italy. In 224 they subdued Transpadane Gaul, and advanced to the Alps. To safeguard their conquests, they built the via Flaminia, a road to the north, and established colonies along the Po River (in Latin, Padus), to check the Gauls in the future.

During one of those battles, M. Claudius Marcellus, the consul of 222, defeated Viridomarus, leader of a Gallic tribe, in hand-to-hand combat, and thus became eligible to offer *spolia opima*. Only two Roman generals, Romulus and A. Cornelius Cossus, had accomplished that before Marcellus, and nobody accomplished it after him.

CHAPTER 14

The Second Punic War

After the end of the First Punic War, the Carthaginians recovered from their losses in Sicily, Corsica, and Sardinia by extending their power in Spain. Suspicious of the Carthaginians' reasons for fighting in Spain, the Romans made a treaty with them, by which Carthage would not advance its power beyond the Ebro River in Spain. Rome also promised help to the people of the Spanish town Saguntum, which lay on the Carthaginians' side of the Ebro, if the Carthaginians attacked them.

In 221 B.C. Hasdrubal, the general of the Carthaginian army, died and his brother-in-law Hannibal succeeded him. Hannibal's father Hamilcar had been a general in the first war with Rome and was very bitter about Rome's victory and double-dealing over Corsica and Sardinia. Hannibal inherited the hatred that his country and father felt for Rome.

"They say that when he was almost nine years old, Hannibal, seeing his father Hamilcar giving a sacrifice before taking his army to Spain, tried, like a child, to sweet-talk his father into taking him along; after being taken to the altar, Hannibal touched the sacred objects there and was made to swear an oath that he would be an enemy of the Roman people as soon as he could" (Livy XXI.1.4). Hannibal did not disappoint his father.

Hannibal continued Carthage's conquests in Spain, moving ever closer to Saguntum and the Ebro River. Finally, in 219 he attacked Saguntum itself. The Roman Senate protested to the Carthaginian government, but the Carthaginian nobles supported their general, and the Senate's inaction let Hannibal conquer and enslave the town. Before the town was stormed, many of the townspeople built a huge fire and threw their riches in it, rather than let Carthage have them; then they threw themselves into the fire. While his soldiers were subduing the town, Hannibal ordered them to kill all Saguntine men of military age. He gained an enormous amount of loot from the city, in spite of the citizens' sacrifices.

The Senate sent another embassy to Carthage to ascertain whether or not the city still supported its general. When the Carthaginians maintained that Hannibal had acted legally and with their support, the Roman ambassador, Q. Fabius, gathered together the folds of the part of the toga covering his chest, so that they appeared to contain something, and said, "Here we offer you peace or war. Take which you will."

"You can give whichever you want!" shouted the Carthaginian senate. Fabius let the folds of his toga drop and said that he brought war. The Carthaginians roared, "We accept! You can be sure that we'll fight the war as courageously as we declared it!" (Livy XXI.18.13).

HANNIBAL CROSSES THE ALPS

With his army of perhaps fifty thousand men, which had bonded into a tight and cohesive force through the many years of fighting in Spain, Hannibal seized the initiative and marched on Italy. An advance Roman force under P. Cornelius Scipio sailed to Massilia (modern Marseille), in southern Gaul, to await Hannibal, but Hannibal fooled the Romans by moving much more quickly than they expected. When Scipio arrived at Massilia, Hannibal had passed by three days earlier and was already approaching the Alps. Scipio then returned to Italy to meet Hannibal there. Then Hannibal fooled the Romans again: They expected him to cross the Alps in the easy places, close to the sea, but he headed toward the part of the Alps closer to central Gaul. He lost some soldiers and many elephants in his legendary crossing of the Alps, but he achieved his goal: He surprised the Romans, who had not had enough time to prepare for the upcoming war. Before him lay an open path into Italy.

BATTLE AT THE TREBIA

The Romans lost a minor engagement to Hannibal in 218 B.C. at the Ticinus River, where the consul Scipio, wounded and surrounded by enemy cavalry, was saved by his seventeen-year-old son. Seeing his father in danger, the young Scipio ran away from the soldiers who had been assigned to protect him, and rescued his father. This boy, P. Cornelius Scipio, later earned the honorary title Africanus for his conquests.

Later that year the Romans faced Hannibal at the river Trebia. Here the weakness of the Roman system of consuls showed itself, for one consul, Scipio, was still wounded and did not wish to have a battle, but the other consul, Sempronius, urged him to go ahead and engage with the Carthaginian forces, which had been augmented by Gauls. Hannibal, knowing of the Romans' divided command and of the proud and passionate personality of Sempronius, worked to lay a trap for the Romans.

A stream separated the two armies. The night before the battle, Hannibal hid his brother Mago, with a thousand cavalry and another thousand of his toughest foot soldiers, behind the bushes and shrubs of the stream. At dawn he ordered his Numidian cavalry to lure the Romans to battle with an attack, but then to quickly withdraw. At dawn the Numidian cavalry attacked the Roman camp and quickly retreated. The Romans, without eating breakfast, surprised by the attack, hurried out into the December cold to pursue the attackers. In their pursuit they crossed the frigid, swollen waters of the stream, so deep it reached their necks. Hannibal's soldiers, meanwhile, sat in front of their campfires, leisurely eating a hot breakfast and rubbing themselves down with warm oil.

The two sides—one cold, hungry, wet, and tired, and the other warm, rested, and ready to fight—met for battle. Hannibal's elephants immediately scared off the Roman cavalry; when the Romans found a way to defend themselves from the elephants, Hannibal had the elephants attack Rome's Gallic auxiliaries, who fled at the elephants' attack. The Romans, already suffering from cold, hunger, and exhaustion, and worn down by the tough Carthaginian troops, then were attacked in the rear by Mago and the troops that had been hiding behind the bushes; the Romans were surrounded.

Part of the Roman army fought its way through the Carthaginian center, only to find itself trapped by the river and unable to return to camp. Those who hesitated to jump in and swim to the camp were cut down by the Numidian cavalry, while those who braved the river risked death by drowning or exposure. Hannibal's victory was complete and devastating. The Romans lost approximately thirty thousand men.

TRASIMENE: "PUGNA MAGNA VICTI SUMUS"

In the next year Hannibal did not relax after his stunning victory. He learned that the Roman consul Flaminius had arrived at Arretium, in Etruria; instead of taking a long but easy path to Arretium, Hannibal chose to travel through swamps. For four days he and his men struggled through the swamps, able to snatch only a few moments of sleep on the heaps of dead pack animals. Hannibal himself, riding his last surviving elephant, came down with an eye infection and lost sight in that eye. Nonetheless his sudden arrival surprised the Romans, and he was able to seize more strategic ground. After a few days' rest, his troops then ravaged the countryside, in full view of the Romans, to anger Flaminius and his troops. Despite his officers' advice that he should wait for the other consul and his army, Flaminius ordered his troops to prepare for a battle with Hannibal. All the omens for battle were bad: When Flaminius jumped onto his horse, it threw him from the saddle, and the standards could not be pulled from the ground—they would not budge.

Hannibal then marched into an area by Lake Trasimene. On one side was the lake, and on the other side were the mountains, with only a small path for an exit. Along that small path the Romans followed Hannibal, not knowing that the night before he had hidden some troops in the mountains north of the lake, and that he had stationed his cavalry to block the path once the Romans had come into the trap. The Romans blindly followed him.

The Carthaginians suddenly swarmed down from the hills, catching the Romans unprepared for battle. The Roman army, which was not able even to see where the enemy was coming from, because of the mist rising from the lake, disintegrated into chaos. More than fifteen thousand Romans—not counting allies— were killed in the battle, including the consul Flaminius. Again, Hannibal had won a smashing victory. Nor was this the last of his exploits: The worst was still to come.

Q. FABIUS MAXIMUS CUNCTATOR: "UNUS HOMO NOBIS CUNCTANDO RESTITUIT REM"

"In Rome, at the first news of the disaster [at Trasimene], the people in terror and panic rushed into the Forum. Mothers wandering through the streets asked those passing by what unexpected disaster had been visited upon Rome, or what the fate of the army was. When a mob, like a packed assembly, summoned the magistrates, the praetor M. Pomponius, just a little before sunset, said only this: 'We have been conquered in a great battle'" ("'Pugna magna victi sumus'"; Livy XXII.7.6–8).

The situation in Rome was clearly desperate enough to warrant appointing a dictator. After some difficulties—only a consul could do so, but one consul was dead and the other was away from Rome—the Senate appointed as dictator Q. Fabius Maximus (later called Cunctator, from the verb *cunctor*, "to delay").

Seeing that Hannibal had defeated the Romans in two set battles, Fabius realized that the wiser approach would be not to engage Hannibal in a battle; instead, the Romans would follow him, harassing his troops with guerrilla-type warfare, working to keep the Italian allies loyal, and trying to isolate Hannibal from supplies and reinforcements. This policy of attrition was successful, for Hannibal could inflict no more losses upon the Romans, while the Romans simply attacked Hannibal's men as they sought water, firewood, and food for their horses (with four thousand cavalry, Hannibal needed a lot of fodder for the horses). Hannibal quickly understood Fabius' intention, and tried to lure him into a trap, but Fabius was too wary and cautious. His characteristic caution gave rise to an adjective in English, *Fabian*, meaning "cautious, dilatory."

At one point, Hannibal was penned in a valley by the Romans, who controlled the surrounding mountain passes. Hannibal could not get provisions for his army and cavalry, while the Roman armies had easy access to food and water. Nor could Hannibal fight his way out of the predicament, for the Romans had the superior position. So the wily Hannibal devised still another brilliant plan to extricate himself:

Pieces of dry wood, collected from the fields all around, and bundles of dry twigs and brushwood were tied onto the horns of the many cattle that he had among the loot taken from the countryside. After that had been done to nearly two thousand cattle, Hasdrubal [one of Hannibal's officers] was assigned the task of setting the cattle's horns on fire that night and driving them toward the mountains and most of all (if he could) above the passes held by the enemy.

They broke camp in silence after nightfall. The cattle were driven some distance in front of the standards. When they arrived at the foot of the mountains and narrow passes, the signal was immediately given to light the cattle's horns and to drive them toward the mountains. The beasts' fear of the flames burning on their own heads, and the heat, by now reaching the skin and nerves, drove the cattle on in a frenzy, as if they had been whipped.

Their sudden scattering made the forest and mountains appear as if they had been set on fire, and the brushwood all around was blazing. The desperate shaking of their heads fanned the flames, giving forth the appearance of men scattering everywhere. When the men who had been stationed to block the passes saw the fires in the peaks of the mountains and above themselves, they concluded that they were surrounded, and left their posts. (Livy XXII.16.7–XXII.17.4)

In the confusion, Hannibal and his men managed to escape from the valley.

Fabius, despite the wisdom of his policy, was becoming unpopular among his countrymen. His master of the horse, Minucius, urged him to fight a battle with Hannibal and maligned Fabius' strategy in public and in private. When Fabius had to return to Rome briefly, to attend to a religious matter, Minucius won a minor engagement with Hannibal and became even more self-assured. His criticism of Fabius intensified. The people of Rome, moreover, feeling more and more confident because Rome had suffered no recent catastrophes, urged the Senate to have the troops fight a set battle with Hannibal and his army. Finally, the Senate split the command between Fabius and Minucius. When the two commanders were discussing how they would manage one army, Fabius insisted that they split the army and that each be in full command of his half, rather than alternating days of command over the whole army. Thus, Fabius figured, Minucius would destroy only half the army if he made a mistake. The two split the army and cavalry, and even constructed different camps.

Fabius was right. Minucius was promptly led into a trap by Hannibal. Fabius, seeing Minucius' army in great danger of being destroyed, rescued the errant commander and his troops, and inflicted great losses upon Hannibal's forces. ("The cloud," Hannibal is reported to have said after the battle, "which has been accustomed to resting among the mountain peaks, has produced a gale and a terrific storm.") After the battle, Minucius returned to Fabius' camp, called him *pater*, and said, "Dictator, I owe my existence to my parents, to whom I just compared you by calling you father, but to you I owe my safety and the safety of all these men here. Therefore I now renounce the people's decision, which has brought me more distress than honor, and renounce my position, and return under your power and authority, and restore these standards and legions to you, so that it may be beneficial to these armies of yours and to me, the one who was saved, and to you, the one who saved" (Livy XXII.30.3–5).

The two men shook hands, and Fabius graciously allowed Minucius to remain his master of the horse. News of the event was brought to Rome, and Fabius' reputation rose higher than ever. Years later in his *Annales*, a poetical treatment of Roman history, the poet Ennius wrote of Fabius, "unus homo nobis cunctando restituit rem" (one man saved the state for us, by waiting).

When Fabius' dictatorship lapsed, the Romans elected as consuls L. Aemilius Paullus and G. Terentius Varro. Varro swore that he would beat Hannibal and his army on the first day that he saw them. His colleague, Paullus, preferred Fabian tactics. Since the two could not agree on strategy, they alternated their days of command.

DISASTER AT CANNAE

In 216 B.C. Hannibal took up a position near the village of Cannae. The Romans had amassed an army of more than fifty thousand men, hoping to smother Hannibal's army of forty thousand. The Romans, now wary, made sure that there was no place in which Hannibal could conceal troops; nonetheless, Hannibal had other plans for defeating the Romans. On his day of command Varro led the army out to battle, without even consulting Paullus.

Hannibal placed the bulwark of his troops, his veteran Africans, in the rear center of his army and kept his first lines thin. Once the Romans had cut their way through Hannibal's thin front center, Hannibal's flanks closed in on the Romans. Now the tired Romans were not only surrounded but also facing Hannibal's toughest veterans, fresh from sitting out the morning's battle. The Romans were again crushed by Hannibal, losing more than forty-five thousand men, including the consul Paullus, who had advised against a battle with Hannibal, and the two consuls of the previous year. Varro survived; when he returned to Rome from the disaster at Cannae, throngs of citizens came out to meet him, and despite his responsibility for the disaster, they thanked him because "he had not lost hope for the republic."

Rome was in a panic. Not only had the Romans lost a hundred thousand men in the recent battles, but even some Italian allies were deserting Rome: Capua, a city not much inferior to Rome in wealth and population, was one Italian city that revolted. The Gauls in the north were taking Hannibal's side. Many of the Greeks in the south, including those of Tarentum, revolted. The Samnites sided with Hannibal. Sicily and its chief city Syracuse, ruled now by Hiero's grandson, also joined Hannibal. Nonetheless, most of Rome's Italian allies remained loyal, even though its power in Italy seemed to be collapsing. So desperate were the Romans that they performed a human sacrifice, killing two Gauls and two Greeks. Two Vestal Virgins were found to have broken their oaths of chastity and were punished with being buried alive; the man involved in the scandal turned out to be a minor official in the college of priests. He was beaten to death by the *pontifex maximus* in a public assembly. Roman women were sweeping the pavements of the temples with their hair. The Romans declared a Ver Sacrum, or Sacred Spring, in which all first fruits of the season were dedicated to the gods. After consulting the Sibylline books, they instituted games in honor of Apollo. They dedicated to Jupiter a golden sculpture of a thunderbolt, weighing fifty pounds. To put an end to these expressions of panic, the consuls decided that women should be forbidden to appear out of doors, family mourning should be checked, and silence should be imposed everywhere. The government of Rome then bought eight thousand slaves from their owners and armed them; later, the Romans even opened their jails, with offers of freedom and forgiveness for the criminals and debtors, if they would join the army.

Despite the emergency in Rome, the Romans maintained their courage and discipline. The Senate decided not to pay the ransom for those soldiers held by Hannibal after Cannae, and even forbade the soldier's families to pay. Hannibal sent a group of Roman prisoners to beg the Senate to pay the ransom of the thousands of Romans whom he was holding prisoner; before letting them leave, he made them swear that they would return to his camp. One of the prisoners, while leaving Hannibal's camp, claimed that he had forgotten something in the camp and returned to get it; then he went to Rome to address the Senate. After addressing the Senate, he did not return to Hannibal's camp with the others, for he had already fulfilled his obligation of returning to the camp. When the Senate learned of his deceit, it had him arrested and taken in chains to Hannibal. Those soldiers who managed to escape Cannae with their lives were punished for bad soldiering by being sent to Sicily, where they spent most of the war, begging for an opportunity to redeem themselves and regain their honor.

Many stories of the Romans' courage and character explain how they were able to survive the war and eventually to conquer Hannibal. For example, the former dictator Q. Fabius Maximus was overseeing the election of new consuls for the year 214; the first tribe voted for Marcus Aemilius Regillus and Titus Otacilius Crassus, the latter of whom was the husband of Fabius' niece. Fabius objected to both decisions and asked the tribe to reconsider:

Regillus was a priest and could not leave the city, while Otacilius had not seen enough action to be an excellent general.

"Citizens," Fabius said, "I urgently advise you to elect consuls today in the same spirit that you would if *you* were the ones standing in battle formation, armed and ready for battle: under whose leadership and control would *you* want to fight? Let your sons take their oaths to the same men you would want to, let them gather at those men's orders, and let them fight under such men's care and oversight. Remembering Lake Trasimene and Cannae is painful, but provides useful lessons for avoiding similar catastrophes in the future." (Livy XXIV.8.18–20)

The voters reconsidered their decision and elected as consuls Fabius himself (for the fourth time) and Marcus Marcellus (for the third time), both of whom had ample experience in battle. Later, in 210, Manlius Torquatus, although elected to the consulship, refused the honor because his eyes were too weak, and ordered the tribe to vote again.

Another example of the Romans' courage and character is the consuls' edict in 210 for citizens to pay more money for oarsmen in the fleet. The people were already heavily taxed to pay for the war, and many had little or no income, either because their farms had been destroyed by Hannibal's foragers or because the men were serving in the army. The people protested. The consul Laevinus summoned the Senate and said, "Just as it is necessary that the magistrates lead the Senate and the Senate lead the people, because we are more honorable, so it is necessary that there be a leader for enduring all things harsh and bitter. If you wish to impose some order on a person lower in rank, if you first impose it on yourself and your kin, you will have other people obeying you more readily" (Livy XXVI.36.1–3). He adjourned the Senate; the senators went home and then returned, bringing their gold, silver, and bronze. The knights learned of the senators' contributions and brought their wealth, too; and last, the common people likewise brought in theirs. The government had ample money for the ships' crews and was able to repay that loan from the citizens a few years later.

THE SCIPIOS IN SPAIN

The Romans at this time were also fighting in Spain, to deprive Hannibal of supplies and reinforcements coming from Spain and to prevent the great wealth of Spain—mostly in metals—from falling into Carthaginian hands. The two Roman generals there, Gn. Cornelius Scipio and his brother P. Cornelius Scipio, had made use of arms and diplomacy to slowly detach the Spanish people from loyalty to Carthage. Unfortunately both Scipios were defeated and killed in two separate battles in 211. The Spanish then returned to supporting Carthage. The Romans elected the son of Gnaeus, Publius Cornelius Scipio (who as a boy had saved his father's life at Ticinus), to succeed the two dead generals, although he was only twenty-four years old. Publius Cornelius Scipio surpassed his relatives in fame and accomplishments.

After arriving in Spain in 210, Scipio did not dally. He immediately attacked and sacked the strongly fortified and wealthy city of New Carthage, the capital of Carthaginian Spain. He won an immense amount of loot that the Carthaginians had stored there and by his diplomacy won some allies as well: He let the citizens of New Carthage go free, retain their property, and live in their city. An example of his diplomacy involves a beautiful young woman whom his soldiers brought to him, perhaps so she could be his concubine; Scipio asked her her name, and where she was from. She told him that she was engaged to Allucius, the chief of a nearby tribe. Scipio sent for her family and fiancé; he handed the young woman over to her family unharmed, refused the ransom that they offered, and gave her and her fiancé the gift (a weight of solid gold) that her parents had begged him to take. The young man, in gratitude, returned to Scipio a few days later, accompanied by fourteen hundred cavalry, to serve in Scipio's army. As another example, Scipio learned that among the African prisoners from New Carthage was a boy of royal blood. The boy, who had been raised by his grandfather, had joined the cavalry to fight against the Romans, against the orders of his uncle Masinissa. Scipio gave the boy many gifts— among them a gold ring—and an armed guard to escort him as far as he needed to go. Masinissa was the ousted king of the Numidians, whose help was invaluable to Scipio in later battles.

One battle that Scipio won deserves notice because it gave rise to an important word in Latin. The story goes that after defeating the Carthaginians in one battle, Scipio set free ten thousand Spaniards whom he had taken captive. To honor Scipio and show their respect and gratitude, the Spaniards began calling him *rex* (king); Scipio knew that under no circumstances could he allow himself to be called king (recall that the early Romans had driven out their kings to establish the republic), yet he wanted the peoples he defeated to have some term of respect and honor for him. He thanked them for the honor, but asked them to call him *imperator* instead; from then on, *imperator* became the word used to honor victorious generals, and an army would not honor its general (*dux*) with the title *imperator* (conquering general) until he had won a major battle.

ROME REGAINS MOMENTUM: "VICTORIA UTI NESCIS"

The Romans had a little bit of luck in the middle of all the catastrophes. When Hannibal's friends were congratulating him at Cannae, Maharbal, Hannibal's commander of cavalry, urged him to attack Rome immediately. He said, "Hannibal, so you may understand the significance of this battle, let me tell you this: on the fifth day, you'll be enjoying a victory feast on the Capitol. Come after me; I'll go first with the cavalry, so that I will arrive before they even know that I'm coming" (Livy XXII.51.2).

Hannibal replied that he needed some time to think about it. "Hannibal, you know how to win a battle, but you don't know how to use your victory [victoria uti nescis]," Maharbal replied. Hannibal missed his great opportunity; the Romans later believed that his indecision saved Rome.

By dogged persistence and unflinching courage the Romans regained the upper hand. Hannibal was in hostile territory, which made it difficult for him to get supplies for his army and cavalry. The Italians were not deserting from the Romans to his side as he thought they would. He could not besiege Rome, for he needed always to be moving, simply to secure food and supplies for his soldiers and horses, and in any case he lacked siege equipment. He was losing men through many small battles with the Romans and

from the ravages of disease and hunger. He and his troops spent
the winter of 216 B.C. in Capua, where they lost their fighting edge
and discipline; so changed was Hannibal's army after the winter
spent in that decadent city that one Roman general, Marcellus,
called Capua "Hannibal's Cannae." (Imagine an army bivouacked
in the French Quarter of New Orleans for the winter. How sharp
would the soldiers be, come March?) Eventually Rome regained
Capua, Tarentum, and Sicily. When Hannibal at last marched to
the gates of Rome and waited for the battle to begin, he learned
through a prisoner that the land on which he had pitched camp
was sold that day in Rome, with no reduction in price.

The Romans regained the momentum partly through the successes of their general M. Claudius Marcellus (the winner of the
spolia opima; see chapter 13). He had the caution of Fabius, but
combined with a greater boldness; the Romans called Fabius the
Shield of Rome, but to Marcellus they gave the nickname Sword of
Rome. After Capua revolted to Hannibal's side, Marcellus prevented
Hannibal from attacking another large Campanian city, Nola.

In 214, when Sicily revolted from Rome, Marcellus was sent to
reconquer the island. He attacked Syracuse by land and sea, but
was foiled by its most brilliant citizen, the famous geometrician
Archimedes. It was Archimedes who figured out the principle of
the lever, saying, "Give me a place on which to stand, and I will
move the Earth." He also discovered the principle of displacement
of water, which caused him to exclaim, "Eureka!" (I have found it!).
Archimedes used his great knowledge to build various engines to
defend his city. Some of his devices threw quantities of rocks at the
Roman army, killing soldiers and throwing the army into
confusion. Another device was a huge beam, hanging out from the
city walls over the sea, where the Roman navy was attacking. Some
beams dropped great weights on the Roman ships, sinking them,
while others, with iron claws at the end, simply picked up the
Roman ships and hauled them out of the water; the beam then
either released the suspended ship, allowing it to fall into the water,
or else was swung around, dashing the ship against the rocks.

Marcellus was forced simply to starve Syracuse into giving up.
While besieging Syracuse, he also reconquered the rest of the
island. He finally took Syracuse in 211. Archimedes was killed by

a Roman soldier; according to the story, the soldier commanded Archimedes to accompany him to Marcellus, but Archimedes refused to move until he had finished the problem he was working on. Enraged, the soldier killed him.

After reconquering Sicily, Marcellus returned to Italy, and from 210 to 208 he kept Hannibal's activities under control. Hannibal tried many times to lure Marcellus into a trap, but Marcellus was his match in wits. Under Marcellus' leadership the Roman army inflicted many small losses on Hannibal, killing thousands of his soldiers and reestablishing morale in the Roman army. Marcellus was killed in 208 B.C., while on reconnaisance.

In Spain too the pendulum had swung to the Romans' side. Scipio had been so successful in conquering Spain for Rome that the Carthaginian government abandoned its hope of a Carthaginian empire in Spain and ordered Hasdrubal, Hannibal's brother who led the Carthaginian forces in Spain, to take his armies to Hannibal in Italy. Hasdrubal started his march.

THE BATTLE AT METAURUS

The Romans and the Italians were alarmed by the news that Hasdrubal was approaching Italy; his army was as large as Hannibal's, and his own reputation only slightly less than his brother's. One consul, Marcus Livius, had been assigned to northern Italy to intercept Hasdrubal; the other consul, G. Claudius Nero, had been assigned to southern Italy to check Hannibal's progress. After an engagement with Hannibal's troops, in which the Romans inflicted heavy losses upon the Carthaginians, Nero decided to leave half of his army with a praetor to guard Hannibal, while he with the other half would secretly slip away at night to lend help to Livius and his troops. He and his soldiers then marched 400 kilometers in seven days, to join Livius in the north. Both Carthaginians had been fooled: Hannibal thought an entire consular army was still dogging him, and since Livius and Nero shared the same camp, Hasdrubal did not know—until it was too late—that the Roman forces facing him had been augmented by six thousand soldiers.

The battle at the river Metaurus, in 207, avenged Cannae for the Romans. Hasdrubal was killed in the battle, his army annihilated, and an immense amount of gold and silver taken; Hannibal would not receive reinforcements now. The Roman populace was hysterical with joy, for the Romans had won their first major engagement against the Carthaginians in Italy; every shrine and temple in the city was garlanded with flowers and wreaths. Nero returned to his army in southern Italy and had Hasdrubal's head thrown in front of the outposts of Hannibal's camp, to be taken to Hannibal.

SCIPIO CARRIES THE WAR TO AFRICA

While briefing the Senate on affairs in Spain, Scipio brought up the idea of invading Africa; his reasons were, first, to punish the Africans and cause them to suffer, for Italy had been the battleground long enough; second, and more important, to force the Carthaginians to recall Hannibal to Africa to defend Carthage. The wisdom of his proposal was not apparent to all the senators; it was vigorously opposed by Q. Fabius Maximus, who argued that Scipio and the soldiers should stay in Italy to eliminate the real and present danger of Hannibal.

In spite of opposition, Scipio received the Senate's grudging approval, but he was not given permission to enlist new soldiers, and the Senate supplied him with only thirty-five warships for his expedition. Scipio sought volunteers and contributions of war materials, and the Italians responded: Seven thousand soldiers immediately volunteered, eagerly joined by the twelve thousand survivors of Cannae, who were still desperate for an opportunity to regain their honor, and more allies joined them as well. Contributions of various war materials—iron, cloth for sails, timber for ships, wheat—poured in. When Scipio landed in Africa the next year, he was joined by Masinissa (Rome's ally from Numidia), and the army numbered approximately thirty-five thousand soldiers. Scipio and Masinissa ravaged the countryside.

Hasdrubal (not Hannibal's brother, who had been killed) and his ally Syphax from Numidia encamped a few miles from the Romans. Scipio, using Hannibal-like tactics, first played a deadly trick on Syphax: Scipio had sent some centurions, disguised as slaves, along with his envoys in the customary attempts at negotiating peace before a battle; Scipio learned from his spies that the buildings in Syphax' camp were made of reeds. This gave Scipio an idea, and he took his officers aside, explained the plan, and made it clear that everything had to go just right.

Laelius, Scipio's good friend and lieutenant, went forth first that night, and soon afterwards Scipio left with other soldiers and stopped not far from Syphax' camp. Scipio then saw that Laelius had succeeded in his mission: Syphax' camp was on fire. When the whole camp was ablaze, Scipio and his men rushed forward, massacring the men who ran out to escape the flames. Hasdrubal's men too rushed from their camp to help put out the fire; they too were butchered (but not in such great numbers). They never suspected that the fire had been set deliberately. The Carthaginians lost approximately forty thousand men. The Carthaginian government was then forced to recall Hannibal from Italy so he could defend Carthage.

Hannibal with difficulty escaped from Italy—the Romans were doing their utmost to destroy his army—and returned to Carthage. He faced Scipio at Zama in 202 B.C. Masinissa and his cavalry ran the Carthaginian cavalry off the battlefield, and the Roman light-armed troops so scared the elephants that they rampaged and turned on the Carthaginian troops. The Roman infantry then engaged the Carthaginians in a hard-fought battle; with the battle undecided, Masinissa and his cavalry returned, surrounding the Carthaginians and cutting them down. Hannibal escaped the Roman soldiers and forced his government to sue for peace.

The terms of the treaty allowed the Carthaginians a fleet of only ten ships, forbade them to wage war without Rome's consent, forced them to pay a war indemnity of ten thousand talents of silver, and barred them from keeping war elephants.

Rome was now a world power, having conquered its sole rival in the western Mediterranean. It had made allies in Africa, to help in the defeat of Carthage, and thus held Carthage in its grip. Further, it had conquered much of Spain and parts of southern Gaul, to disrupt Hannibal's supply lines; these areas soon became the provinces of Hispania and Gallia Cisalpina. Since King Philip V of Macedon had made a treaty with Hannibal during the war, and might have delivered some assistance to him, Rome soon found itself in wars with Macedon, which involved Rome in affairs Hellenic. Rome's relations with Greece and the East led to the conquest of Asia Minor. The defeat of Carthage launched Rome into world prominence, from which position it would not fall for more than seven hundred years.

CHAPTER 15

Rome Encounters the East

After defeating Hannibal and Carthage, and in the process becoming masters of the western Mediterranean, the Romans wanted peace and quiet, but with security. Instead, they became involved in the political troubles of the eastern Mediterranean, which threatened not only their recent conquests, but also their very existence. The politics of the kingdoms of the eastern Mediterranean are somewhat complicated; some background information will be helpful.

THE HELLENISTIC EAST

Alexander the Great, king of Macedon, during his short life (356–323 B.C.) had united the Greeks in an invasion of the Persian Empire. Supposedly, the reason was to get revenge for the Persians' invasion of Greece and destruction of its houses and temples in 491–479, but the real reason was economic. The young men of Greece, seeing no future at home, found work as mercenaries in the army of the Persian king, Darius III, thus strengthening Greece's mortal enemy while weakening Greece itself.

After crossing the Hellespont (present-day Dardanelles, the narrow strait that separates Asia from Europe) in 334, Alexander and his army marched along the western coast of Asia Minor (modern Turkey), defeating Darius in two separate battles, at Granicus and Issus. Alexander and his army then continued marching south though Syria, Palestine, and Israel, and entered Egypt. There Alexander founded a city off the westernmost tributary of the Nile, and named it Alexandria. Then he continued east in pursuit of

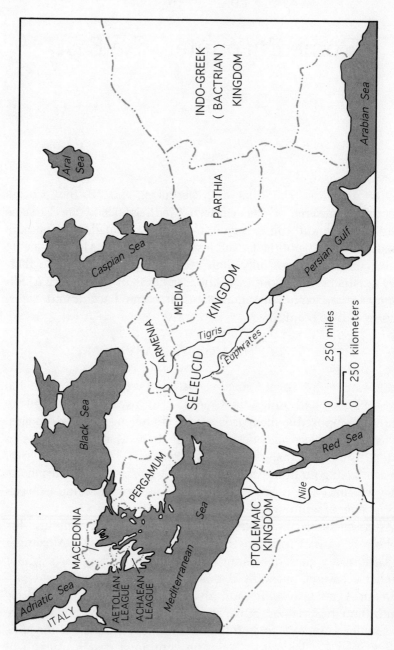

The Hellenistic kingdoms, 185 B.C. (Drawn by John Cotter)

Darius and defeated him once again, at the Battle of Gaugamela. Darius, now a fugitive, was murdered by his own attendants, and Alexander was acknowledged king of Persia. King Alexander continued his march east, occupying the famous cities of the East—Babylon, Susa, Persepolis, and Ecbatana—and carrying off Darius' treasure.

Some historians say that Alexander then started dreaming of placing all mankind under the rule of law, united by Greek culture; therefore, at strategic locations throughout his conquests he planted colonies of his soldiers, who spoke Greek, and encouraged them to marry native women to blend the Greek and Persian peoples. Eventually Alexander entered India and defeated the Indian prince Porus; so impressed was Alexander by Porus' dignity and bearing that he made him his ally. He then continued his march east, his dream being to see Ocean and the end of the earth. When Alexander reached the Hydaspes River (present-day Jhelum River), he and his soldiers heard that there was still a great river to be crossed (the Ganges) and much more land beyond that. Hearing this, the soldiers revolted and refused to go any farther: It is estimated that they had marched fifteen thousand miles. Alexander reluctantly turned back to the west; he died in Babylon in 323.

At Alexander's death his former generals—all Greeks—established control over different parts of his empire and waged incessant warfare with each other for control over the rest or for protection from aggression. Thus his empire disintegrated into what we call the Hellenistic kingdoms, of which these were the most important:

Macedonia, which sometimes included Greece, ruled by the Antigonid line;

Thrace, ruled by Lysimachus;

Seleucid Empire (included present-day northern Syria, Jordan, Palestine, Israel, Iran, and Iraq), whose kings were named Antiochus or Seleucus;

Egypt, ruled by the Ptolemies, who treated all Egypt as their personal farm and factory, thus making themselves fabulously rich (with some of their riches they built the famous library and museum of Alexandria, and encouraged scientists, philosophers, and poets).

Two other Hellenistic powers should be mentioned: Pergamum, close to what was once Troy, ruled by kings bearing the names Attalus or Eumenes, and the island of Rhodes, with its powerful navy and commercial interests. These Hellenistic powers, despite their common Greek language and culture, were constantly at war with one another in frequently shifting alliances. Into this bees' nest the Romans wandered after finishing the war with Hannibal.

THE SECOND MACEDONIAN WAR

Shortly after Cannae (216 B.C.), King Philip V of Macedon had made an alliance with Hannibal, and taking advantage of Rome's current troubles, he had even tried to expand into Illyricum (modern Albania) by taking over Dyrrhachium and Apollonia, both of which Rome had won in the wars against the pirates after the First Punic War (see chapter 13). In 215 Rome sent an army to drive Philip away, and encouraged his Greek neighbors and enemies, specifically the Aetolians, to wage war on him. But since Rome was at the time busy with Hannibal, the Gauls, Spain, and Africa, the war with Philip (First Macedonian War) was waged with little dedication on Rome's part. Rome abandoned the Aetolians, who were conquered by Philip in 206; the Aetolians never forgave the Romans for deserting them. Rome made peace with Philip in 205.

Enter Antiochus the Great, king of the Seleucid Empire. He was rightly called "the Great" because he had restored to his kingdom lands and territories that his predecessors had let slip away; in addition to most of modern Syria, he acquired Armenia, regained Parthia (the country from the Euphrates to the Indus) and Bactria (northern Afghanistan, southern Uzbekistan, and Tadjikistan) as vassal kingdoms, and expanded into the Cabul Valley. He and Philip made an agreement by which they were to wage war on their common enemies and to split the gains. Antiochus had his eye on Egypt's holdings in southern Syria (called Coele-Syria) and Thrace, Egypt itself (at this point very vulnerable because its king, Ptolemy V, was only six years old), and parts of Asia Minor. Philip wanted Thrace, the islands in the Aegean Sea, Pergamum, and part of Egypt.

Antiochus conquered Coele-Syria, while Philip attacked Thrace and other towns allied to Rhodes and Pergamum; at one point he even attacked Pergamum itself, but quickly withdrew his army. Rhodes and Pergamum declared war on Philip and fought a naval battle with him; the outcome was inconclusive. Rhodes and Pergamum then asked Rome for help against Philip.

The Romans did not have a good legal reason for declaring war on Philip. He had not attacked Rome or any of its allies, except for Pergamum, and they were tired of war; yet they feared that Philip and Antiochus, with all the resources of the Seleucid Empire, would join forces and invade Italy, using Macedonia as a base. The Romans did not want another Pyrrhus or Hannibal in Italy. The proposal for war against Philip was rejected by the Comitia Centuriata, because the Romans were tired of war; in response the consul Publius Sulpicius gave a speech that convinced them to declare war against Philip after all. "Citizens," he said,

"it seems to me that you don't know that you are not being asked to decide whether you'll have peace or war; Philip—who even now is working on a war on land and sea—is not leaving that decision up to you. You are deciding whether you'll send legions over to Macedonia or whether you'll let the enemy into Italy. After the recent war with Carthage, you are certainly well familiar with how much is at stake. Who, after all, has any doubts that if we had immediately brought help to Saguntum, when it was under attack and begging our help, as our ancestors had done to the Mamertines, that we would have fought the whole war in Spain? As it was, because we acted slowly, we let the war into Italy, at great suffering and destruction of our people. . . . Let Macedonia, not Italy, have the war; let the cities and fields of the enemy be destroyed by fire and the sword." (Livy XXXI.7)

Wanting to avert another destructive war in Italy, the Romans declared war on Philip. To justify the declaration of war, the fetials set impossible conditions for Philip to meet, if he wanted to avoid war with Rome: He had to free his Greek subjects and not wage war on the Greeks in Asia Minor. Philip ignored the fetials, as the Romans knew he would, and promptly attacked the Greek city of Abydus in Asia Minor. His lieutenant attacked Athens, and the

Athenians asked Rome for help: Now Rome had the justification it had been looking for. The consul P. Sulpicius and an army crossed over into Greece in 200 B.C.

After invading Macedonia, the Romans were joined by Philip's old enemies, the Aetolians, Pergamum, and Rhodes. Then the Achaean League, an alliance of cities in the Peloponnese, also joined; the Greeks were angry with Philip for his brutal actions, such as selling the people of a conquered city into slavery or killing all the males of military age. Macedon's enemies the Dardanians invaded from the north, while Rome and its allies invaded from the west and south, and the Roman and Rhodian navies blockaded Macedon on the east; Macedon was surrounded.

The Roman and allied victory at Cynoscephalae (Dog's Heads) in 197 B.C., under the leadership of T. Quinctius Flamininus, ended the war. Philip was beaten, and he asked for peace. According to the treaty he had to abandon all his holdings outside of Macedonia and leave the Greeks free of Macedonian rule. The Aetolians, whom Rome had deserted during the First Macedonian War, again found ample reason to be unhappy with Rome: They did not regain the territory that Macedon had taken from them in earlier wars.

In contrast to the sullen and bitter Aetolians were the remaining Greeks, who were ecstatic over Flamininus' declaration, at the Isthmian Games in 196, that the Greek city-states were now free of foreign rule. The Greek city-states were fanatically devoted to their individual autonomy (so much so, in fact, that they were regularly at war with each other to preserve their liberties and independence) and suffered under the political domination of Macedon and the various powers directing affairs in Greece before Macedon (most recently Persia, and before it Thebes, Sparta, Athens, and Sparta). Once free of Macedonian domination, however, the Greeks would return to their regular warfare with each other, which would occasion their finding a new master: Rome.

WAR WITH ANTIOCHUS OF THE SELEUCID EMPIRE

Antiochus had stayed out of the war between Philip and Rome, but he had not been idle. He had taken Coele-Syria from Egypt, and had even taken cities from Philip while he was occupied with Rome. Now Antiochus was attacking Asia and Pergamum; in fact, Attalus, the king of Pergamum, had had to leave the Romans in their war against Philip to protect his kingdom from Antiochus. Soon Antiochus attacked Thrace. He was encouraged in his hopes of power in Europe by the Aetolians, who invited him to liberate Greece from Roman oppression. When the Romans warned him to stay out of Europe, Antiochus asked the Romans what business they had in Asia Minor and claimed that he himself was simply reconquering territories that his predecessors had lost (and it was true that one of his ancestors had once controlled Thrace). The Romans had no real reason to wage war—other than his attacking Pergamum—but plenty of reason to fear, for a certain fugitive from Carthage had come to Antiochus to help him arrange the war against Rome: Hannibal. Hannibal advised Antiochus to establish a base in Greece, while he himself attempted to incite Carthage to invade Italy. The Romans once again told Antiochus to stay out of Europe.

Antiochus therefore brought the war to the Romans via Greece. The Aetolians had promised him that all Greece, groaning under Roman oppression, would welcome him, and he promised the Aetolians that he would bring all the resources of his empire to free them. After withdrawing all its soldiers from Greece in 194 B.C., Rome sent an army back to Greece in 192, to await Antiochus.

Antiochus and his Greek allies were soon disappointed with each other. The Greeks did not revolt from Rome as Antiochus had hoped they would. His only significant Greek allies were the Aetolians; the other Greeks fought on the side of Rome. The Aetolians, after hearing reports of how Antiochus would bring the wealth of Asia against the Romans, were disappointed when he appeared in Greece in 192, leading an army of only ten thousand men. Later, however, he was joined by more soldiers from his empire.

Antiochus subdued small parts of Greece before the Romans and their allies beat him at the Battle of Thermopylae in 191 B.C. Students of ancient history may remember that in 481 King Leonidas and his three hundred Spartans had heroically held the pass of Thermopylae against Xerxes' Persians, and had even refused the opportunity to flee when they learned that soon they would be attacked in the rear; all three hundred Spartans, including Leonidas, then fought to the death to hold the pass. The Romans and their allies won their Battle of Thermopylae when M. Porcius Cato led a detachment of two thousand soldiers in a surprise strike upon the Aetolians; this successful tactic allowed Cato to attack Antiochus' army from behind. Antiochus, deserted by the Aetolians, now found himself fighting a war of liberation for the Greeks who were fighting against him. Beaten, Antiochus fled to his kingdom.

The Romans sent L. Scipio, brother of Africanus, in pursuit of Antiochus. (Africanus, having served as consul in 194, was ineligible for another seven years but nonetheless joined his brother's staff.) After defeating Antiochus' navy at Myonessus, the Romans offered Antiochus the terms for peace; he did not like the terms, but the Roman and allied victory over him at Magnesia in 190 forced him to seek peace. According to the terms of the treaty Antiochus was to stay out of Europe, withdraw from Asia, and hand over Hannibal. He complied with the first two demands, but let Hannibal escape to Prusias, king of Bithynia. (Hannibal later commited suicide when the Romans demanded that Prusias hand him over.)

The Romans were not quite finished in Asia Minor, however. They also waged war against the Galatians in central Asia Minor. As the name implies, the Galatians were Gauls; they had been marauding over central Europe and had crossed into Asia, where they settled down. They had given help to Antiochus during his war with Rome, and the Romans wanted revenge. They understood that the Gauls threatened the peace and security of their allies in Asia: Antiochus and the Galatians could cause great trouble for Pergamum and Egypt if they were not taken care of. Defeated in two battles, the Galatians sued for peace.

THE THIRD MACEDONIAN WAR

After Cynoscephelae, Philip of Macedon had fulfilled most of the obligations of his treaty with the Romans, even helping them against Antiochus. Yet he was bitter about how the Romans treated him. The Romans took the side of Pergamum during the boundary disputes between Pergamum and Macedon. Philip started planning for another war with Rome, and accordingly consolidated his kingdom, storing up huge reserves of money, supplies, and soldiers—grain for thirty thousand infantry and five thousand cavalry for ten years, cash on hand for ten thousand mercenaries, and weapons for armies three times as large. Small but frequent expeditions against Thrace and other enemies kept his soldiers experienced and well trained, but did not deplete their numbers. During those expeditions, Philip conquered Thrace, and now had its supply of soldiers to draw from as well.

Philip died before he could carry out his plans. He is said to have died of a broken heart after having murdered his innocent son. Philip had two sons, Demetrius and Perseus. Perseus was older, but illegitimate, supposedly born of a slave woman. Demetrius, five years younger and born of a noble Macedonian woman, was popular with the Romans, for during the three years that he had spent as a hostage in Rome (to ensure his father's good behavior after Cynoscephelae), he and the Romans had come to understand and appreciate each other. The Romans were hoping that Demetrius would succeed Philip as king of Macedon.

Consequently, as Philip became increasingly resentful of the Romans, he began to dislike and distrust Demetrius, who seemed pro-Roman. At the same time his affection increased for Perseus, who played upon his father's hatred of the Romans; Philip's feelings are clear from his choice of the name Perseis for a city that he founded in 183 B.C. Perseus then played upon his father's fears and his distrust of Demetrius, alleging that with the help of the Romans Demetrius was trying to take over the kingdom. He offered proof of the conspiracy with a forged letter to himself from Flamininus; thus in 181 B.C. he convinced his father to have Demetrius killed as a traitor. With Demetrius dead, Perseus' position was secure.

Eventually Philip was informed of Perseus' deception, and was devastated to learn that he had ordered the death of his innocent son. He wanted to have another man—anyone but Perseus—succeed him as king, but Perseus was too strong for him. When Philip died in 179, Perseus became king.

Perseus inherited the stores of weapons, grain, cash, and veteran soldiers from his father, along with his hatred of Rome. He now had everything he needed for waging a successful war; the extent of his preparations induced many northern and southern Greeks to revolt from Rome, and his charisma won many to his side. The Romans were alarmed by his preparations and aggression, and incensed by his attempts at assassination: Perseus had planned to assassinate Eumenes, the ruler of Pergamum, and had tried to get an Italian friend to poison Roman officials. The Romans declared war on Perseus in 171 and sent an army to Macedonia. When Perseus heard that the Romans had arrived in Macedonia, in a frenzy of worry and fear he jumped out of his bathtub and ran away, shouting that he had been conquered without even a battle. Shortly after that, he ordered his friends to throw the treasury from one of his cities into the sea, so the Romans could not seize it. Later, when he calmed down, he had divers recover the money, and then, fearing that they would tell everyone of his foolishness, he had them killed.

Perseus' panic was unnecessary. The Romans were slow in their preparations for the war; one consul even granted a truce to Perseus, on the pretext of allowing further negotiations for peace, when, in fact, the consul knew that his troops were all new recruits and no match for the well-trained and experienced Macedonians. The older Romans decried the way the younger generation had let the Roman army deteriorate so that Rome now granted truces out of lack of preparation, whereas in the past Roman commanders had had so strong a sense of honor that they agreed with the enemy upon a day of battle, just to prove without a doubt who was the superior soldier. When the Roman army crossed into Macedonia in 171, the Roman consuls feared risking a battle with new recruits on unfavorable ground against the experienced Macedonians who held the strategic hills and mountain passes. The war dragged on, with little fighting and no progress.

In 168, however, the new consul was Lucius Aemilius Paullus. One of his first acts as consul was to convene a meeting of the citizens, who, seeing the lack of progress in the war, accused the generals of incompetence. He told the assembled citizens, "If there is anyone who trusts that he can give me advice in the war that I am about to wage, let him not deprive the republic of his services, but let him come along with me to Macedonia. I will take care of his passage, horse, tent, and traveling money. If that person, however, does not find that a very inviting proposal, and prefers the leisure of the city to the toils of being a soldier, he shouldn't command our armies in Macedonia while he is safe at home in Rome" (Livy XLIIII.22). We can assume that none of the armchair generals took him up on his offer. With that done, Paullus crossed over to Macedon. He immediately made some changes in the operation of the army, which brought about an improvement in the soldiers' discipline, confidence, and morale. The soldiers now felt confident and courageous, ready to take on the Macedonian phalanx (the Macedonians' particularly deep and strong formation of foot soldiers, each armed with a *sarissa*, a pike nearly 4 meters long).

In fewer than three months Paullus accomplished what the previous generals had failed to do in three years. At the Battle of Pydna, in 168 B.C., the Roman army destroyed Perseus' army. The victory was so overwhelming that within a few days—just long enough for the report to have gotten out—most of the cities of Macedon surrendered to Paullus. For a while Paullus refused to respond to Perseus' letters proposing peace, as Perseus was still calling himself king. He was captured shortly after, with his wife and son.

When Paullus first saw before him in tears a man who had been a rich and powerful king but was now a helpless suppliant destined to march in Paullus' triumph in Rome, he said to his soldiers, "You see here before you an excellent example of the change in human affairs. I'm talking especially to you young men: during good times it is right to make no arrogant or impetuous decision against someone or to put too much stock in the luck of the moment, since you never know what will happen later. He, then, is a true man, whose character is not changed by prosperity or adversity" (Livy XLV.8).

The terms of the treaty broke Macedon into four independent republics, so that it could not cause trouble for Rome again. The Macedonians retained their basic freedom and self-government, but now had to pay Rome one-half the taxes that they had paid to Philip and Perseus. Paullus made a walking tour of Greece, to inspect the country and make treaties with different Greek cities, according to their degree of support of the Romans during the war with Perseus. Greece was fairly calm, for a while.

While assessing the help that the Greeks had contributed to the Romans during the war against Perseus, the Romans were dissatisfied with the Achaean League, a confederacy of cities in southern Greece. The Romans deported to Rome a thousand prominent Achaeans as hostages, for investigation. One of the Achaean hostages, named Polybius, became the good friend of leading Romans (including Scipio Aemilianus, the adopted son of Scipio Africanus's son) during his years there and came to admire Roman government and character. He then wrote a history that explained Rome's rise to empire. Polybius' writings give us much valuable information about Mediterranean history in the third and second centuries B.C., including the Punic Wars, the Macedonian Wars, and the war with Antiochus, as well as the nature of Roman government.

THE FOURTH MACEDONIAN WAR

Despite the partition of Macedon, the Romans were not yet finished with this enemy, for a man named Andriscus, pretending to be the long-lost son of Perseus, started a rebellion against the Romans in Macedon. He made many raids on Macedon's neighbors, who appealed to Rome for help. Rome conquered Macedon again in 148 and this time annexed it as a province, installing a governor who had sway over affairs in Greece. Perhaps inspired by the uprising in Macedonia, the Achaean League also rebelled. The Romans conquered its forces in 146 and, under the leadership of L. Mummius, sacked and destroyed the city of Corinth in 146, dissolving the Achaean League.

ANOTHER WAR WITH CARTHAGE: "CARTHAGO DELENDA EST"

The Carthaginians had recovered much of their city's previous prosperity since Zama in 202 B.C. (see chapter 14) and had aided the Romans in their wars against Philip and Antiochus. They had also lived according to the terms of the treaty and had caused the Romans no trouble. Masinissa of Numidia, a neighbor of Carthage and an ally of Rome, took advantage of Carthage's inability to defend itself by encroaching upon its territory and capturing more than seventy towns. The Carthaginians frequently complained to Rome about Masinissa's acts, but he was able to create sufficient doubt about the Carthaginians that the Romans always sided with him. The Carthaginians were finally forced to declare war on Masinissa in 150, and were beaten.

In declaring war on Masinissa, the Carthaginians technically broke one of the terms of the treaty, which specified that Carthage could not wage war without Rome's permission. This gave the hardliners in the Senate the opportunity they had been looking for. One of these hardliners was M. Porcius Cato, who ended all of his speeches in the Senate with the phrase "Carthago delenda est" (Carthage must be destroyed). Other senators, however, noticing that the newfound wealth of empire was corrupting conservative Roman mores, thought that Carthage should be spared, so its continued existence would present a constant threat to Rome that would keep the Romans vigilant and strong.

In 149 the Senate delivered its ultimatum: The Carthaginians must vacate their city and move further inland. Since Carthage was a commercial and trading power, moving away from the sea would destroy its prosperity; the Carthaginians decided to fight instead. Being a wealthy, well-fortified city, Carthage endured a siege of four years before the consul P. Cornelius Scipio Aemilianus stormed the city in 146, sold the surviving Carthaginians into slavery, and sowed the land with salt, so Carthage would never again pose a problem for Rome. The area, roughly modern Tunisia, became the Roman province called Africa.

ANOTHER ANTIOCHUS

In 168 the Romans had an incident with Antiochus Epiphanes (Antiochus God Manifest), the son of Antiochus the Great and king of the Seleucid Empire. When Ptolemy VIII drove his elder brother and co-ruler Ptolemy VI from the kingdom of Egypt, Antiochus Epiphanes invaded, supposedly to secure the throne for the ousted Ptolemy, but in reality to do so for himself. He had already taken over much of the country except for Alexandria, when Roman envoys came to him. One of the envoys was G. Popilius Laenas.

When the envoys approached Antiochus, the king stretched out his hand and greeted them; Popilius did not shake his hand and said nothing, only handing him the Senate's orders to leave Egypt alone. Antiochus read the decree and replied that he needed time to consult with his friends; at that point Popilius took his staff, drew a circle in the ground around the king, and said, "Before you leave this circle, give me an answer to take back to the Senate." Antiochus hesitated, shocked by Popilius' rudeness and directness. He then replied he would do what the Senate had decreed. Then Popilius stretched out his hand in friendship and treated the king like a friend (Livy XXXXV.12.5).

OTHER WARS

All the time that Rome was fighting those wars against Philip and Perseus, Antiochus, and the Galatians, it was also fighting in Spain. Spain was by no means a unified country: Numerous tribes existed in the mountains, each ruled by its own chieftain. Rome fought constantly in Spain during the second century B.C., until its victory over Numantia in 133 (under the leadership of Scipio Aemilianus) ended Spain's organized opposition. Even after this victory the Romans still waged almost continuous warfare in Spain, for after a period of peace one tribe would revolt, followed by others; the reason for the revolts was frequently the Romans' unfair rule and taxation. It was in Spain in 62 B.C. that Julius Caesar himself first learned the art of military leadership, one hundred fifty years after Rome first brought its arms against the Spanish.

After gaining the provinces of Africa, Spain, and Greece by bitter fighting and gloodshed, the Romans were given Asia Minor, for in 133 B.C. Attalus III of Pergamum died without an heir. He bequeathed his kingdom instead to the Roman people, who declared it the Roman province Asia.

IMPERIUM ROMANUM

How did Rome manage its farflung territories? After all, the Romans did not have a full-time, professional government filled with paper-pushing bureaucrats, armed with various stamps and forms to be filled out in triplicate—a civil service, in other words. Lacking a civil service, the Romans had neither the desire nor the manpower to extend the range of their government and their responsibilities. They avoided the extension of their government as long as possible.

Instead, the Romans allowed many allies simply to rule themselves. Being legally outside the system of provinces, three privileged types of allies enjoyed great freedom and autonomy as a reward for their faithful service to Rome. One type was what we call client kings and the Romans simply called friends (*amici*) of the Roman people. These were kings of territories that the Romans had not conquered, did not want to conquer, or had no reason to conquer; the Romans left these kings alone because the kings cooperated with them, maintained good relations with them, and helped Rome in its time of need. Similarly, Rome provided aid to the client kings when necessary, for "manus lavat manum" (one hand washes the other). These client kings paid no taxes to Rome, kept their own laws, and were not under the power of any Roman magistrates. Still, despite the appearance of equality in the relationship, the wise client kings recognized their lower status and adapted themselves to it. One client king, Prusias of Bithynia, wore a freedman's cap (the cap that freed slaves wore after being manumitted) when he addressed the Senate, just to show that he knew who was boss.

Other free allies were *civitates foederatae*, or "states allied by treaty." They too were technically outside the provincial system, for they paid no taxes to Rome and were independent of Roman magistrates. They had full judicial powers over their own citizens and perhaps over Roman citizens in their territory. They had to provide military assistance to Rome when it was requested, and they could ask the Romans for help when needed. They did not have to quarter Roman troops. Similar to *civitates foederatae* were *civitates sine foedere liberae*, "free states without a treaty," which enjoyed all the same privileges as those bound by a treaty with the exception of security: The free states without a treaty were granted their free status by a decree of the Senate, which (unlike a treaty) could be revoked at any time, for any reason.

The last class is what people usually think of when they think of a Roman province: Called *stipendiarii* (payers of a stipend) by the Romans, these peoples were ruled by a Roman governor stationed in their territory, who had the support of a force of Roman soldiers. They paid taxes or a stipend to Rome.

When the Romans decided to annex a territory as a province, the conquering general or a consul, in conjunction with a commission of ten, would write the *lex provinciae*, "the law of the province." This functioned as a charter of sorts, determining the level of taxation, boundaries, and laws, and served as a constitution. Then the Romans would install a governor. Since the governor would be in charge of a force of Roman and Italian soldiers (its size depending upon how peaceful the province was), he would have praetorian or consular status; therefore he was called a *proconsul* or *propraetor*, meaning that he was sent out with the authority of a consul or praetor. Eventually it became customary that one would go to a province as a governor the year after serving as a consul or praetor in Rome. The governor would have his staff, usually a group of his friends, and a quaestor to help him in his work. The governor would then manage the affairs of the province in accordance with the *lex provinciae*, edicts of the previous governors of the province, instructions from the Senate, and the custom not only of Roman government but also of the community. The Romans generally tried to work within the social framework that existed in the province before they took over.

The trial and crucifixion of Jesus Christ in the province of Judaea (annexed in 59 B.C.) gives a good example of the Romans' attitude toward preexisting institutions. Jesus was put on trial by the Sanhedrin, the council of Jewish priests, for breaking Jewish law; he broke no Roman law, but had committed blasphemy against the Jewish religion. Pontius Pilate, the Roman magistrate overseeing the trial, "washed his hands" of the matter and allowed Jesus to be condemned by the Jewish court. The Romans tried to interfere in such matters as little as possible, both out of respect for other peoples, their institutions, and their religions, and also out of a sense of realism, knowing it would be futile and disruptive to try to force Roman ways on others. One exception to this was the case of the Druid religion in Gaul, which the Romans sought to eradicate, since it used human sacrifice and symbolized Gallic resistance to Rome.

The governor had a great deal of power over his subjects, and his exercise of it was not closely scrutinized by the Roman Senate. If the governor was corrupt and evil, those in his province were in for a rough year, the usual term for a governor, though longer terms were not uncommon. The sad truth is that there were many such corrupt governors, who simply stole all that they could, making themselves filthy rich off the helpless provincials. The local people could not fight the governor, for he had an army and the backing of Rome, and they had no legal recourse except in far-off Rome, where the welfare of the provincial peoples was not high on the list of priorities. Their only recourse was to complain to the corrupt governor's political enemies in Rome, who might charge him with extortion in a special court set up for judging cases of extortion in the provinces (called a *quaestio de repetundis*, "court for recovering monies"). But the corrupt governor would be tried in Rome by men like himself: governors who had already enriched themselves at the expense of the provincials, or those who looked forward to enriching themselves while governor someday, or those who were susceptible to bribes. For example, the Roman writer Cicero tells how the corrupt governor Verres had earmarked the proceeds of his first year as governor for his estate, the second year's proceeds for his legal team, and the third year's proceeds for bribing the judges (*In Verrem* I.40). If convicted (and some were), the corrupt governor simply went into exile or paid restitution. Despite the appearance of a totally corrupt system, there were good, honest and fair governors; the bad ones (like Verres, convicted of extortion in Sicily) were more sensational, while nothing was written about the good ones.

The provincial peoples who paid taxes paid them either as a war indemnity, or as upkeep of the Roman army which guarded their borders, or as a percentage of the year's produce. The system that the Romans devised for collecting taxes in Sicily and Asia Minor was horrible. Since Rome lacked a civil service to perform official functions, such as collecting taxes, the censors would sell the right to collect the taxes to the *publicani*, or "publicans," middle-class businessmen (hated in the New Testament), who would pay the taxes on the spot and then troop off to Asia Minor and Sicily to collect what they had paid, plus a profit. When the provincials could not pay their taxes, the *publicani* were happy to lend them the money—with a healthy interest charge, of course. The provincials were more likely than not to have no protection against the *publicani* from the governor, for the *publicani* whose rapacity was held in check by the governor would get their revenge on him in a Roman court when he returned from his province. Such was the fate of P. Rutilius Rufus, who was convicted for extortion, even though he had actually protected the provincials. This terrible system of collecting taxes in Asia was created in 133 B.C. and largely abolished almost a century later by Julius Caesar; Augustus created a new system that was fair to the provincials.

THE THREAT TO THE OLD WAYS

In the space of approximately 130 years Rome went from a position of leadership only in Italy to that of world power with dominion over many lands bordering on the Mediterranean. The Romans attributed their success to their adherence to *mos maiorum*, "the custom of our ancestors" or "the way our ancestors did things"—in short, the old ways. The Roman poet Ennius (239–169 B.C.) wrote, "Moribus antiquis res stat Romana virisque" (the Roman state remains strong because of its men and its ancient customs). Some of the chief customs and virtues that had made Rome great and powerful were *virtus* (courage), *pietas* (dutifulness to gods, community, and family), *gravitas* (seriousness), *constantia* (perseverance), *continentia* (self-control), and *pudicitia* (sense of shame, mostly for women).

The new and changing conditions of Roman life put great stress on the Romans' adherence to *mos maiorum*; in the view of many ancient historians this time period, the second century B.C., marked the beginning of the decline of Rome's morality, which resulted in the fall of the republic. The ancient historian Sallust (86–35 B.C.) wrote,

But once the republic had become great because of work and fair dealing, great kings were conquered in war, wild nations and vast populations were subjugated by force, and Carthage, the threat to the Roman power, was destroyed to its very foundations; all seas and lands lay open, but Fortune grew angry and began to throw things into confusion. Those who had easily suffered labors, dangers, and matters of great stress and uncertainty, were hamstrung by peace and quiet and wealth, things usually hoped for. Therefore, for the first time in Rome there grew the longing for money and then power; from this developed all the troubles. For greed perverted trustworthiness, propriety, and other honorable ways, and instead taught arrogance, cruelty, neglect of the gods, and the habit of considering all things for sale. Ambition compelled many men to lie, and to have one thing secret in their hearts, while saying something different, to judge friendships and hatreds not according to the facts but according to expediency, and to put forth a good appearance more than a good character. (Sallust, Bellum Catilinae X)

Allowing for some exaggeration on the part of historians such as Sallust, we can safely say that prodigious amounts of money from loot, tributes and taxes from the provinces, proceeds from the sale of slaves captured in war, and bribery flowed into Roman hands; some Romans, who by now had seen in Syracuse and Asia the amenities and luxuries that money could buy, used their new-found wealth with abandon. The censors enacted legislation to curb the love of wealth and luxury, but to no avail. Cato remarked that people in his day were spending on a jar of pickled fish what they once paid for a pair of oxen (the reason was not inflation, but simple extravagance). The cook, says another ancient historian, at one time the least valuable of the domestic slaves, now became the most highly prized.

The number of slaves in Rome and Italy also increased dramatically. Rome captured approximately seventy-five thousand slaves during the First Punic War and approximately two hundred fifty thousand more from 200 to 150 B.C. (Scullard, *History of the Roman World*, p. 358). As a point of comparison, the census of 164 B.C. counted 337,452 adult male citizens in Rome. The slaves now were Spaniards, Greeks, Gauls, and Asiatics, whose foreign ways inevitably threatened traditional Roman ways. They also posed an internal threat to the security of Rome and the Italian countryside, for runaway slaves resorted to crime, simply to live. The availability of slaves also decreased employment for freemen and citizens alike. The slaves from Greece and Greek Asia Minor were frequently better educated than their Roman masters, and thus became the tutors and teachers of their masters' children; this meant that the children were less likely to receive an education in the traditional Roman virtues from their mother and father.

Another area to suffer was religion. In one famous incident in 186 B.C., a Bacchic cult was discovered in Rome, with Roman citizens as inductees. We do not know exactly what happened in the Bacchic get-togethers, but it was sufficiently shocking for the consuls to convene an emergency meeting of the Senate to discuss what should be done. Seven thousand people in Rome are said to have been involved in the Bacchic cult; many of them were executed and some detained. Nonetheless, foreign religions continued to enter Rome. Astrologers also began appearing in Rome. In 139 the consuls expelled the astrologers from the city, but they returned; later, although they were periodically deported, they always returned.

"GRAECIA CAPTA FERUM VICTOREM CEPIT"

This time period also saw the beginnings of Latin literature. While conquering the Greeks of mainland Greece and Sicily, the Romans also encountered the glories of Greek civilization. They were rightly overawed by the immense literary and artistic achievements of the Greeks; this occasioned the famous statement of the Roman poet Horace, "Graecia capta ferum victorem cepit" (Greece, although captured, took its wild conqueror captive). The Romans were not slow to learn from the Greeks and to adapt Greek ways to fit their needs.

The first Roman poet of record is Livius Andronicus (mid-third century B.C.), a Greek slave from Tarentum, who translated the *Odyssey* into Latin in a rough poetic meter called the Saturnian, and adapted the content to Roman ways. His *Odyssia* became a textbook for Roman schoolboys. Other epic poets followed; one was Ennius, who first used the Greek poetic meter called the dactylic hexameter for Latin verse. Ennius' most famous poem (fragments of which survive) was the *Annales*, a history of Rome in verse. Soon followed, among others, Plautus (254–?184 B.C.), who wrote comedies (another Greek genre) for the stage; he took as his models the writers of Attic New Comedy, and an ancient critic said that if the Muses spoke Latin, they would speak Plautine Latin. Twenty of his plays survive. Plautus' younger contemporary was Terence (195–?159), who had come to Rome as a slave from Africa; Terence may have been the first known black writer, as he is described as having a dark complexion (*fuscus* is the Latin adjective, which in other contexts is used to describe a crow, the wings of night, or the cloak of sleep). Six of his plays survive; Julius Caesar, himself famous for his simple and elegant writing style, praised the purity of Terence's Latin. Terence's plays were more genteel and Greek in manners than those of Plautus, which were rougher and more boisterous, and therefore more popular with the Roman spectators. Rome also had composers of tragedy (another Greek genre); the most famous were Naevius, Pacuvius, and Accius. Only fragments of their works survive. Scipio Aemilianus and his friend Laelius may have formed a group with other intellectuals interested in Greek literature and thought, and they may have become the patrons of poets. Modern scholars call the group the Scipionic Circle and believe that Polybius and Terence, among others, may have been associated with it.

The Romans also started writing history during this time; while they had always recorded the year's events on linen sheets stored in the *aerarium*, now they began to write history as a literary genre, again following a Greek model. The first Roman historian, Q. Fabius Pictor (fl. 225), actually wrote in Greek, supposedly to justify Roman policy to the Greek world. During this time period a purely Roman type of literature arose, called satire. Satire fit Rome perfectly, for in it the poet could poke fun at faults and vices and thereby spur people to moral improvement. The first Roman satirist we know of is Lucilius (d. 102/1).

The Romans were not yet writing philosophy, but they were reading it, for the Romans by this time were receiving a Greek education in philosophy, logic, and rhetoric. The Roman mind was not much given to the kind of abstract thought that forms a large part of philosophy. The philosophy the Romans liked most was Stoicism, which emphasized values and a strong sense of duty to community, family, and gods. Romans tended to be suspicious of other schools of philosophy. For example, Epicureanism, which advocated that one withdraw from society to lead the quiet, stress-free life of contemplation, conflicted with a Roman's love of Rome and pursuit of glory. But it was a Roman poet, Lucretius (94–55 B.C.) who wrote the longest surviving document on Epicureanism, a poem entitled *De rerum natura* (On the Nature of Things). The Greek philosophy called Cynicism, which held that governments and norms were evil, was simply incomprehensible to Romans.

Perhaps the Roman fear and distrust of philosophers can best be seen in the case of the second-century philosopher Carneades. In 155 B.C. he made a series of speeches in Rome, and all the Roman young men in attendance were deeply impressed by them. To the traditional Roman ways of thinking, however, Carneades must have embodied all that was evil about Greek philosophy: On one day Carneades spoke on behalf of an issue, and on the next day, to show his dexterity, he spoke against the very same issue, with equal effect. To traditional Romans this was undoubtedly very dangerous cleverness, allowing one to "make the worse cause appear the better"—which could only lead to agnosticism or atheism, dishonesty, and moral confusion.

CATO VS. SCIPIO

The social turmoil of the times can be summed up in the dispute between M. Porcius Cato and Scipio Africanus. Cato (234–149 B.C.) was born of peasant background in Tusculum, a city long allied to Rome that had been the first Latin city granted Roman citizenship. Despite his lack of training in rhetoric, Cato was very gifted at public speaking, and represented in court whoever needed his services (he did this for free, since Roman advocates were prohibited by law from receiving pay for legal services). He was also a formidable soldier, seeing his first action in 217. He later fought at Metaurus and served as consul in 195, governor in Spain in 194 (where he won many battles and later celebrated a triumph), and censor in 184.

Early on Cato dedicated himself to a life of simplicity and self-discipline. He worked among his slaves in the fields, ate the same bread and drank the same wine, and lived in a simple cottage. He wore simple clothes; once he was bequeathed an embroidered Babylonian robe, but immediately sold it. When governor in Sardinia, he did not milk his expense account (which was paid for by the provincial peoples) for all that he could, but imposed an unheard-of economy on his staff. When his army won loot from the enemy, Cato says he never took any of it for himself, but let his soldiers have it all. A good summary of his way of thinking is this: The Romans had won their territory by means of virtue and self-restraint, not self-indulgence and vice, which tended to destroy empires. Which path should one then take?

Cato worried, seeing the Romans being swept up in wealth, luxury, and the rush of all things Greek. It all threatened *mos maiorum* and the moral simplicity of earlier times. So while other Romans employed Greek slaves to tutor their children and sent their young men to learn Greek rhetoric and philosophy, Cato himself undertook the education of his son, teaching him to read and to understand Roman law, to throw the javelin, to fight in armor, to ride a horse, box, and swim. Seeing a lack of good literature in Latin that dealt with Roman topics, Cato wrote his *Origines* (Beginnings), a history of Rome, including its various myths and legends.

When Cato was a candidate for the censorship in 184, most of the nobles were frightened and vehemently opposed his candidature. He promised them that he would be a harsh doctor to their sickness of vice and luxury. Not only did they see the austerity and asceticism of his personal life, they also remembered that as consul in 195 he had spoken against the repeal of the Lex Oppia, which forbade women to own more than a half-ounce of gold, to wear multicolored dresses, and to ride in two-horse carriages (the law had been passed during the war with Hannibal). What would he do as censor?

The Roman populace, with the exception of the corrupt nobles, gladly elected Cato, thinking that they needed a harsh physician. Once elected censor, he put heavy taxes on luxury items, expelled Lucius Scipio (brother of Africanus) from the knights, and expelled another man for embracing his wife during the day in the presence of their daughter. He also concerned himself with Rome's infrastructure, by reconstructing sewers, destroying the pipes that some had illegally connected to the aqueducts to bring water into their houses, tearing down houses that had been built illegally on public land, and raising the rent on public land. Consequently he became very unpopular with some Romans, but others erected a statue of him in the Temple of Salus, for he had tried to restore Rome's health.

Unlike Cato, Scipio Africanus was fond of Greek culture and ways. In 204 B.C., while he was in Sicily preparing for the invasion of Africa (see chapter 14), he was under attack by his political enemies in the Senate. Cato had been Scipio's quaestor, and he reported to the Senate that Scipio was wasting money on theater amusements for his men and on athletic contests. We also hear that "the general's style of living was not only not characteristically Roman, it was not even real army. He would hold his parades in the exercise area, wearing a Greek cloak and Greek slippers, and he spent his time and energy on books and Greek wrestling. His whole staff also just as indolently and lazily was enjoying the pleasantries of Syracuse, having totally forgotten about Carthage and Hannibal. He had let the whole army be corrupted by all that indulgence" (Livy XXIX.19.11).

Scipio was exonerated of charges of wasting money, being extravagant, and sacrificing Rome's better interests to secure the safety of his son (whom Antiochus had captured and returned without ransom). However, in disgust at Rome's treatment of him, he retired in self-imposed exile to his estate in Liternum, ordering in his will that his body not be buried in ungrateful Rome. His brother Lucius fared worse: He refused even to give an account of the finances of the campaign against Antiochus and thus fell under suspicion of receiving bribes; for this he was expelled from the knights.

Yet despite his victory over the Scipios, Cato lost the war against Hellenism. The next two centuries saw a Golden Age of Latin literature, which became an amalgam of Greek, Roman, and Italian elements. This Greco-Roman literature shaped the intellectual development of western Europe.

CHAPTER 16

The Gracchi
The Beginning of the End
of the *Res Publica*

The period of the brothers Tiberius and Gaius Gracchus, who held tribunates in 133 and 123–122 B.C. respectively, inaugurates a century of incessant civil strife in Rome, with occasional outbursts of civil war. The struggle culminates in the civil wars of 49–31 B.C. and in the final destruction of the republican form of government. A century after the Gracchi, Rome was governed by the principate, a type of monarchy, created by Octavian (Augustus).

Tiberius and Gaius Gracchus came from a plebeian family that was well known and respected; their father had twice been a consul and once a censor, and their mother Cornelia, who personally supervised the education of her sons, was a daughter of Scipio Africanus. Tiberius, the elder of the two brothers, had a past that he and his family could be proud of. As a very young man, he had been honored with an augurship. Accompanying P. Cornelius Scipio Aemilianus (adopted son of Scipio Africanus) to Carthage in 149 B.C., Tiberius had won the *corona muralis*, a crown awarded a soldier for being the first to climb over the walls of a besieged city. When he was a quaestor in Spain, his personal influence and reputation for fair dealing had helped save the lives of twenty thousand fellow Roman soldiers trapped by enemy troops; for that he should have been awarded the *corona civica*, a crown of oak leaves awarded to a soldier for saving the life of a fellow soldier. His early accomplishments presaged an illustrious career in service to Rome. Yet Tiberius was murdered in political strife, and his body dumped into the Tiber; his name to some Romans came to symbolize attempts at tyranny frustrated by patriots.

The trouble began when Tiberius was elected tribune in 133 B.C. He immediately called for reforms to address several problems:

1. *Decline of the peasantry.* Since its beginnings, Rome had been a city-state of peasant farmers working small farms, who served in the army in Rome's time of need. The number of family farms not just in Rome but also in all Italy had declined as Rome's increasing involvement in overseas wars required that the citizen-farmers leave their farms to fight in Spain, Greece, Gaul, Africa, or Asia. The family farmers typically did not own slaves who would work the land while the masters fought Rome's battles, and they did not have the money to live on while they restored their farms after long periods of neglect. Before Rome had overseas entanglements, the farmer-soldier could quickly return home when the war was finished, and work on the farm, although the story of the former centurion (see chapter 8) shows how difficult survival was even when Rome waged wars with immediate neighbors.

When these family farmers quit farming, they typically sold their land to wealthy men, who combined their purchases of many small farms into plantations worked by slaves; these large enterprises, called *latifundia*, also concentrated on raising sheep and cattle, thus increasing Rome's dependence on grain imported from Sicily and Africa.

The displaced peasants could try to make a new start by farming the public lands, which were lands Rome had confiscated either from its conquered enemies during its expansion in the fourth and third centuries or from those towns and cities that had taken Hannibal's side. A law, the Lex Licinia, forbade one man from farming more than 500 *iugera* (300 acres) of public land, but the rich landowners used their superior knowledge of the law and their powerful connections to drive the peasants from the public lands, which they then incorporated into their *latifundia*. The displaced farmers then drifted to the big city, Rome, to become craftsmen, tradesmen, or, more likely, one of the growing mass of the unemployed. Since there was no significant industry in ancient Italy and no demand for free labor, since servile labor was so cheap, the displaced farmers could no longer meet the property qualification for being a soldier. Rome's military might therefore suffered.

2. *Slave rebellions.* While traveling through Etruria on his way to Spain, Tiberius had noticed the great numbers of slave gangs working the fields and the dearth of peasants working family farms. The large numbers of slaves in Italy, if united under a capable leader, could cause great havoc in Italy. Such slave rebellions had already occurred in Asia, Greece, and, as recently as 135, in Sicily (a rebellion that the Romans overcame only with great difficulty).

3. *Agitation of the Italian allies for suffrage.* Ever since Rome and its allies had gained control of Italy early in the third century B.C., there had been roughly three classes into which the Italians could fall in their legal relations to Rome. First were the Roman citizens; second were those who held Latin rights (*Latinum nomen*), which meant Roman citizenship except for the right to vote and to pursue political office in Rome; third were the *socii Italici*, who had no rights in Rome and no say in the government of Italy or of the other Roman territories. Although liable for military service, the *socii* could not vote for the generals under whom they would serve and had no say in whether war should be declared. The Italians had long been pressing the Romans for some type of representation in governing Italy and the republic.

To address these problems, Tiberius proposed the following reform. He reaffirmed the old limit set by the Lex Licinia of 500 *iugera* of public land per man; to appease those already illegally farming public lands, he allowed the man, if a father, to claim an additional 250 *iugera* (150 acres) per son, with a maximum of 500 *iugera* for two sons. The rest of the illegally farmed land was to be confiscated and distributed to the landless poor, who could claim land according to the provisions of the Lex Licinia. The goals of this reform were to revive the family farmer in Italy, to relieve Rome of its unemployed poor, to increase the number of men eligible for service in the army, and to lessen the number of slaves in Italy.

Tiberius had the support of a few powerful men in the Senate, such as the consul Mucius Scaevola and Appius Claudius Pulcher, the *princeps senatus*; he would certainly need their help against the nobles who were illegally farming the public lands. Laelius, Scipio Africanus' friend, had made a similar but more radical proposal years earlier, but he had promptly withdrawn it upon encountering opposition from some members of the aristocracy, who did not want to lose what they had invested in the illegally farmed lands. Tiberius encountered the same opposition, but did not bend to it; he pressed forward with the bill.

Tiberius created more opposition and hostility to his plan than would have been expected. Instead of bringing his plan to the Senate for its advice and approval, as was customary before bringing a bill before the Popular Assembly, he immediately brought his plan to the Popular Assembly, without first consulting the Senate. His snub of the Senate alienated many who might have supported him; they fought the bill for political reasons, simply to avenge the insult. They succeeded in getting another tribune to veto Tiberius' law; when Tiberius could not persuade that tribune to withdraw his veto, he convinced the Assembly to approve a law deposing the other tribune. Thus Tiberius removed the tribune and his veto, and the bill passed. A commission began to distribute the land.

The members of the Senate were alarmed. Tiberius had bypassed them in proposing the bill, and with measures of questionable legality he had squashed their legal attempt to defeat his bill. Was he aiming at making the Assembly and the tribunes the rulers in Rome? If he could simply eliminate the Senate's legal opposition to him, what would prevent him from becoming a tyrant and starting a social revolution with cancellation of debts and redistribution of land?

The senators had one more trick up their sleeves: They would deny Tiberius the money he needed to finance the land commission. But Tiberius got lucky: Attalus III, king of Pergamum, died and bequeathed his kingdom to Rome, including his substantial treasury. Tiberius then proposed a law to distribute Attalus' money to those who had been allotted public lands. The Senate relented and gave him the money for the land commission.

Tiberius' hardball politics had turned still more senators against him. He realized that he needed to be tribune for another year, both for his own protection and for the preservation of his laws, which the senators would doubtless declare illegal once he was out of office. Being elected to an office two years in a row was illegal for magistrates, although it was unclear whether the law applied to tribunes. To help his bid for reelection, he proposed more laws that would strengthen his popularity among the common people.

Tiberius' proposals compelled some members of the Senate to take action. Led by Scipio Nasica—Gracchus' cousin and one of the largest owners of the public lands—they ordered the consul Scaevola to put down the tyrant; Scaevola responded that he would not be the first to use violence and would put no citizen to death without a trial. So a group of senators, led by Nasica—who, as pontifex maximus, was supposed to remain free of bloodshed—fearing that Tiberius was aiming at a tyranny, attacked and killed him and three hundred of his supporters. They dumped his body into the Tiber and denied Gaius permission to bury his older brother. Some of Tiberius' supporters survived the attack and soon found themselves on trial, while others were driven into exile without a trial. Those who had murdered Tiberius were not brought to trial; eventually the Senate, embarrassed by Nasica, sent him to Asia as head of some mission, where he later died. Nonetheless, the land commission continued distributing land.

Gaius, nine years younger than his brother, had been a member of the land commission. Some years after Tiberius' murder, Gaius had a dream in which the ghost of Tiberius said to him, "Gaius, what are you waiting for? There is no escape. We have both been given but one life and one death for fighting for the good of the common people" (Plutarch, *Tiberius and Gaius Gracchus* I). Gaius was elected tribune for 123 and reelected for 122. Gaius was more passionate than his brother; when he gave a speech, he was often so swept away by his emotions that his voice became high and grating, at which point he had a slave blow a little whistle, as a sign that Gaius should calm down. The senators feared him even more than his brother. He continued Tiberius' work and proposed some reforms of his own:

1. *The establishment of many colonies.* One of these was at the former site of Carthage, which had been destroyed in 146. Besides addressing a need to free Rome of many idle and unemployed people, establishing colonies would also make Gaius immensely

popular among the masses, and therefore very powerful, for the colonists would henceforth regard him as their *patronus*, and he would have many *clientes* to summon when he needed help.

2. *A law for the regulation of the sale of grain in Rome.* The price of grain fluctuated widely, and this caused the poor to suffer. Gaius wanted the government to buy grain in bulk and then to sell it at unchanging prices.

3. *Changes in the makeup of juries.* Since the jurors in the courts for judging Roman governors' conduct in the provinces were recruited from the nobles, the courts were ineffective in ensuring ethical administration (see chapter 15). Gaius wanted to abolish the juries of senators and to replace them with juries of members of the equestrian class, the knights, who would not have such sympathy for the accused.

4. *A grant of Roman citizenship to allies of Latin status, and Latin status to the Italians.* Rome could not have obtained its vast territories without the help of the Latins and Italians, yet did not show its gratitude to them by granting them some political rights and power. In 129 Scipio Aemilianus had tried to help the Italians, but failed; four years later the Latin colony Fregellae, which had stayed loyal to Rome during the Pyrrhic and Hannibalic wars, revolted and was destroyed. The consul of 125, M. Fulvius Flaccus, proposed a law giving citizenship to the Italians, but the Senate conveniently sent him on a military expedition to Gaul when his proposal was to be voted on. As one of Gaius' colleagues in the tribunate in 122, Flaccus continued his attempt to give the Italians the vote, or at least the *ius provocationis*.

5. *Miscellaneous reforms.* Gaius passed a law making seventeen the minimum age for military service, and another providing that soldiers' clothing should be paid for by the state, with no reduction in the soldiers' pay. He also passed legislation for the construction of roads to serve the needs of agriculture, not necessarily those of the military, as before. If he were to make a provision that the roads would be built by paid, citizen labor, instead of servile labor, that law would have made him extremely popular with the unemployed common people.

Gaius encountered opposition not only from the Senate, which wanted its power left unshaken, but also from the urban citizens, who did not want to share the privileges of citizenship with non-Romans; before the proposal was voted on, the consul drove all non-Romans out of the city, so they would not put pressure on the voters. Gaius faced opposition also because of religion: The area of Carthage had been cursed (see chapter 15), and rumors spread that the colony, to be called Junonia, was on cursed ground and therefore contrary to the will of the gods. During the founding of the colony, terrible omens were seen, such as gales of wind blowing the sacrificial victims from the altars beyond the stakes demarcating the boundaries of the colony and even blowing away the stakes themselves.

With opposition growing, and plans being made to repeal the legislation, Gaius' supporters made a fatal mistake. They occupied the Aventine Hill (once public land, the Aventine had been given to the common people for settlement back in 456 and now was the plebeian quarter of Rome), thus causing the Senate to pass the *senatus consultum ultimum*, "the final decision of the Senate," which in effect declared martial law. The consul called forth armed citizens, who attacked Gaius' supporters, killing thousands and eagerly seeking Gaius himself, to earn the reward of the weight of his head in gold. While trying to escape, Gaius committed suicide. Dead bodies were thrown into the Tiber, and Opimius the consul condemned three thousand of Gaius' supporters to death without a trial. Their estates were confiscated, and their families were forbidden to wear mourning.

The affair of the Gracchi shows many faults in Roman government, which were left unsolved and eventually led to the Social War; the pacification of the unemployed urban masses by "bread and circuses"; the war with Spartacus; the growth of the professional army; and the fall of the republic. Among the immediate effects, the *equites* had been granted political power without political responsibility, and they frequently would use their wealth to guide Roman politics in a way advantageous to them, but not to the republic. Further, Roman politics was now sharply split between the *boni* (also called Optimates), who favored senatorial rule, and the *populares*, who wanted to rule Rome through their control of the popular assemblies. It is tempting for us to see the *populares* as democrats and the *boni* as republicans, but this is inaccurate, for the *populares* were themselves aristocrats who had failed to break into the senatorial power group. The *populares* merely used the popular assemblies to gain the power they could not secure within the Senate. Were the Gracchi selfless reformers or radicals aiming for a tyranny? The truth probably lies somewhere between the two extremes. Either way, the next century of Roman history gave proof of their foresight.

CHAPTER 17

The War against Jugurtha
and the Rise of Marius

Numidia had become an ally of Rome during the Second Punic War, when together they waged war on Carthage, and had been steadfast in its loyalty to Rome. Despite that longstanding alliance, Rome fought a war with Numidia.

The king of Numidia, Micipsa, had two sons by marriage, Adherbal and Hiempsal, and a third by adoption, Jugurtha. When Micipsa learned that he was dying, he summoned his three sons to his bed and asked them to divide the kingdom into three parts and to live in peace with each other. He would not live to see his hopes disappointed.

Soon after the death of Micipsa in 118 B.C., Jugurtha had his brother Hiempsal killed. He then attacked the kingdom of Adherbal; after losing the battle, Adherbal fled to Rome to seek assistance against Jugurtha, who now was king of all Numidia. Jugurtha had foreseen what Adherbal would do and had accordingly bribed many senators to reject Adherbal's pleas. The Senate then decided to divide Numidia between Jugurtha and Adherbal. Three years after the division, in 112, Jugurtha again attacked Adherbal's kingdom and besieged its main city, Cirta, where thousands of Italian merchants lived. Trapped in the city, Adherbal sent an embassy to Rome to beg for help against Jugurtha; the Senate then sent a commission to summon Jugurtha to address the Senate. The Italian merchants in Cirta felt it was now safe to surrender the city to Jugurtha, for, they thought, the authority of the angry Senate would prevent him from harming them. With the city in his hands, Jugurtha tortured and killed his brother and ordered his soldiers to kill all the adult males in the city. That included the Italians.

Outraged at the massacre, the Romans declared war on Jugurtha in 112 B.C. and sent the consul Bestia with troops to Africa to deal with Jugurtha. After Bestia had destroyed a few small towns, Jugurtha sent an embassy to him to seek a treaty. After receiving an enormous bribe, Bestia agreed to a treaty, by which Jugurtha surrendered only some elephants, some cattle, and a small amount of money.

Bestia returned to Rome, where the common people were outraged at his tender treatment of Jugurtha; Jugurtha, after all, had massacred thousands of Italians. They accused Bestia and other nobles of receiving bribes from Jugurtha. Jugurtha was summoned to Rome to give testimony about bribery, but his testimony was blocked by a tribune whom he had bribed. This further inflamed the anger of the common people; they suspected that Jugurtha's testimony would have implicated many nobles. With the Romans hating him and wanting to install a different king as ally in Numidia, Jugurtha had a rival claimant for the throne killed in Rome; he was then ordered to leave the city. Upon departing, he exclaimed, "Now that's a city available for a price, and it will fall soon enough, once it finds a buyer" (Sallust, *Bellum Iugurthinum* XXXV).

The war was resumed. The Romans sent the consul of 110, Postumius Albinus, to Africa to conquer Jugurtha, but he failed to finish the war, despite his eagerness to do so before his term ended. When he left Africa to oversee the elections in Rome for the next year, he left his brother Aulus in charge as acting praetor. The foolish Aulus then allowed the army to be trapped by Jugurtha; to avoid the massacre of the army, he was forced to agree to a treaty by which his soldiers, after being sent under the yoke, would evacuate all Numidia within ten days. He too returned to face Rome's angry citizens, who demanded action against Jugurtha.

THE RISE OF MARIUS

The next consul, Metellus, had to restore discipline and confidence to his troops when he arrived in Africa, for they had been demoralized and humiliated by Jugurtha. Metellus had some success in the war against Jugurtha—he captured towns and won some battles—but could not capture Jugurtha. He was assisted in his victories by his legate, Gaius Marius.

Marius, born to an equestrian family in a village outside the town of Arpinum, had won awards while serving under Scipio Aemilianus at Numantia and showed himself fearless in carrying out whatever orders he was given. The common soldiers who served under Marius loved him, for he ate the same type of food, slept on the same type of bed, and did his share of drudge work alongside them, such as digging trenches. Despite his lack of illustrious ancestors—to the Roman nobles, Marius was an outsider—he decided to campaign for the consulship.

When Marius asked Metellus for permission to go to Rome to pursue his political ambitions, Metellus (a noble) at first responded that he should not seek things that he could not get and should not try to go above his station in life. When Marius asked again, Metellus told him to wait until after they had finished the business of the state. Marius made his request a third time; Metellus then told him that quite soon—in another twenty-three years—he could seek the consulship with Metellus's son, who was then twenty years old. Marius, who was forty-nine years old at the time, was not amused; Metellus' insult unleashed his latent fury against the arrogant nobles. He started badmouthing Metellus, especially to the traders, probably so that they would repeat his words the next time they were in Italy, and he spread the rumor that the war could be finished within a few days if Metellus were not so fond of power.

Marius was finally allowed to return to Rome, where he won a consulship for 107; he thus became a *novus homo*, "new man," a consul who could not boast of an ancestor who had been consul. He won the consulship because he was *not* a noble; the common people had seen other nobles waste Rome's manpower and resources in the war against Jugurtha, and the scandals of bribery left them even more bitter against the nobles. Here, instead, was a commoner with many awards for valor who gave speeches in plain Latin—the nobles had long before learned from the Greeks the art of giving fancy speeches—and castigated the nobles for their inefficiency, loose morals, and arrogance toward the common people. The plebeians found in Marius something of a folk hero and made him consul. In one of his speeches, Marius told the common people:

"Those men, they're so arrogant, they have it all wrong [in thinking that their noble birth alone warrants special respect]. Their ancestors left them all the things they could leave them, such as wealth, wax masks, the memory of their brilliant deeds. They didn't leave them manliness, though, and they couldn't. That's the only thing that isn't given and received like a gift. They think I'm uncouth and trashy because I don't give an elegant enough dinner, or I don't have some actor or a cook who's worth more than a slave who manages a farm. My fellow Romans, I'm happy to admit it, because I got it from my father and other upstanding men that pretty things are right for women, but work is a man's job, and that having a good reputation is worth more than money, and that one gets glory not with household objects, but with weapons." (Sallust, *Bellum Iugurthinum* LXXXV.38–40)

Marius returned to Africa to take over Metellus' command. Metellus refused even to meet with Marius upon his return, for Marius had maligned him in particular, despite the help that Metellus had given him in advancing in his career.

While drafting troops, Marius disregarded the property qualifications necessary for becoming a soldier; thus he accepted many men who had no money or property at all. By taking these men as soldiers, Marius started the development of the professional army in Rome, which eventually had tremendous consequences in the fall of the republic. These soldiers had no land to return to upon the end of the war, and the Roman government did not provide any type of pension. As a result, such soldiers became dedicated not to the republic, but to their generals, who as leaders and patrons of their soldiers/clients would provide for their retirement. Thus the generals had whole armies to call upon for help in their political squabbles with the Senate or with other generals.

Marius proved to be an excellent general. He repeatedly defeated Jugurtha in battle, sacked many towns and a few large cities, and captured large numbers of slaves and immense amounts of loot; one of the cities he sacked held Jugurtha's treasury. Still, he was unable to catch the elusive Jugurtha. Finally, when one of Jugurtha's allies saw that Jugurtha would eventually lose, Marius forced him to give up Jugurtha, dead or alive. Jugurtha was handed over to Sulla, Marius' quaestor (about whom we will hear more), and the war with Jugurtha was finished in 105 B.C.

While Marius was finishing off the war against Jugurtha, the Romans were threatened by the Cimbri and Teutones, Germanic tribes from central Europe that were descending upon Italy. These tribes had already inflicted enormous defeats upon many patrician consuls and their armies. Worried, the Romans elected Marius consul in absentia (which was illegal) for 104 and summoned him to Rome to defend Italy against the Germans. During 104 Marius was lucky, for the Germans went to Spain instead; the Romans reelected him consul for 103, again wanting an experienced general to deal with the Germans. During 103 the Germans failed to appear; Marius then managed to be elected consul again for 102, with the tribune Saturninus promoting his candidature.

In 102 the Germans started their advance on Italy. Marius crossed the Alps to oppose them. For a long time he avoided battle, which the Germans interpreted as cowardice; while marching past the Roman camp, the Germans, laughing, asked the Italians if they had any messages for their wives and daughters, as they would be with them shortly. Once Marius' soldiers started begging him to allow them to fight the Germans, he let them fight; they won that skirmish, and the next day they inflicted a crushing defeat on the Germans, capturing or killing a hundred thousand of them at Aquae Sextiae (modern Aix-en-Provence). The next year, as consul yet again, Marius, with his colleague Catulus, conquered another part of the German armies at Vercellae, taking sixty thousand captives. For that victory Marius was called the third founder of Rome.

THE TRIBUNATE OF SATURNINUS

Since Marius had taken into his army men who owned no land that they could retire to, he needed land for his veterans. However gifted a general Marius was, he was not adept at politics; therefore, he benefited from the help of the tribune Saturninus. Although born to a plebeian family, Saturninus could boast that one of his ancestors had been a praetor. While quaestor, Saturninus had been in charge of securing a supply of grain (the *cura annonae*), in accordance with the laws passed by the Gracchi. Owing to a shortage in the grain supply, however, he was removed and replaced by a patrician who relieved the shortage and received the credit and popularity. Angry at this, Saturninus then turned violently against the oligarchy of the Senate.

Saturninus was elected tribune for 103 and tried to pass a law offering land in Africa to Marius' veterans upon their discharge from the army. Another tribune tried to veto the bill; Marius' soldiers, throwing rocks at him, ran him out of the assembly, and the proposed bill became law. Saturninus may have passed a grain bill as well; whether or not he did so, just the attempt would have made him more popular and powerful.

Saturninus was elected tribune again for 100. He proposed another land bill, this one to give allotments of land in Gaul to the veterans of the German wars and to found colonies in Sicily and Greece. The bill was unpopular with the common people of Rome; they saw it as too narrow and too favorable to non-Roman Italians, who were to receive land in the colonies. The Senate objected to the bill because one of its clauses required that senators swear an oath to abide by the law; senators who refused to swear would incur a fine and exile. When the bill was being voted upon, the tribunes who tried to veto it were run off by the soldiers; no one else dared oppose the bill at risk to his life. Therefore, the bill passed, and Marius' soldiers in the German wars received land in Gaul.

Many people—including Marius, who had supported him— were now angry at Saturninus for using violence to get the bill approved. Popular opinion against Saturninus peaked when his friend Glaucia, who was running for the consulate, had his main rival assassinated. The Senate passed the *consultum ultimum* and entrusted Marius with preserving the safety of the state. In the ensuing violence Saturninus, Glaucia, and their supporters were killed.

CHAPTER 18

The Italian Wars
and the Career of Sulla

By the start of the first century B.C. almost two hundred years had elapsed since Rome had gained control of peninsular Italy. During those years Roman power had spread over many of the Mediterranean lands, a phenomenal success that the Romans could not have achieved without the help of the Latins and the Italian allies.

During that time, however, little change was made to reflect the important role that the Latins and Italian allies had played. The Latins still could not vote in Rome, and the Italian allies had no rights at all against the power of Roman magistrates. Consequently the *Latinum nomen* became less a sign of honor, and more a stigma of second-class status. The conduct of the Roman magistrates was also becoming more obnoxious, and this emphasized to Latins and Italians their inferior position with regard to Romans. In 123 Gaius Gracchus had spoken about this glaring example of the magistrates' abuse of power:

Recently the consul came to Teanum Sidicinum. His wife said that she wanted to bathe in the men's baths. The job of driving out those who were using the baths was given to M. Marius, the quaestor of Sidicinum. The consul's wife announced to him that the baths had not been given up to her quickly enough and that they were not clean enough. Consequently a stake was put in the forum and M. Marius, the most eminent man in the city, was led to it. His clothes were ripped off, and he was flogged. When the people of Cales heard about this, they passed the decree that no one should use the baths when a Roman magistrate was nearby. At Ferentinum, for the same reason, our praetor ordered the quaestors to be brought forward: one threw himself from the city wall [committing suicide], and the other was seized and flogged. (Aulus Gellius X.3)

In 91 a new tribune, Drusus, wanted to propose a law giving Roman citizenship to the Latins and Italians. He encountered opposition from the Senate, whose members feared encroachments upon their power; from the Roman people, who did not want to share with the allies the benefits of Roman citizenship (free grain, land in the colonies, freedom from direct taxes, higher pay in the army, and shorter term of military service); and even from some of the Italians themselves, who feared that his plans for creating colonies might take their land. Drusus' legislation for colonies, which had already been approved, was declared invalid, and he was murdered before he could bring to a vote his legislation to grant citizenship to the Italians. The knights then coerced the tribunes into passing a law prosecuting all those who tried to help the Italians get the vote, and many eminent Romans were driven into exile.

The Italians could find no more patience. The first rebellion of the Italians against Rome had occurred years earlier at Fregellae, a city long faithful and steadfast to Rome, but pushed too far; it revolted in 125 B.C. and was quickly subdued. Asculum was the next to rebel; in 91 its citizens killed a Roman praetor (who had been sent there precisely to prevent a rebellion) and all Romans residing there. Both sides prepared for war.

The rebel Italian confederacy was concentrated in the south of Italy, among Italy's most formidable fighting men, the Samnites, Marsi (hence another name for the war, the Marsic War; it is also called the Social War), Paeligni, and others. Many of their soldiers had fought under Roman commanders. They chose Corfinium as their capital, and renamed it Italia; they coined their own money, on which their symbol, the Italian bull, was represented goring the Roman wolf. The Etruscans and Gauls in the north of Italy did not revolt, nor did the Latins and the Greek cities in the south.

If the Romans had any doubts about the ability of the Italians to wage a successful war without Roman leadership, they were soon corrected. The leadership of the rebel confederacy proved to be excellent; the rebels defeated the Roman armies in the first battles, even killing two Roman commanders. Sulla and Marius helped turn the tide for the Romans, who were aided also by Pompeius Strabo from Picenum (we will hear more about his son). The rebels had made it clear to the Senate that the war would be fierce; seeing that Rome could eventually lose, or that a victory would be too costly, the consul L. Caesar (uncle of Julius, who was then ten years old) passed a law that gave Roman citizenship to all the Italians who had remained loyal to Rome. The next year, the Lex Plautia Papiria was passed, giving citizenship to the rebels who stopped fighting. The laws had the desired effect, and no more towns and cities joined the rebels' side. The vote was further given to the peoples in Transpadane Gaul.

Some fighting remained, with the Romans eventually gaining control through the victories of Sulla, who used this opportunity to try to exterminate the Samnites. By 88 B.C. most of the fighting was finished, and by 84 all free-born Italians had Roman citizenship. One condition of their citizenship was that they had to adopt Roman government as the model for their local government. The newly enfranchised were still at a political disadvantage, for few would come to Rome to vote, and even then their enrollment in the tribes (where they would vote) was manipulated so as to dilute their voting power.

SULLA TAKES OVER ROME

Although Italy was peaceful, Rome itself became the scene of much fighting and bloodshed. Sulla and Marius, despite having served together in successful wars against Jugurtha, the Germans, and the rebellious Italians, had long nursed a bitter hatred of each other. Marius was envious of Sulla because Sulla had received much of the credit for the capture of Jugurtha: A statue had been placed on the Capitol depicting Jugurtha's being handed over to Sulla, not Marius. Sulla, a cultured man from an aristocratic family, had the lukewarm support of the Senate, even though he had been raised in poverty and his family had not gained high office in two centuries. Marius, however, who came from an equestrian family from outside the town Arpinum and who disdained the arts, was dear to the common people. The differences between the two soon led to bloodshed, because Marius wanted the command in a war against Mithridates, king of Pontus in Asia Minor, while the Senate had voted that Sulla, consul of that year (88), should receive the command.

Mithridates had taken advantage of Rome's involvement in the Italian Wars by conquering much of Roman Asia Minor and was busy now with the islands in the Aegean Sea. At the same time, one of his sons was reducing Thrace and Macedonia. From his base in Athens he was also inciting revolt in Greece; some Greeks and peoples in Asia Minor looked to him for liberation from Roman oppression. Worst, he had arranged a massacre of all Italians and Romans living in Asia Minor; at least eighty thousand Romans and Italians were killed on the appointed day.

To gain the much desired command against Mithridates, Marius sought and received help from the tribune Sulpicius. Sulpicius had no scruples about using force to get his legislation passed; he maintained a private army of three thousand swordsmen and used a gang of young knights, whom he called the Anti-Senate, to intimidate the assemblies. His Anti-Senate forced one assembly to change the command against Mithridates from Sulla to Marius, and in the ensuing riot the son of the consul Pompeius and many enemies of Marius were killed; Sulla, his family, and his friends were forced to flee for safety.

Sulpicius had sent his men to Campania, where the army was located, to bring it to Marius in Rome, but Sulla arrived first and brought the army back to Rome. This was the first time that Roman soldiers invaded Rome. Marius did not have time to organize effective opposition, but Sulla and his soldiers did have to engage in a few hours of street fighting to take the city. During the fighting, people on rooftops were throwing ceiling tiles down on Sulla and his troops below; Sulla ordered his soldiers to burn down the buildings, and even threw the first torch himself. Marius fled to Africa, where he started collecting a force of his veteran soldiers to fight against Sulla.

Sulla now held power in Rome. He had the Senate set a price on the heads of Sulpicius and Marius, and had Sulpicius hunted down and killed. One story says that one of Sulpicius' slaves killed his master; Sulla rewarded the slave with his freedom, and then had him thrown from the Tarpeian Rock for killing his master. Sulla made some changes in the Roman constitution: the Popular Assembly could no longer legislate, and legislation from the Comitia Centuriata would need the Senate's approval. Then he went east, to fight Mithridates.

MARIUS AND CINNA TAKE OVER ROME

During Sulla's absence from Rome, Marius returned to Rome with his veterans, where he joined the new consul, Cinna. They took over Rome and had a reign of terror in which they murdered many leading members of the aristocratic party as well as Sulla's supporters and family. Metella, Sulla's wife, fled with their children to Sulla (who was besieging Athens, which supported Mithridates) and brought him the news that their house in Rome and their villas had been burned down. Marius soon died, having drunk himself to death.

Sulla, meanwhile, was working to deprive Mithridates of his base in Greece. To do this he had to conquer Athens, which was obstinate in its support of Mithridates; Sulla captured Athens in 86 B.C. and let his soldiers loot and kill in Athens as they wished, for during the siege the Athenian tyrant Aristion had shouted obscene jokes about Metella to him, complete with gestures. Sulla then joined forces with the governor of Macedonia, and together they defeated Mithridates' troops in Greece in two separate battles. Sulla and Mithridates met in the Troad, in the northwest corner of Asia Minor, and concluded a treaty, which was lenient to the Asian king. Sulla's soldiers were angry that Mithridates, after organizing the massacre of many thousands of Italians, should even retain his kingdom, but Sulla was too preoccupied with problems in Rome to spend much time bickering with Mithridates.

SULLA RETAKES ROME

While Sulla was in Greece and the East, his enemies in Rome had solidified their opposition to him, so that Sulla had to fight to return to Italy in 83 B.C. In this he was helped by his lieutenants

Crassus and Pompey. Then only twenty-three years old, Pompey on his own initiative had raised a force of more than six thousand armed men and joined forces with Sulla. Sulla and his allies defeated the consul Norbanus and Marius' son in battle. The opposition that Sulla faced from the consul Scipio was easily removed when Scipio's troops deserted him for Sulla. Sulla again defeated the younger Marius, who committed suicide; he then almost lost his last battle outside of Rome, at the Colline Gate. Crassus saved the battle for Sulla, who had had to take refuge in his camp.

Having gained control over Rome, Sulla killed his enemies with a vengeance that was even more bloodthirsty than that of Marius; his victims were mostly *equites* and *populares*. When someone complained to him that people did not like living in uncertainty over whether or not executioners would be coming after them, Sulla responded by drawing up proscription lists: A reward of two talents was given to the person bringing Sulla the head of a person whose name was on the list. Sulla's victims in the proscriptions are estimated to have numbered around six thousand.

Sulla, although fierce in his revenge, nonetheless saw that Roman government needed to be reformed. He had himself appointed "dictator for the sake of reestablishing the republic," with immunity for his past acts and the power of life and death over others. Then he began to reform the republic. To the Senate, which needed new men after all the recent executions and wars, and whose quality of leadership had, to say the least, stagnated, Sulla added three hundred new members, all from the equestrian class; he also hoped that the mix of the two orders, patricians and equestrians, would lessen future conflict between them. He probably also had in mind the unification of Italy, for many of the new members were non-Roman Italians. Another reform put certain restrictions in the *cursus honorum*: The minimum age for consuls was now forty-two; for praetors, thirty-nine; and for quaestors, thirty. He further passed the requirement that a man must wait ten years between his first and second consulship; the same applied to tribunes. Other changes voided the tribunes' unlimited ability to legislate in the Popular Assembly and put restrictions on the tribunate: A man becoming tribune was now barred from further political office. He restored the law courts to senatorial control. After making those reforms and others, L. Cornelius Sulla Felix (Lucky) retired in 79 B.C., after having been dictator for three years. He died the next year.

LEPIDUS AND SERTORIUS

Sulla's reforms and the restored senatorial rule were immediately challenged in the year after his retirement. The two consuls elected for 78 were Catulus, who was pro-Sulla and pro-Senate, and Lepidus (father of the future triumvir), who was opposed to Sulla and the Senate. Through their year in office, the two argued so frequently and vehemently—Lepidus wanted to repeal Sulla's reforms, and Catulus did not—that the Senate compelled the two to swear that they would not resort to violence against each other.

Once Lepidus learned what province he would govern as a proconsul, he left Rome before supervising elections for the next year. He enlisted soldiers to take to the province he was to govern, but never actually left Italy; instead, he stayed in northern Italy with his soldiers. The Senate eventually called him back to Rome to oversee the elections; Lepidus returned, but he came leading his army against Rome and demanding a second consulship for himself and the restoration of the tribune's powers.

The Senate passed the *ultimum consultum* and called upon Pompey for extra help. Catulus defeated Lepidus outside Rome, while in Mutina Pompey defeated and (despite having given a promise of safety) killed Brutus, Lepidus' lieutenant (and father of Julius Caesar's murderer). Lepidus soon died, and his soldiers fled to Spain.

The challenge that Lepidus posed to senatorial authority in Rome was small, because he was inexperienced. All too soon the Senate learned what problems a brilliant opponent could cause. Their teacher was named Sertorius.

Sertorius, like Lepidus, was opposed to Sulla and oligarchic government. He had given his support to Cinna and Marius, but disagreed with them over the murders of their political enemies. When Sulla returned to Italy after conquering Mithridates, and was winning his battles against his Roman enemies, Sertorius went to Spain as governor, to hold out against Sulla and his supporters.

In Spain Sertorius found the local people bitterly resentful of Roman rule. He managed to make himself popular among the Spanish by ruling fairly and reducing taxes. Nonetheless, after becoming dictator, Sulla sent one of his supporters to govern Spain in Sertorius' place. Sertorius and the replacement governor fought a battle for control over Spain; Sertorius lost, and fled. After spending some time with pirates in Africa, he was invited by the natives of Lusitania (modern Portugal) to command their army. It did not take him long to win the hearts and minds of the people with his fair dealing and his magical fawn.

It happened that a hunter had scared a doe, which had just given birth to a milk-white fawn. The doe escaped from the hunter, but left the fawn alive for the hunter to capture. The hunter gave the fawn to Sertorius; soon he had the fawn so well trained and accustomed to him that it would follow him, show no fear of people and crowds—even in the middle of the camp—and come when he called. Sertorius convinced the local people that the fawn was a gift from the goddess Diana and that it told him secrets. For example, he would receive secret scouting reports and tell the people that the fawn had told him; with that divinely given information, he would then conquer the enemy. Or he would secretly hear of a victory by one of his lieutenants; he would then crown the fawn with garlands and tell the people that good news was on the way—news that eventually arrived. The people believed he was some kind of god and followed his every command.

Sertorius did not disappoint the people: His brilliant strategies and use of guerrilla warfare led him and his small army of fewer than ten thousand to win battles against overwhelming odds. He defeated many Roman commanders and inflicted many defeats on Metellus (son of the Metellus who had fought against Jugurtha), the latest Roman to be sent against him. Desperate, the Senate ordered Pompey (who, wanting another command, hesitated to disband his army after defeating Brutus) to go help Metellus against Sertorius.

About the same time that Pompey arrived in Spain to help Metellus, the remnants of Lepidus' army, twenty thousand soldiers led by one Perperna, arrived too and joined Sertorius' side; Sertorius now had a large army, and all the Spanish tribes from the Ebro River to the Pyrenees Mountains were on his side.

Sertorius greeted Pompey by inflicting a humiliating defeat. Pompey was supposed to protect an allied town, which Sertorius was besieging; Sertorius tricked Pompey, so that Pompey could neither attack Sertorius nor help the allied town—he could only watch as Sertorius besieged the town, let the inhabitants escape alive, and then burned down the town. In another battle, Pompey's forces were defeated, and Pompey himself narrowly escaped being captured by leaving his horse—with its golden ornaments and expensive equipment—to the enemy. The morning after another battle, as Pompey was wounded and his forces scattered, Sertorius readied his forces for the final blow to Pompey when he learned that Metellus had arrived to help Pompey. "If that old woman [Metellus] had not been there, I would have spanked that child [Pompey] before sending him off to Rome!" said Sertorius (Plutarch, *Sertorius* XIX).

Pompey, desperate, sent a letter to the Senate, demanding more money and soldiers; otherwise, he wrote, he would leave Spain. Rumors in Rome said that Sertorius would arrive in Italy before Pompey did. Metellus, also desperate, offered a reward of a hundred talents of silver and twenty thousand *iugera* (twelve thousand acres) of land to the person who killed Sertorius. Sertorius had even been invited by Mithridates to enter into an alliance against Rome, yet Sertorius did not like the provision that if victorious, Mithridates would gain the Roman province of Asia; Sertorius thought that would be dishonorable to himself.

Despite his success, Sertorius too was in trouble. His fawn disappeared, and he lost a few skirmishes; his hold on the people was slipping, even after the fawn had returned. When Pompey's reinforcements—two legions and a large sum of money—arrived from Rome, the morale of the Spanish plummeted. They had been fighting Rome for more than a century. Rome's resources seemed infinite. As their morale collapsed, Sertorius became more imperious, which caused more resentment among his followers. His very successes in military and political matters filled some of his officers with envy.

A conspiracy was formed against his life. His officer Perperna assassinated him and took over the command. But Perperna was no match for Pompey, who soon returned to Rome, victorious.

SPARTACUS

Rome soon faced another rebellion, this one in Italy. In 73 B.C. a Thracian gladiator named Spartacus led other gladiators in Capua to revolt, and soon many other slaves joined him. The slave army grew so large—numbering seventy thousand men—that Spartacus was able to divide it into three different bodies. Spartacus had the realistic goal not of sacking Rome but simply of making it to the Alps and from there escaping to freedom. Under his leadership the slave army won battles over three different Roman commanders, even capturing one praetor's camp and another praetor's lictors and horse. Eventually the slave troops defeated a consular army of ten thousand soldiers.

Finally, the Senate put Crassus (Sulla's former lieutenant) in charge of the Roman forces, and he won some battles against the slave army. Crassus was eager to complete the war before Pompey arrived from Spain, for he feared that Pompey would get the credit for the victory. Crassus won the last major battle with Spartacus' army, but the fugitives from Spartacus' forces fell in with Pompey's army, which destroyed them; six thousand of the Spartacans who survived were crucified along the Appian Way, to serve as a warning to other slaves. Pompey sent a letter to the Senate with the information that while Crassus had defeated the slave army in a pitched battle, Pompey had "ripped the heart and soul out of the rebellion" (Plutarch, *Crassus* XI). What Crassus had feared became true: Pompey got the credit for the defeat of Spartacus.

CHAPTER 19

The Rise of Pompey

Upon his return to Rome in 71 B.C., after destroying the remnants of Spartacus' army, Pompey did not immediately disband his army; he simply camped his troops outside of Rome while he asked the Senate for a triumph and for permission to run for the consulship of 70. Since people were worried about his intentions, Pompey replied that he would disband his army as soon as he had celebrated his triumph. Pompey had to ask the Senate for permission to run for the consulship because he had not gone through the *cursus honorum*: to run for the consulship, one had to have served as a quaestor and praetor, and the minimum age was forty-two.

In his thirty-six years of life, Pompey had not been elected to any of the offices in the *cursus honorum*. He had fought in his father's army during the Social War, and after his father's death, he had gathered an army of his father's ex-supporters and joined Sulla. Sulla sent Pompey to fight in Gaul, Sicily, and Africa, where he earned the title *imperator*. Upon Pompey's return to Italy, Sulla himself rode out to meet Pompey along the way to Rome, and even addressed him as *magnus* (great), yet at first he refused Pompey's request for a triumph, citing a law that the man holding the triumph must be at least a consul or praetor. Pompey reminded Sulla that people worship the rising, not the setting, sun. Pompey was the first knight to be granted a triumph. He wanted his chariot to be pulled by four elephants, instead of horses, but had to abandon that plan when it was discovered that the elephants would not fit through the city gates. After Sulla's death, Pompey fought Brutus, Lepidus' lieutenant (and father of Caesar's future assassin); Sertorius in Spain; and the remains of the Spartacan slave army. Pompey had not been elected quaestor, and by Sulla's reforms he was not eligible even for the Senate; Sulla had probably had just such cases in mind when he passed his reforms.

The Senate hoped to play Crassus and Pompey off against each other, but Crassus, who likewise had not disbanded his army, overcame his suspicion and hatred of Pompey for taking the credit for the victory over Spartacus and took Pompey's side. The Senate, lacking an army, gave in and allowed Pompey to run for the consulship. Crassus and Pompey were then elected consuls for 70. Pompey, who did not even know the rules of procedure in the Senate, had the scholar Varro write him a handbook on how to conduct Senate meetings.

Although they were former partisans of the pro-Senate Sulla, Pompey and Crassus immediately restored to the tribunes the power that Sulla had abolished. Now the tribunes could again pass legislation in the popular assemblies, and the tribunate was no longer a deadend office. Why did they restore the tribunate? They wanted to make themselves popular with the common people, and they wanted the power that came from control of the Popular Assembly; perhaps they also understood that the Senate, after being pressured to allow Pompey to run for the consulate, would not be well disposed toward them in the future and would find ways of getting revenge.

The tribunate performed the valuable function of protecting the common people from the magistrates' abuse of power and ensuring that they had a voice in the government. Since the Gracchi, however, the tribunate had become more of a legislative organ, a function for which it was not originally designed. The tribunes led the Popular Assembly; the decisions it passed, called *plebiscita*, automatically became law, regardless of the Senate. The people attending meetings of the Popular Assembly did not have the wide scope of vision necessary for deciding important issues. Most lacked an elementary education, had no knowledge of or experience in foreign affairs, no knowledge of law, no experience in politics and the machinery of government. Many of those who voted in the Popular Assembly were Rome's unemployed and idle masses, who lived from day to day on subsidized grain: "the scum of Romulus," the writer Cicero called them in one of his letters. The Popular Assembly had voted against giving the *socii Italici* the right to vote because they did not want to share the privileges of Roman citizenship with non-Romans; only a threat to Rome's existence convinced the mob to do what was right. Led by an unscrupulous tribune, like Sulpicius or Saturninus, the Popular Assembly could ruin Rome. We will see later what trouble an evil tribune like Clodius could cause in Rome.

Other than restoring the tribunate, Pompey and Crassus accomplished little during their consulship. The rivalry and hostility between them led to inaction and suspicion. At the end of their year in office, they had a public reconciliation.

WAR AGAINST THE PIRATES

Pompey soon benefited from restoring the tribunate, for a tribune friendly to him created an extraordinary command for him against the pirates who now ruled the Mediterranean Sea. Their forces are said to have numbered more than a thousand ships, with which they are said to have sacked more than four hundred cities. They even raided and sacked Ostia, the port of Rome, in 68 B.C. Pirates would capture people and sell them into slavery or else hold them for ransom; they captured two praetors and their lictors, and the daughter of a former consul. One of their most famous victims was the young G. Julius Caesar, whom they held for a ransom of twenty talents. He is said to have ridiculed them, saying that they obviously did not know whom they were holding, and he volunteered to pay fifty talents. Once his ransom was paid and he was released, he gathered together some friends, returned to the pirates who had held him hostage, and crucified them all.

Since merchants feared to sail the seas, the price of grain sky-rocketed; led by the tribune Gabinius, the Romans rightly voted for an enormous effort to clear the Mediterranean of pirates, but wrongly voted the command to Pompey. The command of the war against the pirates encompassed great powers: three years' command over the entire Mediterranean, even fifty miles inland into the many provinces, with the commander having equal authority with the governors of those provinces; six thousand talents for expenses; two hundred ships; and as many men as necessary. The terms of the command were later enlarged to five hundred ships, one hundred twenty thousand men, five thousand cavalry, and twenty-four *legati* with praetorian power. Once the voters entrusted this huge command to Pompey, the price of grain plummeted; people said that just the *name* Pompey had ended the pirates' domination.

With such a force at his disposal, an unscrupulous commander could have devastated Italy and Rome. Rome was lucky: Pompey was not unscrupulous, only vain. When he addressed the Senate after being given the command, he admonished the senators for overloading him with onerous duties: "Do not conclude that I am still a young man, and don't simply add it up as so many years since I was born. If you count up the armies that I have led, and the risks that I have run, you will find that they are more than my years. Consequently you will be more ready to believe that I can still be steadfast through the labors and stress" (Dio XXXVI.25).

In spite of the stress, Pompey yielded to the demands of his country and began his operations against the pirates. Within three months he had cleared the Mediterranean of pirates. His forces had seized ninety warships with bronze prows and had captured more than twenty thousand pirates. Instead of executing the prisoners, Pompey settled them inland in underpopulated areas.

WAR AGAINST MITHRIDATES

The tribune G. Manilius, with help from Cicero (whose speech on the matter survives) and Caesar, next helped Pompey by bestowing upon him another command as well. Mithridates, king of Pontus, with whom Sulla had reached a hasty peace in 83 B.C., was again stirring up trouble in Asia. He was not breaking any treaties with Rome in doing so, however, for the Senate had never ratified Sulla's treaty with him. Mithridates now occupied most of Asia Minor, and the people of the Roman province were glad to see him come, for he was rescuing them from oppression by the *publicani*. So rapacious were these tax-collectors that local people are said to have had to sell their adolescent children in order to pay their creditors.

By 67 B.C. the Roman general Lucullus had had some success against Mithridates, and by cutting taxes and outlawing exorbitant interest rates he managed to regain the local peoples' allegiance to Rome. Lucullus was not allowed to complete the victory over Mithridates, however, for although he was loved by the local peoples for his fairness and justice, he had made himself very unpopular with the *equites* and his own soldiers. The knights disliked him because he protected the provincials from their depredations, and his soldiers hated his harsh authority and the fact that he had kept them active during two winters. Lucullus' soldiers even mutinied and not infrequently refused to follow orders. Therefore, the *equites* worked to have the command against Mithridates transferred to Pompey, who, they supposed, would let them squeeze as much tax money from the provincials as they could. The bill passed, and Pompey took over the command against Mithridates. He is said to have remarked, upon hearing that he had been given the command, "Damn these neverending labors—it's just one thing after another! It would be so much better if I were a nobody, if I can never stop leading armies and, free from others' envy and jealousy, just live with my wife in the country" (Plutarch, *Pompey* XXX.6). Of course, Pompey was actually thrilled to be given the command.

Pompey replaced Lucullus in Asia and, to spite him, deliberately changed all the arrangements that he had made; upon which Lucullus called Pompey some type of crazy vulture, for he always swooped down upon nearly dead victims to claim the prize and glory. Although he too defeated Mithridates in many battles, like Lucullus Pompey could not capture the slippery Pontic king. Pompey chased Mithridates all over Asia before Mithridates finally committed suicide in 63 B.C. Pompey had received vast powers to settle affairs in the East after conquering Mithridates; his settlement of Asia created the new Roman provinces of Syria, Judaea, Bithynia, and Pontus. Rome already had the provinces of Asia and Cilicia, and client kings in Armenia and Cappadocia. The triumph that Pompey celebrated upon his return to Rome lasted for two days, which was not long enough for the whole procession, and marked the first time in Roman history when a general had had triumphs for victories in three different continents. Pompey had

celebrated triumphs for victories in Africa (Libya, as Sulla's lieutenant), Europe (against Sertorius in Spain), and now Asia.

THE CONSPIRACY OF CATILINE

While Pompey was fighting Mithridates, the situation in Rome
was tense because of the political ambitions of L. Sergius Catilina
(called by the English form of his name, Catiline). Of Catiline's
early career, we know this: As a lieutenant under Sulla, Catiline
killed his own brother-in-law and then asked Sulla to add the
name to one of the proscription lists, as if the man were still alive.
When a woman whom he fell in love with refused to marry him
because she feared his full-grown son, Catiline killed his son.
Supposedly he had also had relations with a Vestal Virgin. After
serving as praetor in Africa, he was brought to trial for extortion,
but escaped prosecution with the help of the prosecutor, P. Clodius
Pulcher, whose name will be mentioned again when the topic is
corruption.

Catiline had failed in his bids to become consul for 65 and 64
B.C. As a patrician, he felt it both his right to hold a consulship and
a pollution of the consulate when a nonpatrician was elected
consul. After losing twice, Catiline was urgent in his third attempt
to become consul, for the year 63. His urgency was increased by
his penchant for living beyond his means; he was hopelessly in
debt. To increase his chances of being elected consul for 63,
Catiline ran on the platform of *novae tabulae* (cancellation of
debts) and redistribution of land. The severely impoverished men
who, like Catiline, lived beyond their means and had spent their
inheritances, gravitated to him and his revolutionary program:
They included impoverished nobles, young men of the equestrian
class, and those of Sulla's ex-soldiers who had squandered what
they had earned during their military careers. Among his followers
were the consul of 71, Lentulus, who had been expelled from the
Senate in 70 but elected praetor again for 63, and Publius Sulla, a
relative of the dead dicator.

Quintus Curius, one of Catiline's supporters, told his mistress
Fulvia about Catiline's plans not just for *novae tabulae*, but also for
proscription of the rich and their estates; alarmed, Fulvia talked,

and rumors spread. The rumors of Catiline's revolutionary program alarmed the nobles and the *equites*, who were most often the creditors, and they succeeded in getting two safe candidates elected consuls in 63. They were G. Antonius and a *novus homo* of equestrian family from Arpinum, M. Tullius Cicero.

Cicero had made his first real splash in Roman politics in 70 B.C. by successfully prosecuting Verres, a governor of Sicily, on charges of extortion of his province. Cicero managed to win the case despite the machinations of Verres' friends; failing to delay the case until 69, when it would be tried under a friendly praetor, they nonetheless managed to delay the beginning of the case until the very last day of the term of the praetor Manius Acilius Glabrio, who apparently was incorruptible (we can assume that attempts at his integrity had been made). Seeing that time was short, Cicero skipped the customary opening speeches and immediately called his witnesses. His case was so overwhelming that Verres did not even bother to defend himself but after only one day of the trial went straight into exile. Cicero differed from other consuls in that he was not primarily a military man. Although he had served as quaestor, aedile, and praetor, and had won honors and a good reputation both in the military and in civilian life, Cicero based his future in Roman politics on his knowledge of law and on his eloquence—that is, his ability to compose and express logical and sensible arguments in language pleasing to the audience's ear, the goal being to persuade his audience to follow his recommendations. After winning his case against Verres and publishing the speeches against him—speeches he had never actually delivered— Cicero was acknowledged the best orator in Rome and became known as someone who espoused the conservative values of Italy outside Rome and who supported the rule of the Senate against the *populares*.

In 63, after being delayed because of threats from Catiline, elections were held for 62; Catiline again failed to win the consulate; he was by now a desperate man. He now formed a plan to assassinate Cicero. It was the custom that patrons would open their doors in the morning to receive their guests and clients, who would come to see what assignments the patron had for them; Catiline's accomplices planned to wait outside Cicero's house and kill him when he opened his doors the next morning. Gaius Curius, however, became alarmed for Cicero and told Fulvia, who warned Cicero; Cicero foiled his would-be assassins by barring his doors.

Cicero then informed the Senate of the danger, and the Senate passed the *ultimum consultum*. Cicero lacked hard evidence, however; he could only convene the Senate and deliver his "First Oration against Catiline" (still a staple of third- and fourth-year Latin classes), in which he ordered Catiline to leave the city. To further dramatize the danger, Cicero made sure that everyone saw the breastplate that he was wearing under his toga. Without hard evidence, Cicero and the Senate could do little more than post guards, raise an army, and offer rewards for information. After exclaiming to the Senate that he would extinguish the fires of his own destruction with the ruin of the city, Catiline left Rome for his army in its camp in Etruria and had lictors carry *fasces* before him, as if he were a consul or proconsul.

Catiline proceeded with his plans, which now encompassed open war and chaos. This was his plan for seizing power:

Statilius and Gabinius, with a large band of men, were all ordered to set fire to twelve important parts of the city at the same time, so that during the ensuing confusion they could more easily get at the consul and others whom they were plotting against. Cethegus, meanwhile, would wait at Cicero's door and attack him while someone else killed the other consul. The young men in the conspiracy—most of whom were from the noble families—would kill their parents. When all the Romans were reeling from the slaughter and fire, the conspirators would dash out to Catiline. (Sallust, *Bellum Catilinae* XLIII)

One source reports that they planned also to kidnap Pompey's children and hold them for ransom. They would have needed something extraordinary to control Pompey the Great when he returned to Rome with the army that had just conquered Mithridates.

The hard evidence that Cicero needed soon came. Catiline was trying to incite rebellion in different parts of Italy and accordingly approached a Gallic tribe called the Allobroges, who had many reasons to hate Roman rule. They decided to reject Catiline's offers to join the conspiracy, and instead they told Cicero of Catiline's offer. Cicero asked the Gauls to play along with Catiline and to fool him into giving them more information about the conspiracy. The Gauls did as they were asked: They pretended to be interested in joining the conspiracy and asked Catiline and the other conspirators for written instructions of what they were to do and written promises of what they would gain, so they could discuss the proposal with other members of their tribe. The Gauls dutifully handed the letter over to Cicero's agents.

Some of the conspirators were then caught. Upon interrogation, they gave more information about the conspiracy. Cicero had the captured conspirators executed; among them was Lentulus, who had been consul in 71 and was praetor this year. The praetor Metellus Celer then defeated Catiline's forces in Etruria; Catiline himself was killed in the hard-fought battle.

Cicero had saved Rome from Catiline, and the victory was important—so important, in fact, that Cicero reminded the Romans of his heroism in practically every speech he gave for the rest of his life. He, a *novus homo* without a great army to back him, had conquered Catiline without disrupting life in the city and without causing a huge uproar. For a while he managed to unite the nobles, *equites*, and common people behind him in defeating Catiline; for that he was given the honorary title *pater patriae* (father of his country). After this victory, Cicero proposed a program that he called *concordia ordinum* (harmony among the classes), by which he hoped to appease the different classes in the city, so that the republic would survive. His program failed, but it did so for reasons beyond his control. He also later paid for that victory over Catiline; despite the *senatus ultimum consultum*, which was supposed to give him more power to save the state, years later he was sent into exile for having executed Roman citizens who had not had an appeal. In fact, on the last day of his term, Cicero was prevented by the tribunes from swearing the oath, customary for a departing consul, that he had not violated the constitution. Instead, Cicero swore that he had saved his country.

THE BONA DEA SCANDAL

The following year, 62 B.C., a scandal broke out among the nobility in Rome that had political repercussions a few years later. It was the custom to have an annual celebration of the Bona Dea (Good Goddess, a goddess probably of health), who was worshipped exclusively by women. The celebration was hosted by the wife of one of the consuls or praetors, with all male creatures (human and animal) leaving the house during the celebration. That year, it was hosted by Pompeia, the wife of Julius Caesar, who was a praetor. The noble P. Clodius Pulcher (Catiline's "prosecutor"), who was in love with Pompeia, dressed himself as a female flute player and had himself brought into the house, to have a tryst with her.

Clodius was discovered inside the house and eventually was put on trial for sacrilege. Caesar refused to give testimony against Clodius, but he did divorce his wife, saying, "Members of my family must be as free of suspicion as of accusations" (Plutarch, *Caesar* X). Cicero did give evidence against Clodius and wrecked his alibi. Nonetheless, Clodius was acquitted because, some say, Crassus had bribed the jury. Clodius did not forget the fact that Cicero had given testimony against him.

CHAPTER 20

The First Triumvirate

While Pompey was in the East fighting Mithridates in 65 B.C., the Romans—and especially Crassus—worried: Would Pompey return to Rome as Sulla had? Crassus busied himself with finding a military command for support. The first opportunity was a vacancy in the praetors in Spain. Crassus managed to have Gn. Calpurnius Piso sent as a replacement; Piso hated Pompey. But Crassus' hopes for military support from Piso were dashed when he was killed by the Spanish, who could not bear his arrogance, cruelty, and injustice. Next, Crassus tried to have Egypt annexed as a province, with himself as governor; there he would have a small army and an almost impregnable city, along with the treasury of the Ptolemies. But again he was disappointed. Then Crassus tried to enfranchise Transpadane Gaul, so the Gauls there would be his clients and thus more eager to support him in a showdown with Pompey. That too failed. Last, Crassus contributed money to Catiline's bid for the consulship in 65, so he would have a friend with an army. Catiline was not elected consul. Crassus was so worried that when Pompey was approaching Italy, he packed up his family and left Rome.

Crassus' fears turned out to be unwarranted. Pompey returned in 62 and immediately disbanded his army; he also divorced his wife Mucia who, according to rumor, had been having an affair during his absence from Rome. His triumph lasted for two days. He had captured no fewer than a thousand fortified places, nearly nine hundred cities, and eight hundred pirate ships, and he was bringing twenty thousand talents of gold and silver to the public treasury, in addition to the pay and rewards that he had already given his soldiers. Pompey was now truly deserving of his nickname Magnus (the Great).

The Senate too had been afraid of Pompey's return, but in fact he attempted nothing revolutionary. Pompey had only two requests of the Senate: that it ratify his settlement of the East and that it approve a bill to give his veterans land. Since Pompey had enriched the treasury with millions, his requests were not excessive or unrealistic.

Lucullus, whom Pompey had replaced in the command against Mithridates and whose arrangements he had spitefully overturned, now got his revenge. Helped by the consul Metellus, brother of Pompey's ex-wife Mucia, Lucullus led the Senate against Pompey's requests, and the tribunes vetoed the laws that Pompey's associates brought before the Comitia Centuriata. Pompey's enemies in the Senate won: Pompey's veterans did not get their land, and his settlement of the East was not ratified. Pompey is said then to have regretted disbanding his army and leaving himself vulnerable to his enemies.

Pompey was soon approached by Julius Caesar, who saw in the frustrated general an excellent resource for countering his own Optimate enemies in the Senate. Caesar had been praetor in Spain in 61 and hoped to be elected consul for 59; he would need all the allies he could get if he wished to have an effective consulship, for many in the Senate thought him dangerous and would doubtless oppose him, as they had Pompey. Consequently Caesar entered into secret negotiations with Pompey, Crassus (the richest man in Rome), and Cicero (who now was becoming nervous over threats from Clodius) about an alliance by which they would work on each other's behalf against the senatorial opposition. With Pompey's fame and loyal soldiers, Crassus' immeasurable wealth (he once said that a man was not truly wealthy unless he could support an army of forty thousand from his own funds), Cicero's eloquence and respectability, and Caesar's consular power, the four would be unstoppable. Cicero did not join him in the alliance, but Pompey and Crassus did. The alliance, which we call the First Triumvirate, was cemented by the marriage of Caesar's daughter Julia to Pompey in April 59, the year of her father's first consulship.

JULIUS CAESAR'S FIRST CONSULSHIP

Caesar had not had good relations with the Optimates and nobles in the Senate. Early in his career he had declared himself a *popularis*. His aunt Julia had been Marius' wife; Caesar himself, at the age of eighteen, had at considerable risk to his own life defied Sulla's orders to divorce his wife Cornelia, Cinna's daughter. Furthermore, at the funeral of his aunt Julia, Caesar had dared to have the family masks of Marius brought out and worn although they had not been seen in years, owing to fear of the Sullan party. (The masks, called *imagines*, were wax masks of Romans who had held curule office—that is, any office that imparted *imperium*—and were displayed in the family's atrium and brought out at funerals.) Sulla had considered adding Caesar's name to his proscription lists, but did not do so; he just muttered to his fellow aristocrats (who persuaded him not to have Caesar killed) that in Caesar there were many Mariuses.

During his aedileship, Caesar got himself tremendously in debt by entertaining the public with lavish games—320 pairs of gladiators, banquets, and theatrical performances—to win the love of the common people. So avid was he to win the position of pontifex maximus in 63 B.C. that he vowed to outspend all other candidates in their bribery; when leaving the house on election day, he told his mother that he would return as pontifex maximus, or not at all, meaning that he would not be able to face the creditors whose loans had financed the bribery, unless he won. So heavily in debt was Caesar because of his political ambitions and expensive lifestyle that in 62, when he was leaving Rome for his praetorship in Spain, his creditors prevented him from leaving until Crassus posted bond for him and provided security for his debts.

Caesar spent the year 61 as a praetor in Spain (Hispania Ulterior), where he conquered the tribes of the Lusitani and the Callaeci, earned the title *imperator*, and acquired a great deal of money. Upon his return from Spain, he wanted both to have a triumph for his military victories and to run for the consulship of 59. According to the rules, he could not do both, since a general awaiting a triumph had to wait outside the *pomerium* with his army, while a candidate had to be present in Rome. Cato, a strict constitutionalist and great-grandson of Cato the Censor, kept the proposal from coming to a vote by speaking the entire day; Caesar then abandoned his show of glory so he could seek real power. Caesar had also been suspected of being a member of the conspiracy of Catiline, but supposedly Cicero, not believing that Caesar was a member, saved his life.

For all these reasons the nobles were suspicious of Caesar. He restored the statues of Marius to the Forum, an act that led one noble to exclaim that Caesar was aiming at supreme power in Rome. Supposedly, while he and some of his friends were passing through a squalid and desolate village in the Alps, and his friends were joking that even in such a small and insignificant village men vied in cutthroat contests for political power, Caesar mentioned that he would rather be first man there than second man in Rome. Another story says that Caesar, seeing a bust of Alexander the Great in a temple of Hercules, suddenly groaned deeply, exclaiming that at the same age in his life, Alexander had already conquered the known world while he himself had done nothing of importance.

Upon assuming office, Caesar brought before the Senate the first of his many proposals, one aimed at giving land to Pompey's veterans and ratifying Pompey's settlement of the East. It was immediately obstructed by his political enemies, with Cato (again) filibustering the bill. Caesar had Cato arrested and taken to jail; when many senators, in protest, joined Cato in jail, Caesar had him set free, realizing that Cato was more dangerous in jail than on the rostrum. Since the Senate was blocking him, Caesar took his bills to the Popular Assembly instead. When his colleague Bibulus—Cato's son-in-law and a longstanding, bitter enemy of Caesar—tried to obstruct him there, the crowd attacked Bibulus, broke his *fasces*, and dumped a basket of dung on his head; thereafter Bibulus spent most of his consulate at home, "watching the heavens," and declaring that public business could not be conducted because of bad omens. Consequently, all of Caesar's bills were technically invalid.

While addressing the Popular Assembly about the land bills, Caesar had Pompey standing on one side and Crassus on the other. Caesar asked the people if they liked his proposals; when they shouted yes, he asked them for help in getting the proposals passed.

Pompey then added that if the Senate brought a sword against them, he would bring "a shield and a sword." Pompey also packed the assembly with his soldiers to intimidate those voting. Caesar's proposal granting land to Pompey's veterans, and another law granting more protection to the provincials against the *publicani*, were passed. He regained the good will of the *publicani* by cutting the tax contracts by a third when they claimed that they had overestimated how much they could collect in taxes from Asia and stood to lose money; this act—essentially a huge bribe for the *publicani*—was part of Crassus' reward for joining him and Pompey.

For Caesar, the most important law that he got passed concerned the allotment of proconsular provinces for the year 58. In 61 the Optimates had seen that Caesar would probably win the consulship for 59, and to thwart his ambitions, they voted that the consuls of 59, as proconsuls in 58, should be in charge of rounding up cattle and keeping the forests clear of robbers—not exactly the military command that Caesar had in mind. So Caesar passed a law that disregarded the Senate's allotment of provinces during his proconsulship and gave him the governorship of Cisalpine Gaul and Illyricum with three legions for five years; when the governor of Transalpine Gaul died shortly after, Pompey managed to have Caesar appointed governor of that province as well.

The triumvirate had accomplished its goals: Pompey's veterans got their land and his settlement of the East was ratified; Caesar got an army and the opportunity to use it; and Crassus got the one-third remission on taxes in Asia for the benefit of the *publicani*. Yet the price paid was heavy, for the three men were now deeply hated by Romans and Italians for their domination of politics and their use of force in getting their laws passed. This hatred affected Pompey in particular, for he wanted to be loved by the people; at one performance in the theater an actor turned to face Pompey when he spoke the line, "Nostra miseria tu es magnus" (You are a great part of our misery). Undoubtedly the actor stressed the word *magnus*, and the audience forced him to repeat it countless times (Cicero, *Ep. ad Att.* II.19.3). On another occasion, Caesar was booed when he entered the theater, while Curio, one of the triumvirate's staunch opponents, entered the theater to great applause.

From his house, Bibulus was earning great glory by opposing the triumvirs' *regnum* or *dominatio*. A joke of the day said that the laws had been passed in the consulship of Julius and Caesar. The scholar Varro expressed his opposition to the three by writing a political pamphlet entitled *The Three-headed Monster*. In November of that year Cicero wrote to his friend Atticus, "I have nothing to write you about the republic, except the deepest hatred of all people against those who control everything. There is no hope of a change; but, as you easily see, their hatred bothers Pompey and he regrets it. I don't quite see how this will end, but it certainly seems that things will erupt somehow" (*Ep. ad Att.* II.XXII).

Cicero soon found out how things would erupt because he had angered the triumvirate. In a speech given one morning in late 59, Cicero questioned the legality of the laws that Caesar had passed. Caesar acted with his usual speed and decisiveness: That afternoon P. Clodius, a patrician (from the Claudius family), was adopted into a plebeian family, with Caesar as pontifex maximus and Pompey as augur overseeing the *adoptio*. It mattered not one bit that Clodius was forty-eight years old and his adoptive father twenty years younger. Clodius hated Cicero and had sworn long before to get revenge on him for wrecking his alibi during the Bona Dea trial; after his adoption into a plebeian family, he was eligible for the tribunate, and he was elected one of the tribunes for 58 B.C. Cicero waited nervously, although he was assured by his friends (including Pompey and Caesar) that Clodius could not touch him.

CAESAR IN GAUL

Toward the end of 59 B.C. Caesar departed for his provinces, Transalpine and Cisalpine Gaul, where he would end up fighting for the next nine years. Caesar himself described his experiences there in his *Gallic Wars*, a year-by-year account of his strategies and campaigns, his battles, his soldiers, the countries (Gaul, Germany, and England), and the peoples living there. Written in Caesar's simple and clear style, the *Gallic Wars* contains a treasure of information about the workings of the Roman and allied armies as led by one of history's best generals and writers.

The war for Caesar started in this way. The Helvetii, a Germanic tribe, were migrating into Gaul from their home in the Alps, and were destroying the lands of the Aedui, a Gallic tribe allied to Rome. After conquering the Helvetii, Caesar learned that the Gauls were threatened also by Ariovistus, the king of the Germanic tribe called the Suebi, who already possessed land on the Gallic side of the Rhine. Ariovistus was considered a friend of Rome, but he did not consider the Germans inferior or subordinate to the Romans, and consequently refused to follow Caesar's orders to leave Rome's Gallic allies alone. Ariovistus told Caesar to get his army out of that part of Gaul or he would have them hunted down and killed as enemies—something, he admitted to Caesar, that no doubt would please many nobles in Rome.

Caesar won the battle that soon followed, and next found himself fighting against the Gallic tribes of the Belgae and the Nervii. The battle against the Nervii shows Caesar's great gift for leadership. The Nervii unexpectedly attacked the Romans while they were still constructing their camp, and swarmed onto them unprepared. The Roman army was in great danger, for the soldiers had not had enough time to remove the covers from their shields or put on their helmets before they had to start fighting. At one point, Caesar himself seized a shield and ran to the front lines, inspiring his men, who redoubled their efforts and turned the tide of the battle. Caesar lost many men that day, but won the battle and almost annihilated the tribe of the Nervii. For Caesar's successes the Senate decreed fifteen days of thanksgiving to the gods. (Incidentally, despite what Shakespeare has Mark Antony say, the real Mark Antony was not with Caesar "that day he overcame the Nervii," for Antony did not join Caesar's staff until 54 B.C., three years after the Battle of the Nervii, which was fought in 57.)

THE TRIBUNATE OF PUBLIUS CLODIUS

Clodius became tribune in 58 B.C. and passed several laws, none of which could be said to be in the best interests of the republic. One law substituted free grain for the masses for grain at reduced prices; by giving the grain away, Clodius substantially increased his popularity and power among the masses in Rome. Another law legalized the various clubs that had been banned because the urban masses were using their freedom to assemble to cause political trouble. (Called *collegia*, most of the clubs had originally been religious or vocational in character and had provided the members with social activities during life and a decent funeral upon death.) Again, Clodius had his own interests at heart, for now he could recruit from the clubs to form his own gang, which he later used to intimidate politicians, the Comitia, and the Senate.

Another law, again in Clodius' interests—for by it he got revenge on Cicero—deprived of fire and water (that is, sent into exile) anyone who had put a Roman citizen to death without a trial. Cicero had done just that: During the conspiracy of Catiline he relied on the Senate's *ultimum consultum* as legal authority to put the conspirators to death without a trial and appeal (see chapter 19). The support of Italy, the equestrians, and the Senate did not help Cicero, and Pompey deserted him because he could not afford to have Cicero threatening his land laws and settlement of the East, which had been passed during Caesar's consulship. So when Cicero came to Pompey's house to beg for help against Clodius, Pompey refused to see him and ducked out the back door. Clodius packed the Popular Assembly with his thugs, and the day before the bill passed, Cicero, wretched and wearing mourning, went into exile in Macedonia; the letters he wrote while there show him frequently contemplating suicide. Clodius burned down Cicero's house and villas, and built a temple to Libertas on the site of his house.

Clodius did not stop after sending Cicero into exile; he even attacked Pompey. At one trial, for example, Clodius led his gang in shouting insults at Pompey. Pompey could have taken Clodius' insults, except for the fact that the Senate and crowd enjoyed seeing him humiliated in public; they were angry with him for deserting Cicero to Clodius' wrath. Later, one of Clodius' slaves was caught with a sword making his way toward Pompey during one of the riots in the Forum. The slave confessed that there was a plot to assassinate Pompey. After that, Pompey went into retirement and spent most of his time walking in his park and gardens with his wife Julia.

Eventually, Pompey realized that he needed Cicero and that he could earn Cicero's gratitude if he secured his recall from exile. Pompey therefore called for help from his many clients and organized his own gang under the leadership of T. Annius Milo, to support a law proposed by Quintus Cicero (Cicero's younger brother) to recall his brother from exile. The day before the vote on the law, there was a huge fight in the Forum between the sides of Clodius and Milo; the streets had to be washed to remove the blood. The law passed, and in 57 B.C. Cicero returned triumphant from exile. The Senate voted to have Cicero's house and villas rebuilt at public expense.

Yet Clodius was not finished. A few of Cicero's letters tell us of Clodius' activities:

On November 6 [57] our carpenters [who were rebuilding Cicero's house] were driven from the building site, since Clodius' men had come, bearing weapons. Catulus' portico, which was being repaired in accordance with a decree of the Senate, was destroyed; it was near completion. Quintus' house was first damaged by rocks thrown from our building site, and then it was set on fire, at the order of Clodius. The city was watching as the fires were tossed on, and all people were groaning and crying [for me]. . . . He rushed around, a madman. After that bit of insanity, he thought of nothing but the slaughter of his enemies, and he went from village to village, openly offering the hope of freedom to slaves. . . . On November 12, as I was coming down the Sacred Way, he and his gang attacked me. There was shouting, rock throwing, clubs, swords, and all this was unexpected. (*Ep. ad Att.* IV.3.2)

In February 56 he writes to his brother Quintus:

Pompey gave a speech [during a meeting of the Senate], or rather, he wanted to, for as he stood up, Clodius' gang started shouting, which lasted though all of Pompey's speech, hindering him not only with the shouting, but also with the curses and insults. As Pompey was concluding his speech, Clodius stood up; such a shout arose from us against him—we had to repay the favor—that he could neither think nor speak. . . . At almost four o'clock, as if upon a given signal, the Clodians began to spit on us. Our suffering flared out; they surged forward, to push us from our seats; we made an attack against them. Then the Clodians fled, and Clodius himself was thrown from the rostrum. (*Ep. ad Quintum Fratrem* II.3.2)

Cicero immediately repaid Pompey for securing his recall by proposing to the Senate that Pompey be appointed dictator of the grain supply, for there was a shortage of grain in Rome. Pompey desperately needed something to restore his public image and popularity, which were being overshadowed by the violence and intimidation associated with Caesar's consulship, his desertion of Cicero, and Caesar's great victories in Gaul. Pompey nonetheless dissimulated, saying he would do whatever the state needed him to do. Clodius said that the shortage had been created by Cicero and Pompey so another extraordinary command could be created for Pompey. During one of the missions to find grain, a storm arose, causing the captains to refuse to sail; Pompey led his men onto the ships and ordered them to set sail despite the weather, saying, "We have to sail—we do not have to live!" (Plutarch, *Pompey* L). He found more than enough grain, relieved the famine, and regained his popularity.

CRISIS IN THE TRIUMVIRATE: CONFERENCE AT LUCA

Meanwhile, relations among the members of the triumvirate were not good. Pompey was angry with Crassus because he thought Crassus had set Clodius upon him. Cicero thought Pompey could rescue the dying republic and was trying to draw him away from Caesar and Crassus. In 56 B.C. Caesar asked Pompey and Crassus to meet with him at Luca, a town in northern Italy, to discuss the situation.

At Luca the three worked things out to the advantage of them all. Crassus and Pompey were to be consuls in 55 and thereafter would receive proconsulships in Syria and Spain, while Caesar gained five more years of command in Gaul. Caesar also convinced Pompey to warn Cicero to be quiet; in his speeches, Cicero had been questioning the legitimacy of the laws Caesar had passed. Cicero therefore retired and wrote philosophical and rhetorical works or defended the triumvirate's friends.

Pompey and Crassus had missed the deadline for filing their candidature for the consulship for 55, but that was no problem. They organized a band of armed men who attacked one of the leading candidates, Domitius, as he was walking home one night, and killed the slave who was carrying his torch. Cato, who was a candidate for praetor, was wounded while trying to defend Domitius. The attack caused the elections to be delayed, thus allowing Pompey and Crassus to submit their names for candidature. Since no one dared to stand for election against Pompey and Crassus, the two were elected consuls for 55 and took office immediately, since the year had already begun, thus rendering themselves immune to prosecution for bribery or the use of violence. When Crassus and Pompey were overseeing the elections for the praetorships, they learned that Cato was winning, but then Pompey heard thunder (a bad omen), so the two dissolved the assembly. Later, after distributing larger bribes than before, they held another election for the praetorships, and Vatinius, one of their friends, was elected praetor instead of Cato. As consuls, Pompey and Crassus passed the laws giving Caesar five more years in Gaul and themselves proconsulships in Spain and Syria respectively. At the end of the year Crassus left for Syria and the glory he hoped to win in a war against Parthia, but Pompey stayed in Rome and governed Spain through his legates, for he wanted to keep an eye on things at home.

MORE TROUBLE IN THE TRIUMVIRATE

Good relations among Crassus, Pompey, and Caesar did not last long. During the elections for the aedileships in 54 B.C., a riot broke out; a man standing near Pompey was killed and his blood stained Pompey's toga. Pompey changed into a clean toga and sent his bloody one home. His pregnant wife Julia, seeing the toga, mistakenly thought the blood on his toga was his own and fainted, then suffered a miscarriage and died. Julia had been a bond between Caesar and Pompey; even though Pompey had married her as part of the bargain of the triumvirate, he loved her, and her death broke a link between him and Caesar. She was so dear to the common people that they insisted that she be buried not on the family estate, but in the Campus Martius.

The triumvirate suffered another blow the next year, when Crassus was killed in Parthia. The war had begun terribly: The tribune Ateius Capito vetoed Crassus' departure from Rome, and when his veto failed, he cursed Crassus and his army for beginning an unjust war (Rome and Parthia had a peace treaty). It was a bad omen for Crassus, but worse was to come. Once in Syria, for example, after winning a small battle, Crassus and his son Publius were leaving the Temple of Astarte (Ishtar), when the son tripped and fell and Crassus fell on top of him—a very bad omen. When Crassus and his army were about to cross the Euphrates, he let slip another bad omen, by telling his troops that he would break down the bridge so that not one of them would return that way. He meant something very different from what his soldiers understood, but the damage to their morale had been done.

In fact, very few of them came back. On the plain of Carrhae (modern Harran, south of Urfa in Turkey), Crassus and his army were surrounded by the Parthian army, which had a neverending supply of arrows to shoot at the Roman army. Ordinarily, enemies using archers would have run out of arrows, allowing the Roman army to engage in their specialty, hand-to-hand combat, but the Parthians were supplied by a long train of camels, bearing baskets full of arrows. The Parthian archers were also trained to shoot while on horseback; thus when the Romans made a charge, the Parthians fled, but still rained arrows on Crassus and his hapless army. Eventually twenty thousand of Crassus' men were killed and ten thousand taken prisoner; Crassus and his son were among the dead.

The three members of the triumvirate had been on their best behavior out of fear that one would join the second against the third. Only Pompey and Caesar now remained, and they were no longer bound by their mutual affection for Julia.

CAESAR IN GAUL, PART TWO

The younger Publius Crassus had been on Caesar's staff in Gaul before joining his father on the Parthian expedition and had even played a crucial role in the victory over Ariovistus. He should have stayed with Caesar, for Caesar's campaigns were as spectacular as his father's was disastrous. In 56 B.C. Caesar fought Rome's first naval battle in the Atlantic, against the sea-faring Gauls called the Veneti. The battle is remarkable because of an amazingly simple tactic that the Romans used to win. The Gauls' ships, constructed from thick oak, were too solid and heavy for the light Roman ships to ram, yet the Gallic ships were propelled solely by wind, while the Roman ships could be rowed or propelled by the wind. The Romans' solution was simple: they attached knives to long poles and cut the cords that secured the Gauls' sails to their ships. That done, the Gauls' ships could only drift until the Romans boarded them.

The next year Caesar did something no Roman had ever done before: In ten days he built a bridge across the Rhine and led an army of Rome across it in a punitive expedition into German territory. Before, Rome and Italy had merely defended themselves from the marauding Germans; now, Caesar explains, "the most convincing reason [for invading Germany] was this: seeing that the Germans were so easily incited to come into Gaul, Caesar [he usually refers to himself in the third person] wanted them too to feel fear for their possessions, since they would understand that an army of the Roman people could cross the Rhine, and would not hesitate to do so" (De bello gallico IV.16). Caesar's audience, no doubt remembering earlier invasions (such as that of the Gauls in 390 B.C. and of the Cimbri and Teutones fifty years earlier), must have thrilled at Caesar's words. Cicero himself, no lover of Caesar the politician, boasted that Caesar's victories rendered the Alps unnecessary. Later that year Caesar accomplished something else never before done: He led a Roman army into Britain, won the battle, and returned the next year to win further battles. He made British kings pay tribute to Rome. For that the Senate decreed twenty days of thanksgiving to the gods. Caesar's forays into Britain brought no lasting results, since he spent the rest of his life fighting civil wars, and Britain quickly reverted to its former status. Almost a century later, however, Emperor Claudius completed what Caesar had intended to do.

In 54 B.C. Caesar thought the pacification of Gaul complete. Yet that winter the Gauls all revolted and attacked the Roman armies in their winter camps, while Caesar was in Italy. The Gauls promised to spare the Romans' lives if they left their camps; one unfortunate Roman commander trusted them and led his army out of the camp, only to be massacred by the Gauls. The officer in charge of another camp, Q. Cicero, the younger brother of the orator, was too smart to trust the Gauls, yet his camp was in trouble since the men were wounded and exhausted after defending it for so long. After getting the reports of the revolt, Caesar sped to the rescue of his camps; he wanted to tell Q. Cicero and his men that he was on the way and to keep fighting bravely, yet the hostile Gauls besieging the camp would catch any messenger. Caesar wrote the message in code, in Greek letters, hid the letter in the shaft of a spear, and paid an allied Gaul an enormous sum of money to take it to the besieged camp. The allied Gaul then approached the camp, as if he were an attacker, and threw the spear into the camp, where it stuck to one of the towers. Two days elapsed before the Romans inside the camp noticed it; Q. Cicero then read the letter to the soldiers and thus revived their hopes and courage. They soon had more reason to cheer, for they saw smoke rising in the distance: Caesar and his army had arrived and were destroying the towns and villages that had revolted. Q. Cicero and his men were saved, and soon the revolt was quashed.

The reason why Caesar, with his army of forty thousand, had been able to conquer Gaul, was the Gauls' lack of unity and concerted leadership. In 52 the Gauls, seeing their freedom being wrenched from their hands, united under a leader named Vercingetorix. Caesar defeated him in battle, and the Gallic army took refuge in the stronghold of Alesia. Caesar's siege of Alesia is particularly noteworthy because while he laid siege to the city by digging a huge trench around it, a Gallic army was attacking Caesar's troops from the outside; to protect the Roman army in the middle, Caesar's men dug another huge trench on the outside, thus ringing themselves off from the Gallic army. Eventually Alesia gave up, and Caesar won both battles, over Alesia on the inside and over the Gallic army on the outside. Vercingetorix was captured and later executed at Caesar's triumph in 46. After Alesia, the hardest fighting in Gaul was finished.

ANARCHY IN ROME

Pompey, who had remained in Rome when Crassus left for Parthia, was soon called upon by the Senate to restore order in the city, where the gangs of Milo and Clodius were causing more and more frequent riots. The year 53 began without consuls, as the elections had been delayed because all the candidates were on trial for bribery. The interest rate doubled before the elections, as the various candidates scurried to finance their bribery. "You really should hurry back to Rome," writes Cicero to Atticus, "and see what remains of the good old Roman republic. You can see the bribes handed out, tribe by tribe, right out in the open, you can see Gabinius acquitted, you can sniff out dictatorship in the air, and enjoy the suspension of public business and the total anarchy" (*Ep. ad Att.* IV.19).

Rome needed a dictator to restore order, and Pompey was the obvious choice. In public he said he did not want to be dictator, but to Cicero he confided that he did want the post. He was instead elected sole consul for 53; even the younger Cato, the strict constitutionalist, agreed to the unusual appointment. Pompey restored order and passed some laws against bribery and disturbing the peace. That year the tribunes passed a plebiscite called the Law of the Ten Tribunes, which gave special permission to Julius Caesar to run for the consulship of 48 in absentia, when his term as governor of Gaul expired; thus Caesar would have another command awaiting him. Since Caesar needed soldiers, and Pompey was not using his, he loaned Caesar a legion.

In 52 Milo and Clodius had another battle, this time outside Rome, at Bovillae, where Clodius had laid a trap for Milo. Clodius was wounded during the fight and was dragged for safety into a nearby inn; Milo found him there and had him killed. When his body was returned to Rome, the urban mob used the Curia, the Senate House, as a funeral pyre for his body, and burned down the building. Later Milo was put on trial for the murder of Clodius, and Cicero defended him. The soldiers whom Pompey had stationed around the Forum to prevent violence could not keep the mob quiet during Cicero's speech; Cicero lost his composure, and

Milo was convicted. He went into exile in Massilia. (Cicero later sent him a copy of the speech he had *intended* to deliver; Milo is said to have thanked him for not delivering the speech he wrote, for otherwise he would not have been enjoying the fine mullets of Massilia.)

Later, Pompey passed a law barring candidature in absentia, which contradicted the Law of the Ten Tribunes. After the law was passed, Pompey added a rider giving an exception to Julius Caesar. The rider, of course, was invalid, as it had not been approved by the voters. The matter was of great importance to Caesar, who needed the dispensation to run in absentia for the consulship of 48, so he could have another command awaiting him upon the expiration of his term in Gaul. Without overlapping commands, he would be vulnerable to prosecution and political violence from his enemies. Pompey betrayed his former colleague in the triumvirate in the same year that he declined Caesar's offer of another marriage alliance, this time with Caesar's niece. Instead, Pompey married Cornelia, the widow of Publius Crassus, Crassus' son, who had been killed at Carrhae. Cornelia was the daughter of Metellus Scipio, one of the Optimates, and after his marriage Pompey started moving in those circles.

CHAPTER 21

Civil War

M. Claudius Marcellus, one of the consuls in 51 B.C., was violently anti-Caesarian. He showed his hatred for Caesar by flogging a Gaul whom Caesar had made a Roman citizen; as a citizen, of course, the man had the right to a trial and an appeal before punishment, both of which Marcellus denied him, as if he were not a citizen. Marcellus told the Gaul that he was giving him proof that he was not a Roman citizen, and that he should go show his scars to Caesar.

During 51 Caesar asked for an extension of his command in Gaul, but the Senate rejected his request. Marcellus then proposed a law that Caesar's command should be terminated and a successor sent out immediately. Pompey and the tribunes vetoed the proposal, since by law Caesar had his command at least until the end of 50. Yet the Senate did approve a measure empowering the next year's consuls to debate a replacement for Caesar in Gaul.

One of the consuls of 50, G. Claudius Marcellus, was Marcellus' cousin and shared his hatred of Caesar. Undoubtedly with his connivance Pompey convinced the Senate to decree that Pompey and Caesar should each relinquish one legion for the defense of Syria, the forces of which had never been brought back to strength after Crassus' catastrophe. Pompey's contribution, however, was to be the legion he had loaned to Caesar in 53. Thus Caesar lost two legions, or approximately eight thousand soldiers. Ever the wise investor, Caesar gave each departing soldier the equivalent of 250 drachmas as a reward for good service. The soldiers were never sent to Syria; they stayed in Italy.

Late in 50, when it became clear that civil war might erupt between Pompey and Caesar, the tribune Curio proposed that Pompey and Caesar should both lay down their commands. Earlier in his career, Curio had been staunchly anti-Caesarian, but now that his massive debts had been paid by Caesar, he was staunchly pro-Caesarian. The proposal was approved by a vote of 370 to 22 by the Senate, yet it was vetoed by the consuls. The next day Marcellus entrusted Pompey with the defense of the republic. Thus Caesar would gain neither an extension of his command nor any special permission to run for the consulship of 48 in absentia. Nor was Pompey exerting himself to help his former colleague in the triumvirate. He told the members of the Senate that he would not defend them if they were not firm in their resolve against Caesar, and he even threatened to leave for Spain, the province he was governing. The threat left the Optimates in a panic: What would they do if Caesar returned?

To Caesar the matter concerned his honor, his political life, and his actual existence. If he were not able to go straight into the *imperium* of the consulship of 48 when his command in Gaul expired at the end of 49, there would be some period of time when he would lack *imperium* and an army; he would then be a private citizen and thus vulnerable to all types of prosecution by his enemies—for using force to pass his laws in 59; for breaking a truce with the Usipetes, a Germanic tribe that was friendly to Rome, and allowing his soldiers to massacre them; or for using bribery. Cato had said that he would prosecute Caesar once he had laid down his command. There was no shortage of nobles wanting to prosecute Caesar, on any charge they could imagine, for Caesar had made many enemies during his career. Caesar thought that his services to the state—such as conquering Gaul, a mighty feat— merited special consideration, especially since Pompey himself had so frequently won special consideration that resulted in all his extraordinary commands.

Why did Pompey seek a war with Caesar? It would be neat but untrue to say that he was fighting for republican principles and against tyranny. Pompey had a great love of power and distinction; he also wanted to be needed and loved by his country. Perhaps his desire for glory—even greater than that of the typical noble, with the masks of the ancestors in the atrium and past great deeds to live up to—became so powerful owing to the hatred he saw people pouring upon his dead father (whose corpse was dragged off the funeral pyre and through the mud) and upon Sulla (whose funeral with honors many wanted to deny). Perhaps Pompey saw that it was better to have power and to be liked than to have power and be hated, as his father and Sulla had been. Pompey always sought power *and* public approval and popularity.

Yet although he was only six years older than Caesar, Pompey (to use his own words) was now the setting sun, and Caesar the rising; Pompey's glory days were from 70 to 62, while Caesar had been earning glory from 58 to 50 by his unexampled military exploits. Pompey was being eclipsed by Caesar. "Pompey," one ancient historian tells us, "did not tolerate anyone being his equal. In matters in which it was necessary for him to be in charge, he wanted to be the only one. In fact, no one ever cared less for all other things but craved glory more than he did" (Velleius Paterculus II.33.3). Caesar was threatening Pompey's primacy in Rome.

Pompey's vanity grew still more. In 50 he came down with a serious illness while in Naples. Plutarch tells us:

When he recovered, the people of Naples gave sacrifices on behalf of his recovery. Their neighbors started doing the same thing, and soon the practice went through all Italy, and cities large and small held festivals for many days. No place could contain those who had come from all over to greet him; the roads, villages, and harbors were full of people partying and giving sacrifices. Many people wearing garlands received him under torches and threw flowers on him as they sent him on his way, making his whole journey a most beautiful and dazzling sight. This, more than any one thing, is said to have been the cause of the war. (*Pompey* LVII.1–6)

Pompey became overly confident, and his allies were similarly misguided. One of the Optimates, Appius Claudius, denigrated Caesar's accomplishments in Gaul, spread malicious stories about Caesar, and told Pompey that he was ignorant of his own power and reputation, for he could easily finish Caesar off with the armies that he already had. Later, one of Caesar's lieutenants, Titus

Labienus, who joined the Pompeians against Caesar, told Pompey and the Senate that Caesar's army was demoralized and that the veterans who had conquered Gaul were dead or retired. When someone asked Pompey what he would defend Rome with, if Caesar invaded, Pompey nonchalantly replied, "Wherever I should stamp my foot in Italy, there will rise up forces of infantry and cavalry" (Plutarch, *Pompey* LVII).

Yet, as the vote on Curio's proposal shows, most people wanted peace. In 50 Cicero wrote to his friend and confidant Atticus, "Up to now I have scarcely found anyone who would prefer fighting it out with Caesar to allowing him what he wants" (*Ep. ad Att.* VII.6). "Even Cato himself," he writes in another letter to Atticus, "prefers to be a slave than to fight [in a civil war]" (*Ep. ad Att.* VII.15). In March of 49 Balbus, one of Caesar's men, wrote to Cicero that Caesar preferred nothing to living without fear, with Pompey the more eminent. Pompey, however, turned down Caesar's numerous requests for a meeting to work things out. Later, Caesar blamed the war's horrible bloodshed on the twenty-two diehard Optimates who had voted against ordering Caesar and Pompey both to lay down their commands and relinquish their armies.

"IACTA ALEA EST"

In 49 the consuls were G. Claudius Marcellus (brother of the consul of 51) and Lucius Lentulus, both hostile to Caesar, but Caesar's lieutenant Marcus Antonius (better known in English as Mark Antony) was elected tribune. Caesar made another offer, to take Illyricum as his province with one legion. That too failed. Another offer from Caesar: He would resign his command if Pompey would resign his. The consuls would not permit a vote on the exact terms.

Metellus Scipio (Pompey's father-in-law) then proposed that if Caesar did not lay down his command, he should be declared a public enemy. Marcus Antonius vetoed the proposal, but his veto was ignored; he and Q. Cassius (not Gaius Cassius, Caesar's future murderer), another tribune friendly to Caesar, were warned that they might meet with violence if they remained in Rome. Fearing the violence of the Optimates, Antonius and Q. Cassius disguised themselves as slaves and fled to Caesar in Ravenna. The consuls' threat of violence against the tribunes gave Caesar another point in propaganda: The Senate was destroying the rights of the tribunes and common people.

After receiving the news that his latest peace proposal had been rejected, Caesar ate dinner with his staff and then said, "Iacta alea est" ("The die is cast" [Suetonius, *Divus Julius* XXXII]). With only one legion (the others were stationed across the Alps), he crossed the Rubicon, the river that separated Italy from the province of Cisalpine Gaul. In doing so, he committed treason against the republic. This act of Caesar's also added a phrase to English: "to cross the Rubicon" is to commit oneself to a course of action from which there is no turning back.

STAMP YOUR FOOT, POMPEY

The party opposed to Caesar did not choose a wise time for giving Caesar the ultimatum either to relinquish his command or to become an enemy of Rome. Although on paper Pompey had all the resources of the republic at his disposal, he had only two legions in Italy, both of which had formerly served under Caesar and no doubt remembered him fondly. Pompey and the Optimates never expected Caesar to attack immediately, but they were now about to experience what the Gauls were already very familiar with: Caesar's *celeritas* (swiftness). Caesar knew to strike immediately, before an enemy could prepare his defense.

Since most of his soldiers were in Spain, Pompey had to recruit in Italy; his new soldiers were inexperienced. Many men refused to enlist, and those who did who were apathetic. Caesar's legions, in contrast, had served under him during the years in Gaul and were devoted to their charismatic and seemingly democratic leader; contrary to Labienus' claims, Caesar's soldiers did not have low morale and constituted an army of great endurance and discipline. So devoted were Caesar's soldiers that, at the beginning of the war, his centurions offered to pay for a cavalryman, each from his own savings, and his foot soldiers offered to fight without pay or rations and to pool resources so no one would go short.

When Caesar invaded Italy, the Senate and Pompey, having no
army with which to mount a defense, fled, with Pompey declaring
that any senators who stayed in Rome would be considered traitors.
One noble, Favonius, when seeing that they could not defend Rome
from Caesar, told Pompey to stamp his foot and produce the promised armies. First they went to Capua, then to Brundisium, on the
Adriatic coast, and then across the Adriatic into Greece. Caesar
pursued but failed to catch them. Backed by only one legion, Caesar
took over Italy and Rome without bloodshed; even Picenum, where
Pompey's family lived and had great influence, surrendered to
Caesar without fighting.

After failing to catch the fleeing senators, Caesar returned to
Rome, where he rifled the treasury, which the consul Marcellus in
his haste to flee had neglected to empty. A tribune tried to veto
Caesar's access to the treasury, but Caesar threatened his life, and
the tribune wisely relented. Caesar was appointed dictator, in
which capacity he oversaw the consular elections for 48; he was
elected consul for 48 and resigned his dictatorship. He then turned
to Spain, where a large contingent of Pompey's forces was stationed. Caesar wanted to prevent their joining Pompey in Greece
or taking Italy and Rome when he himself went to attack Pompey.
As he was leaving, he said that he was first going to fight against
an army that had no general, and after that, against a general who
had no army. On the way to Spain he demanded the surrender of
Massilia, which refused. He left a part of his army to besiege the
city and continued to Spain.

Caesar took over Spain with no large battles, although there
were many small ones and skirmishes. In the endless maneu-
vering for better position, Caesar managed to trap his enemies on
a hill, where they had no access to food or water. The enemy
troops, Romans and Italians, were forced to surrender; Caesar,
showing his *clementia*, let them go free, demanding only that
they disband their army. He even gave them food for a few days'
journey. Caesar's clemency was not without purpose or result:
Since the Optimates had branded him a renegade, he wanted to
prove that he was not a Sulla and was not waging war against
Rome for his own power or profit. He worked extra hard to
restrain his soldiers from plundering the fields and houses of

Italy, for he wanted to win the goodwill of the Italians. His policy was successful, for a number of the Pompeians deserted to his side, and he gave them positions of equal rank and pay. After taking over Spain, Caesar returned to Massilia, which surrendered after a three-month siege.

Caesar then traversed Italy again and crossed from Brundisium to Greece. Crossing the Adriatic was no easy matter, for it was winter and, more important, Pompey had the republic's fleet with which to control the seas. Bibulus, Pompey's admiral, died while attempting to prevent Caesar from landing in Epirus, but Caesar and a small force managed to slip through the blockade. Later, Antony brought four legions to Caesar in Greece.

Pompey had by now consolidated his forces and provisions in the vicinity of Dyrrhachium, where each general tried to outflank the other and to isolate him from food and water. Such was the scale of their defensive works that it took a line of forts and entrenchment more than 25 kilometers long for Caesar to hem in Pompey's army; the line was too long for Caesar's small army to maintain, however, and Caesar had to abandon that plan. Every day the two did not fight allowed Pompey more time to train his recruits. Time was on Pompey's side, for he had ample provisions and superiority in number of foot soldiers, cavalry, and navy. Caesar's troops, however, were so low on provisions that at one point his men were forced to bake bread made from tree roots. They threw some of the loaves to the Pompeians to prove that they were not starving. Upon seeing one of the loaves, Pompey exclaimed, "What beasts we're fighting with!" and ordered the loaves to be hidden, so his soldiers would not learn just how tough Caesar's soldiers were.

Finally Caesar decided to leave for Thessaly, where he could more easily get food for his men. His departure followed a small defeat, in which Pompey could have inflicted a crushing blow if he had not been timid: according to Caesar, "Today the enemy would have had the victory, if they had had a real winner in charge" (Appian, *Civil Wars* II.9). This raised the Pompeians' spirits even higher: Caesar's forces were hungry and sick, had recently suffered a loss, and had to flee. Things looked good for the Pompeians.

"UTERQUE REGNARE VULT"

In spite of these seemingly favorable circumstances, Pompey's army had major problems, namely, divided leadership and purpose. Soon after following Caesar into Thessaly, the Pompeians were joined by Metellus Scipio, who had brought his army from his province Syria to help Pompey. Caesar describes the problems in Pompey's camp:

Once Pompey's army had been enlarged and the two large armies had been joined together, the opinion that they had formerly held was simply confirmed, and the expectation of victory grew so large that whatever time came before the victory seemed simply to delay their return to Italy. Whenever Pompey did something somewhat slowly or carefully, they said the whole war was simply a day's work, but that he reveled in the power and considered men of consular and praetorian rank like slaves. By this time they were vying with each other, out in the open, for rewards and priesthoods, and they allotted the consulship for years ahead. Others, meanwhile, were seeking the houses and possessions of those in my camp. . . . Already Domitius, Scipio, and Spinther Lentulus were resorting to viciously insulting each other in their daily arguments about who would become pontifex maximus after me. (Caesar, *De bello civili* III.82.2)

Plutarch tells us that the Optimates, Pompey's allies and followers, called him Agamemnon and King of Kings.

Still worse was the lack of principles: Pompey was not fighting for republican principles against tyranny; he was fighting for the Optimate party. "I look at it this way," writes Cicero to Atticus (*Ep. ad Att.* IX.7), "we won't have a republic with both alive or even with this one [i.e., Pompey]." He writes in another letter:

Each of them has sought a tyranny; they have never done anything so that the state would be prosperous and respectable. He [Pompey] certainly didn't leave the city because he couldn't guard it or Italy because he was being driven from it. No, he planned this from the start, to get all the lands and seas in an uproar, to arouse foreign kings, to lead to Italy wild, armed nations, and to create huge armies. He's been after that type of Sullan power for a long time now, and many who are together with him want the same thing. Do you really think that those two have nothing in common, and that an agreement was impossible? It could happen today, except that our contentment is not a goal of either of them: each wants to be king [uterque regnare vult]. (*Ep. ad Att.* VIII.11)

Cicero eventually joined Pompey's side, finding him the lesser of the two evils. According to Cicero, Caesar had collected around him "all the criminals, all those afflicted with ignominy, all those worthy of condemnation and infamy, the worthless and hopeless urban masses, all those who can't pay their debts" (*Ep. ad Att.* VII.3) and who were looking for Caesar to cancel debts or to allow them to plunder the property of the wealthy once he became dictator. Consequently, people with property generally backed Pompey.

"HOC VOLUERUNT"

In Thessaly, on the plain of Pharsalus, in 48 Pompey finally relented to the demands of the Optimates: At last, they would settle the issue. Before the battle, Caesar's soldiers destroyed their own camp and its fortifications, to force themselves to fight for victory, since they had no refuge in defeat; in any case, there was certainly nothing left for them in Rome or Italy if they lost. Caesar describes the battle:

When the signal was given, our soldiers ran forward with their javelins ready. When they noticed that the Pompeians were not running to meet them, without being ordered to, they held back, as they were used to doing, and as they had been trained in earlier battles, and stopped, almost in the middle between the two armies, so they would not be exhausted when they arrived. After a while they started running again. They hurled their javelins and immediately drew their swords, as I had ordered them. The Pompeians, on the other hand, met the charge. They received the javelins and the legions' attack without breaking ranks; after throwing their javelins, they too drew their swords. At the same time Pompey's cavalry rushed to attack us from his left wing, as they had been ordered, and the whole mass of archers poured forth. Our cavalry could not handle their attack and little by little retreated; Pompey's cavalry began to bear down all the more threateningly, breaking off into squadrons, surrounding our lines on our vulnerable side.

When I noticed that, I gave the signal to the fourth line, which I had deployed from the number of cohorts [a cohort was a unit of 600 men]. They quickly dashed forward and attacked Pompey's cavalry with such great force that none of the cavalry stood their ground—all of them not only ran away, but even started a general rout to the highest part of the mountains.

All their archers and slingers, left defenseless when their cavalry was run off from the battle, were killed. In the same attack, the cohorts surrounded Pompey's left wing, where the Pompeians—even though surrounded—had not given up fighting and resisting, and we attacked them in the rear. At the same time I ordered my third line to attack; it had been inactive and had stayed behind, up to that time.

Fresh, and not wounded, as they were, they came to battle the weary Pompeians, while others attacked them from the rear. The Pompeians could not bear the attack, and all turned their backs and fled. (Caesar, *De bello civili* III.93)

Pompey fled the battlefield to his camp and sat down, stunned. Soon Caesar's soldiers burst into the camp. "What? Even into our camp?" Pompey said. He took off his general's cloak, found a horse, and fled. While storming Pompey's camp, Caesar's men found the tents wreathed with myrtle, dining couches laid out and covered with flowers, and drinking cups and bowls of wine. The Optimates were ready for the victory celebration, but Caesar and his men enjoyed the feast.

During the battle itself, Caesar had ordered his soldiers, "Spare your fellow Romans!" After the battle he looked at the six thousand Pompeians killed in the fighting (his own army lost only two hundred) and groaned, saying: "They wanted this [hoc voluerunt]. Despite all that I have accomplished, I, Julius Caesar, would have been condemned, if I had not sought protection from my army" (Suetonius, *Divus Julius* XXX). Then he set off in pursuit of Pompey.

Pompey sailed to Egypt, where he expected the king, the sixteen-year-old Ptolemy Auletes (the Flute Player), to offer him safety;

after all, Pompey and Caesar had put Ptolemy on the throne of Egypt. Yet Pompey was killed by the ministers of the king, as his rowboat was nearing the Egyptian shore. "A corpse doesn't bite," explained the king's adviser, grinning, as he recommended that Pompey be killed. Pompey's head was cut off, to be taken to Caesar; one of his former slaves and a former soldier later found his headless body, washed its wounds, and, on a pyre constructed from the wood of an old wrecked fishing boat, cremated Pompey the Great.

When Caesar landed in Egypt, Pompey's head and signet ring were brought to him. Seeing them, Caesar wept and had Pompey's murderers found and killed. Not content with killing Pompey, the king's ministers also attacked Caesar, probably because he demanded payment of 10 million of the 17 million drachmas that the king owed him. Caesar also wanted Ptolemy to receive Cleopatra back into the palace (he had driven her away) and to rule the kingdom jointly with her. Caesar was accompanied by only a few hundred soldiers, and with great difficulty saved his life; at one point he had to escape through the water, holding important documents above the water with one hand and swimming with the other, all the time clenching his scarlet cloak between his teeth, to keep it from becoming a trophy for the Egyptians. Eventually he conquered Ptolemy, made Cleopatra queen of Egypt, and spent some time with her. Later Cleopatra bore a son, whose father was supposedly Caesar; she named the child Caesarion, or Little Caesar.

Caesar next went to Asia Minor, where Pharnaces, the king of Pontus (son of Mithridates), was taking advantage of Rome's troubles by attacking its allies. Caesar and his soldiers defeated Pharnaces in 47 B.C. at Zela; that was the battle that inspired Caesar's famous line, "Veni, vidi, vici" (I came, I saw, I conquered)—a testament to Caesar's legendary speed. Five days after arriving in Pontus, and four hours after catching sight of Pharnaces, Caesar defeated him in battle and destroyed his army. Caesar then commented that Pompey had been very lucky to have had such weak enemies on which to build his military reputation.

Caesar then returned to Rome, where his victorious troops were mutinying. They were tired of waiting both for their general, who had been away for more than a year, and for the lavish gifts that he had promised them. Caesar had only to address them as *quirites*, "citizens" (that is, no longer soldiers), and they then begged him to allow them to continue serving in his army.

Caesar then went to Africa, where some remaining Pompeians, under the leadership of Cato and Scipio, were making preparations to take over Italy and restore the republic. Caesar defeated them at Thapsus (close to Carthage) in 46; after that battle Cato, one of the diehard republicans, committed suicide, much to Caesar's disappointment, for he wanted the glory of extending clemency to this hated enemy. Romans later admired Cato for his dedication and devotion to constitutional government and for his high moral principles, in an age of government by the sword and election by bribery. For example, Cato knew very well that Pompey was not much preferable to Caesar; while making an accusation of bribery against Gabinius, one of Pompey's allies (who as tribune had rewarded Pompey with the command against the pirates), Cato was assaulted and dragged from the rostrum. As he was being dragged away, he called Pompey *privatus dictator*, "a self-appointed dictator." While fleeing to Greece, Pompey appointed Cato to Sicily, knowing that Cato would immediately call upon him (if victorious over Caesar) to disband his army, since the common enemy of the republic had been destroyed—needless to say, Pompey had no intention of rescuing the republic only to leave himself a private citizen, like anybody else. After Pharsalus, Cato joined with Metellus Scipio in Utica; there Scipio decided to execute all the inhabitants of the town for supporting Caesar, but Cato would not allow it and thus saved many thousands of lives. Later, after Scipio was defeated by Caesar, Cato put the safety of the citizens of Utica before his own and allowed them to surrender rather than fight a losing and destructive battle against Caesar. To those men who embraced republican principles during the empire and who were disenchanted with one-man rule and the exclusion of the nobles from positions of power and glory, Cato appeared a martyr for the republic. The poet Lucan (living under the tyranny of Nero) wrote a fine line of poetry about Cato: "victrix causa deis placuit, sed victa Catoni" ("The winning cause [that is, the principate, tyranny] pleased the gods, but the losing cause [the republic, justice] pleased Cato"; Lucan I.128).

In 45 Caesar went to Spain, where he conquered the last remnants of the Pompeian opposition at the Battle of Munda, which he almost lost. Sextus Pompey, the last son of Pompey, survived the battle and continued to cause problems for Caesar's successors. By March 45 Caesar was master of Rome.

CAESAR AS DICTATOR

Caesar's enemies were happy to learn that Caesar did not return to Rome as Sulla did, driven by a desire for revenge. He recalled those who had been driven out during Sulla's proscriptions. Those men who had opposed him before and during Pharsalus were not punished or deprived of their estates; many were given political appointments or received advancement in their careers. Brutus and Cassius, both of whom had fought against Caesar at Pharsalus, received praetorships. Caesar forgave the orator Cicero and later even the ex-consul Marcellus, who had stridently opposed attempts to work with Caesar in 50. So grateful was the Roman populace that it dedicated a temple *clementiae Caesaris*, "to the clemency of Caesar." Those Pompeians who resisted after Thapsus were punished by exile and confiscation of their estates.

With no significant opposition, and having been appointed dictator for ten years, Caesar set himself to solving the many problems in the government. He first relieved the treasury of a burden by reducing the number of those eligible for free grain, from 320,000 to 150,000; 80,000 of those disqualified from free grain were sent to work for their food at overseas colonies. Caesar also sent skilled freedmen as colonists, wishing them to make colonies that would be industrial and mercantile, not just agricultural. To settle his soldiers, Caesar made extensive use of land outside of Italy, a policy with far-reaching consequences. He settled his soldiers in Africa, Spain, and Gaul, thus establishing more outposts of Roman and Latin civilization, in addition to ensuring the stability of those regions. Caesar also granted citizenship to people of Transpadane Gaul and to certain nobles from other towns of Spain and Gaul. Caesar also made certain Gallic supporters senators; jokes of the time reported Gauls, wearing trousers, becoming senators. Caesar made the rulers of Roman lands more truly represent those lands and gave the provincial peoples more of a stake in the survival of the empire.

One of Caesar's most famous endeavors was the reform of the Roman calendar. The Romans used a lunar calendar, which had 355 days in a year. Whenever the seasons had gotten out of synch with the calendar year, the priests would insert a month to realign the seasons with the calendar (this is called an intercalation). Caesar changed that. First, he started using an Egyptian solar calender. Since only one intercalation had been made since 52, he brought the calendar year 46 into harmony with the seasons by adding sixty-seven days between November and December; he added the ten extra days of the solar year throughout the twelve remaining months (*Cambridge Ancient History* 9:696). The calendar remained unchanged until 1582, when Pope Gregory XIII made some minor changes to it.

Another of Caesar's reforms called for at least one-third of the shepherds and herdsmen in Italy to be freedmen. He wanted to minimize the number of slaves in Italy, and he doubtless wanted also to improve the quality of recruits for the army. He also gave citizenship to doctors and teachers living in Rome.

Caesar had great plans. He planned one more epic military exploit, the conquest of Parthia and, on the return trip back to Italy, the conquest of Germany. He planned to organize the code of civil law, which had become chaotic. He wanted to create one library for Greek literature and another for Latin, and even commissioned the scholar Varro to classify Greek and Latin works. He wanted to create more farmland by draining marshes, to build a highway from the Adriatic to Rome, across the Apennines, and to cut a canal through the isthmus of Corinth. He did not live to carry out his plans.

"ET TU, BRUTE?"

After being appointed dictator for life early in 44, Caesar became increasingly unpopular. His triumph after the Battle of Munda angered many, for he was celebrating a victory over fellow Romans, not over barbarians. Another time, the consuls and praetors came to him in the Senate, as he was sitting above the rostrum on his

Bust of Julius Caesar, first century B.C. (Courtesy of the Archer M. Huntington Art Gallery, University of Texas at Austin, William J. Battle Collection of Plaster Casts)

golden throne, to present him with more honors; he did not stand to greet them and even told them that the number of honors given him ought to be decreased, not increased. (We are told that the honor that most pleased him was permission to wear a crown of leaves, for it covered his bald head; otherwise, Caesar tried to comb his few remaining hairs over his bald spot.) This was seen as an insult to all. Then there was the scene at the Lupercalia (a festival held on February 15, in which nearly naked young men— the Luperci—ran around striking people with strips of goatskin; women struck by them were supposed to become more fertile). Three times Marcus Antonius presented Caesar with a crown, and each time Caesar turned it down. Later, tribunes arrested and jailed the individuals who urged Caesar to accept the crown; Caesar had those tribunes deposed from office. Once Caesar was addressed as king; his famous reply was, "Non sum Rex [a cognomen of the Servilii family], sed Caesar" (I am not a King, but a Caesar). The rumor spread that, according to the Sibylline oracles, Parthia could be conquered by none but a king, and that Caesar should be called a king, so he could conquer Parthia. There was also a rumor that he was planning to move the capital to Alexandria and transfer all the wealth and power there. Caesar was also designating those whom he wanted to be consuls and praetors years in advance and was rewarding his friends with such positions. When the consul of 45 died on the last day of his term, Caesar insulted the dignity of the position by appointing another friend consul for the rest of the day. This last episode occasioned the joke of Cicero, when the new consul's friends hurried to the Forum to congratulate him, "Let's hurry, before his term of office expires!" (Plutarch, *Caesar* LVIII). Caesar also angered many by commenting that the republic was just a name without substance or form and that whatever he said should be considered the law.

A conspiracy against his life arose. The conspirators had to act quickly, before Caesar started for Parthia with his legions. Among the conspirators were men whom Caesar had forgiven for fighting against him at Pharsalus and Thapsus, and to whom he had given important posts in the government. They felt it necessary to lure Brutus into joining the conspiracy, for he had a reputation for uprightness and just dealing. Graffiti were written on the statue of

Brutus' remote ancestor, Junius Brutus ("If only you were here now, Brutus!" and "How helpful it would be, if Brutus were alive!"), and on Brutus' own tribunal chair ("Brutus, are you sleeping?" and "You aren't really a Brutus!"), to remind him of his ancestor's famous deed. Brutus joined the conspiracy and opposed plans to assassinate Antony too, arguing that killing Caesar would be a just deed, but that killing Antony was unnecessary, and they must act only with strict justice. Caesar had recently decided that it was better to die than to live his life in fear and accordingly had dismissed his Spanish bodyguard; he also knew that many people wanted him to remain alive, since a worse civil war would erupt upon his death. It was probably simple weariness that prompted Caesar frequently to say, "I have lived long enough either for nature or for glory." (He was fifty-six years old.) In a conversation with friends, concerning the best type of death, Caesar said that the best death is one that comes swiftly and unexpectedly.

Plutarch describes the fateful Ides of March of 44 B.C. (students of Shakespeare will recognize this description):

The Senate rose at Caesar's entrance and a great crowd immediately surrounded him once he had taken his seat. They sent Tillius Cimber, one of their fellow conspirators, to plead on behalf of his brother, who was in exile. The others also started pleading, grasping Caesar's hands and kissing his chest and head. At first Caesar rejected their requests, and then, as they would not stop begging, he used force to stand up. Tillius, with both hands, tore Caesar's cloak from his shoulders; Casca, who was standing behind Caesar, drew his sword and was the first to stab him, next to the shoulder, but the wound was not deep. Caesar grabbed the handle of the sword and shouted loudly, "Damn you, Casca, what are you doing?" Casca shouted in Greek for his brother to come help. By now Caesar was being stabbed by the many men surrounding him and, thinking of breaking through the crowd around him, he saw Brutus drawing his sword against him; he then let go of Casca's hand, covered his head with his cloak, and gave up his body to be stabbed by them. (Plutarch, *Brutus* 17)

According to another source (the biographer Suetonius), when Caesar saw Brutus about to stab him, he said in Greek, "You too, my child?" (Kai su, teknon?).

Rome was not ready for the rule of one man who was above the law or outside it. Another decade of ruinous civil wars made the Romans and Italians more receptive to one-man rule.

LATIN LITERATURE OF THE LATE REPUBLIC

In addition to his military and other achievements, Caesar was one of the great authors of the late republic. His *Gallic Wars* has already been discussed. We also have his *Civil Wars*, the account of his campaigns in Spain, Greece, Africa, and Asia. His other works, which have not survived, included a treatise concerning linguistics, *De analogia* (which he dedicated to Cicero); a poem, *Iter*; and, in response to an encomium on the martyred Cato by Cicero, an attack on Cato, *Anticato*, which served only to further canonize Cato. Caesar's style—clear, simple, and elegant—was praised by no less demanding a critic than Cicero.

Lucretius (94–?55 B.C.) wrote a poem in epic style on the philosophy of Epicureanism, entitled *De rerum natura* (On the Nature of Things). His grand and majestic poetry reflects how passionately he felt for his subject. We are told that he was driven insane by a love potion that his wife had given him, after which he committed suicide. Since only fragments of early Latin epic survive, Lucretius' poem also provides examples of the archaizing and grandiloquent speech of early Latin epic; later Latin epic poetry falls under the sway of Alexandrianism.

The poetry of Catullus (84–?54 B.C.) is very different from Lucretius' grand epic. Like many other young poets of the age (called *novi poetae*, "new poets," also "neoterics"), Catullus avoided writing long poems about heroes and their deeds or about Roman history, another favorite topic for early Latin epic. Instead, Catullus and the *novi poetae* chose for their models the poetry of the Alexandrian scholars, especially Callimachus, with his emphasis on smaller poems featuring charm, cleverness, polish, and learned and literary allusions. Other Alexandrians popular among the Romans were Aratus, Apollonius of Rhodes (author of the *Argonautica*), and Theocritus. Catullus' poetry, much of it written in lyric meters, usually concerns the poet's own feelings: his passionate love (and hatred) for "Lesbia," who may have been Clodia, the sister of the tribune Clodius; his feelings for his friends, ranging from affection to betrayal and rejection; his literary tastes and disputes; his grief at the death of his brother; his humor and simple joy in life. Most Romans saw little use for such personal poetry, as it did not glorify Rome and its great men or instruct people for moral improvement; consequently Catullus refers to his poetry as *nugae* (trifles) or *versiculi* (little verses). His *nugae*, however, exercised a profound influence not only on later Latin poets, but also on European poetry.

The historian Sallust (86–35 B.C.) wrote two monographs that have survived: *Bellum Catilinae*, about the conspiracy of Catiline, and *Bellum Iugurthinum*, about Rome's war with Jugurtha. Briefly a partisan of Caesar, Sallust revealed his bias against the nobles in his *Bellum Iugurthinum* in particular. He also wrote *Histories*, a lost work. He may have been the author of *Invectiva in Ciceronem* (an attack on Cicero) and *Epistulae ad Caesarem senem* (letters of political advice to the dictator). Sallust rejected the oratorical style of the day, instead modeling his style on the great Greek historian Thucydides; he was a major influence on the historian Tacitus.

With the murder of Cicero in the political strife following Caesar's assassination, Rome lost one who is arguably its greatest literary figure, and one of the greatest literary figures in Western literature. His greatest contributions were in oratory, for it was by his ability to give a good speech and sway an audience that he overcame his origins as a novus homo and rose in Roman politics. He is regarded as the greatest orator of ancient Rome. Fifty-eight of Cicero's speeches survive, some only in part, and forty-eight more have been lost; without a doubt, he delivered still more that were never recorded for posterity. His most famous speeches are *In Catilinam, Pro Caelio, In Verrem, Philippicae, Pro Archia, Pro Cluentio,* and *Pro Sestio*. Any student wanting to learn how to write a good speech should study Cicero's use of the periodic style, phrasing, diction, rhythm, manipulation of the audience's emotions, treatment of the subject at hand, and humor (Cicero was famous among the ancient Romans for his quick wit and sharp tongue). He also wrote books on rhetoric and the art of giving a good speech, including *Brutus, De oratore, Orator,* and *De inventione*.

Cicero also wrote philosophy. Although not a particularly original thinker, he did write works with significance for ethics and life's situations. These include *De officiis* (Concerning Duties), *De amicitia* (Concerning Friendship), *De senectute* (Concerning Old Age), *De republica* (Concerning the Republic), and *Tusculanae quaestiones* (Tusculan Disputations). Cicero also wrote some poetry, fragments of which survive. He even wrote an epic poem about his consulship (*De consulatu*), and he is derided for the infamous line, "O fortunatam natam me consule Romam" (O Rome that became lucky when I was consul!). Cicero's reputation for poetry suffers because he is judged by those who followed him, such figures as Vergil, Horace, Propertius, Ovid, and Tibullus; it is a rare poet who does not suffer in such company. Cicero had the ability to manipulate the Latin language, but his special talent lay in prose, not poetry. Cicero's last contribution to literature was unintentional, for eight volumes of his letters to friends, family members, and other persons have survived. Cicero did not know that many of his letters would be published someday, and thus he showed both his more private side and his true opinions of many important Romans of his time. For the student of the Latin language, Cicero's letters also give an example of how educated Romans of the day talked, for many of the letters are informal, chatty, and gossipy—the exact opposite of most Latin poetry and oratory.

Cicero's influence on Latin and Western literature was enormous. Generations of orators and writers in Europe have turned to Cicero for models of good speaking and writing. He set the standard for eloquence.

CHAPTER 22

Renewed Civil War
and the Rise of Octavian

Caesar had predicted that the republic would be plunged into civil war upon his death, and he was right, for the conspirators had made no plans for changing Roman government so that future generals would not seize power. Without a fundamental change in Roman government, one could expect only a repeat of the previous sixty years of government, the only change being in the generals' names.

Their hands smeared with Caesar's blood, the conspirators left the terrified Senate and went to the Capitol, showing the frightened citizens their daggers and informing them that liberty had been restored. Many citizens were not pleased, however, and even threatened the conspirators, who then barricaded themselves on the Capitol. The conspirators feared also the Caesarians Marcus Antonius (Mark Antony), who was consul, and Marcus Lepidus, who was outside the city but in possession of an army and who had been Caesar's master of the horse. Hearing of Caesar's murder, Lepidus returned that night and filled the Forum with his soldiers; Antonius, meanwhile, had received Caesar's cash along with state papers and documents from his widow Calpurnia.

When assurances had been given by Antonius and Lepidus that they would not kill the assassins, and by the assassins that Caesar was their sole target, Antonius convened the Senate in the Temple of Tellus. Heeding Cicero's calls for peace, the two sides reached an agreement: Amnesty was granted to Caesar's assassins, but Caesar's acts—including those he had merely planned, which were recorded in his state papers—received blanket ratification. The ratification of Caesar's acts was crucial, for they granted land to

Coin issued by Brutus after the assassination of Caesar. The Latin EID MAR means "the Ides of March"; the cap between the daggers is a pileus, worn by former slaves after being set free. (Courtesy of the American Numismatic Society)

Caesar's veterans, thousands of whom were present in Rome; the Senate did not want to further antagonize them after the unavenged murder of their beloved general. Antonius further passed a law that abolished the dictatorship. Caesar's acts also allotted provinces for the year 43: Macedonia to Antonius, Cyrene to Cassius, Crete to M. Brutus, Syria to Dolabella, Asia to Trebonius, and Gaul to Decimus Brutus. After reaching that agreement, Antonius and the conspirators even had dinner together. M. Brutus then made a big mistake: He allowed Antonius to plan Caesar's funeral. Here is what happened at the funeral, where the contents of his will were announced:

In his will Caesar had given 75 drachmas to each Roman man, and had left to the people his gardens across the river, where the Temple of Fortune now stands. Then an amazing feeling of goodwill and longing for him took hold of the citizens. Then, when Caesar's body was brought into the Forum, Antonius gave the funeral speech, as is the custom in Rome, listing in full all of Caesar's accomplishments. As he noticed that his speech was touching the hearts of the crowd, he changed his tone to pity; he grabbed Caesar's clothes and showed them, stained with blood, to the crowd, while pointing out the gashes and great number of wounds. One could see then that there was not going to be order any longer: Some people shouted to kill the murderers, while others brought up benches and tables from the workshops into the Forum and, as happened to Clodius the demagogue years earlier, made a huge funeral pyre and set fire to it. They set the corpse on it, in the middle of the temples, shrines, and sacred places. As the fire blazed, some brought forth half-burned torches and scattered in all directions to burn down the houses of Caesar's murderers. (Plutarch, *Brutus* XX.2)

"A GREAT AND BEAUTIFUL DEED, BUT INCOMPLETE"

Fearing the violence of the mob, which went out in search of the conspirators, Brutus and the others fled for their lives. They were right to be afraid, for one man named Cinna, who had had nothing to do with the assassination, was mistaken for a Cinna who had been a conspirator and was torn to pieces by the mob. Caesar's veterans were said to be plotting to kill Brutus. As *praetor urbanus*, Brutus was supposed to remain in the city, but the consul Antonius, probably happy to remove any future obstruction to his own ambitions, allowed him to leave. He and Cassius left Rome, ostensibly for their provinces, Crete and Cyrene, long before their terms were to begin.

As consul, Antonius had possession of Caesar's will, which had received blanket ratification by the Senate. Antonius saw this as a blank check and proceeded to insert his own wishes among Caesar's decrees. Thus he sold exemptions from taxes, freed communities from tribute, and recalled exiles, all in the name of Caesar, benefiting others and enriching himself. He is said also to have stolen a prodigious amount of money from the Temple of Ops.

Nor did Antonius stop with satisfying his tremendous greed, which paid for his parties with actresses, mimes, and jugglers (not polite company for the Roman aristocracy and middle class). He surrounded himself with an armed guard of six thousand men, which was illegal inside the pomerium. He kept armed soldiers inside the Forum and Temple of Concord, and passed laws in disregard of the auspices and through the use of violence. At one point he summoned the Senate to a meeting, with the warning that he would consider those not in attendance to be plotting against him. He then forced a law to be passed that, contrary to Caesar's

wishes, transferred Macedonia from himself to his brother Gaius
and Gaul from D. Brutus to himself. He planned to bring his four
legions to Rome from Brundisium, where they were waiting to sail
to Macedonia; Cicero says that Antonius intended to bring them to
Rome to massacre the hostile senators and to make himself
dictator.

Antonius, however, soon encountered unforeseen opposition.
Before he died, Julius Caesar had adopted Gaius Octavius, the
nineteen-year-old grandson of his sister, and in his will he awarded
the young man three-quarters of his estate. Octavian (Gaius Julius
Caesar Octavianus being his full name after his adoption by Caesar)
had accompanied Caesar to Spain in 46 and had impressed Caesar
with his character and energy. Octavian then had gone to school in
Apollonia and was to accompany Caesar on the Parthian campaign.
After hearing of Caesar's death and his own adoption, Octavian
hurried to Rome to receive his inheritance, which Antonius controlled. Antonius, supposedly bitter because Caesar had omitted him
from his will, treated Octavian with contempt; he called him "boy,"
tried to bar Octavian's adoption into Caesar's family, and tried to
brush aside Octavian's attempts to gain his inheritance (Antonius
was, in fact, holding back 25 million drachmas). Antonius believed
that Octavian lacked the backing and experience to oppose him, a
consul. He was not the only one to underestimate Octavian.

While waiting to receive his inheritance, Octavian, from his own
pocket, paid for the games for the inauguration of the new Temple
of Venus, which had been promised to Caesar. Despite Antonius'
obstruction, Octavian succeeded in placing in the theater a golden
chair in honor of Caesar, which the Senate had promised the
dictator; seeing how popular the chair was with the common
people, Octavian then had a bronze statue of Caesar, with a crown
of stars, placed in the Temple of Venus, the founder of the Julian
family. Soon thereafter Quintilis, the fifth month of the Roman year
(which originally started on March 1), was renamed in Caesar's
honor. After exhausting his ready cash, Octavian sold his estate
and used the proceeds to satisfy the obligations he assumed in
accepting Caesar's will.

Finally, Octavian, now calling himself Caesar and bearing generous cash gifts, made the rounds of Caesar's veterans in Campania,

while his agents in Brundisium (before Antonius arrived) won over to his side still more of Caesar's veterans, who were angry that Caesar's assassins had never been punished: Antonius and Lepidus, Caesar's former lieutenants, had even sat down to dinner with the murderers, but here was Caesar's son, eager to avenge his father's murder. Octavian brought his private army back to Rome, to protect the city from Antonius, who was still on his way to Brundisium to bring the legions to Rome. After arriving in Brundisium, Antonius offered his soldiers only a small percentage of the cash Octavian had offered, which caused them to mutiny. Antonius then performed a *decimatio* on the army, in which one of every ten soldiers was chosen by lot and executed; his wife Fulvia looked on as three hundred men, many of them centurions, were executed. Later, when Antonius had stationed his small army in Tibur, just outside Rome, two of the four legions, at great peril to their lives, deserted their consul Antonius and joined Octavian in the defense of Rome.

Nor was Octavian alone in opposition to Antonius. Many members of the Senate feared that Antonius was trying to take Caesar's place as dictator. Antonius himself was consul and already had an army outside Rome; one of his brothers, Gaius, was praetor, and his other brother, Lucius, was tribune. Lucius could expect to be praetor the next year, since Antonius, as consul, would be overseeing the "elections." The Senate was right to be alarmed; Cicero had foreseen the danger that Antonius presented and, in a letter to Atticus, written in April 44, called the assassination of Caesar "a great and beautiful deed, but incomplete" (*Ep. ad Att.* XIV.12).

So Cicero came out of the semi-retirement he had been in since Pharsalus and took charge. He attacked Antonius in a series of speeches and political pamphlets called the *Philippics*. (These were named after the speeches that Demosthenes, the foremost Athenian orator, had delivered against Philip, king of Macedon, who was threatening Athens' sovereignty from 351 to 341 B.C. In English, the term is used for a tirade against someone.) Cicero urged the Senate to declare war on Antonius:

He has drained Caesar's house of its furnishings, pillaged his gardens, and taken all the beautiful objects from them to his own house. He has

used Caesar's death as an excuse for murder and mayhem. After passing
two or three decrees of the Senate that were beneficial to the republic, he
has made everything simply a matter of profit and loot. He has sold
immunities from taxes, he has freed states, he has freed whole provinces
from the rule of the Roman empire, he has brought back exiles. He has
seen to it that false laws and decrees—passed in the name of Caesar—
would be engraved in bronze and set up on the Capitol. In his house he
has established a market of all things, he has imposed his laws on the
Roman people. With weapons and guards he has shut the people and
magistrates out of the Forum. He has crowded the Senate with armed
men and shut armed soldiers in the Temple of Concord, when he was
presiding over the Senate. He has run down to the legions in Brundisium
and cut the throats of centurions from those legions, despite their
patriotism, and with that army, he tried to come to Rome to destroy us
and to portion out the city. (Cicero, *Philippics* III.12.30–31)

Cicero spoke urgently and passionately, for Antonius at that
time was marching to Cisalpine Gaul, to assume control of the
province that he had had transferred to himself; D. Brutus, who
was governor of Cisalpine Gaul in accordance with Caesar's acts,
refused to relinquish his command to Antonius and shut himself
and his small force inside the city Mutina. Antonius started the
siege of Mutina.

The Senate declared war on Antonius. Octavian was granted a
propraetorship by the Senate, and with Pansa and Hirtius, the two
consuls of 43, he marched to the aid of D. Brutus in Mutina. There
they fought a battle with Antonius, defeated his army, and put him
to flight; he found safety nearby in Lepidus' camp and convinced
the governors of other provinces to support him. In the battle,
however, Hirtius was killed, and Pansa mortally wounded. (D.
Brutus was later deserted by his army and killed.) Octavian was
left alone with the republic's army. He then returned to Rome,
expecting to be treated with deference by the Senate for having
freed Rome from the menace of Antonius. "This is for certain,"
writes Cicero to his friend Trebonius, a conspirator who was killed
by Dolabella in Asia. "If he [Octavian] had not quickly enlisted the
veterans, if two legions from Antonius' army had not brought
themselves under his leadership, and if Antonius had had nothing

to fear, he would not have stopped short of any crime and blood-shed" (*Ep. ad familiares* X.28). Instead of being grateful, the Senate, freed of immediate danger, wished to be rid of him too and refused his request of a consulship, even though he promised to take Cicero as his colleague. Upon the Senate's refusal, he brought his troops into the city, and secured for himself a consulship for the rest of 43, to replace one of the consuls killed at Mutina. He chose for his colleague Q. Pedius, also an heir in Caesar's will. One of his acts as consul declared Caesar's assassins outlaws.

When Octavian entered the Campus Martius on election day, he is said to have seen six vultures, and later twelve, just as Romulus had.

THE SECOND TRIUMVIRATE

Octavian soon understood that he needed the cooperation of Antonius and Lepidus more than he needed Cicero and the Senate. Accordingly, after secretly meeting with Antonius and Lepidus in Bononia, he deserted his former allies and joined the two in an alliance that we call the Second Triumvirate. (The refusal to allow Octavian to run for the consulship shows that Cicero and the Senate fully intended to desert Octavian once he had defeated Antonius; they too underestimated him.) The agreement between these three differed from the First Triumvirate because this alliance was publicly known and legalized by the Lex Titia. In legal terms, Octavian, Antonius, and Lepidus were "tresviri reipublicae constituendae causa" (three men for reestablishing the republic). For five years, the length of the triumvirate, they would be superior to all magistrates and governors, and they would have the power to make laws. They agreed on the following allotment of the provinces: Antonius received Cispadane and Transpadane Gaul; Octavian received Africa, Sicily, and Sardinia; Lepidus got Gallia Narbonensis and all Spain. To cement the deal, Octavian married Clodia, the daughter of Antonius' wife Fulvia by her first husband, Clodius the tribune.

Soon the three embarked on the proscriptions, in which they not only raised the money to finance the purchase of land for the veterans and the pay of their forty-five legions, but also got revenge on their enemies, some of whom were even members of their family. Antonius, for example, let his uncle, L. Caesar, be killed, while Lepidus proscribed his own brother, Paullus. Antonius became as monstrous as Cicero had portrayed him, as the triumvirs killed more than three hundred senators and two thousand knights and confiscated their estates. Antonius insisted upon the death of Cicero, who had insulted him repeatedly in his *Philippics*. Cicero was killed by a man he had once defended in court, and at Antonius' orders the head and hands were cut off his corpse and nailed to the rostrum in the Forum; Cicero's son was safe, being at school in Athens, but Cicero's brother Quintus and his son were killed. The triumvirs were hated because of the proscriptions. Those fleeing the proscriptions joined either Brutus and Cassius in Asia or Sextus Pompey, the last son of Pompey the Great, who with his powerful fleet was harassing Italian shipping and controlling the seas around Italy.

After fleeing Rome, Brutus and Cassius had proceeded to Crete and Cyrene, the provinces allotted to them by Caesar. The two men nonetheless managed to take control of Macedonia, Syria, and Asia. They even captured G. Antonius, Marcus' brother, who had been sent to secure Macedonia; he was later killed, supposedly to avenge the murder of Cicero. Brutus and Cassius were amassing a large army and supplies to rescue the republic, and they established a base in Greece, at Philippi. Their forces were soon augmented by fugitives from the proscriptions. Among the soldiers joining them were M. Cicero, the son of the orator, and Q. Horatius Flaccus (Horace). (Horace became a better poet than soldier; in the one battle he saw in his brief military career, he threw down his shield and fled.)

In 42 Antonius and Octavian sailed to Greece to have a battle with the remaining republicans. Octavian was sick in bed on the day of the battle and narrowly escaped death, as his camp was taken by Brutus' victorious army; nonetheless, Antonius' army defeated that of Cassius. Cassius, thinking Brutus conquered and dead, committed suicide; Brutus then collected his and Cassius' army and faced Antonius and Octavian in a second battle, which he lost to Antonius. Brutus too committed suicide.

ANTONIUS IN THE EAST

After Philippi, Antonius left Italy for the East, to prepare for the invasion of Parthia. While the Romans were fighting with each other, the Parthians, led by T. Labienus, son of Caesar's former lieutenant, had taken over all of Syria except for Tyre and even threatened southern Asia Minor. It probably seemed an excellent idea for Antonius to go east and fight Parthia, for besides the obvious advantage and necessity of rescuing part of the empire, he would win wealth, fame, and glory: He would be fulfilling the dream of Caesar and he would get revenge for Crassus. Antonius' brother Lucius was consul in 41 and could control Octavian; since one of Octavian's tasks was to find land for the thousands of veterans, Antonius could be free of the whole mess. Yet leaving Italy and Rome turned out to be a terrible mistake for, absent from Rome and Italy, Antonius was able neither to see their transformation under Octavian nor to adapt himself to oppose the changes that Octavian was making.

Octavian had to find land for approximately one hundred thousand veterans. To do so, he took land from rightful owners. For this reason Octavian was hated by many Italians. One of the victims of the land confiscations was the young poet P. Vergilius Maro (called Vergil in English), whose ancestral farm near Mantua was awarded to a soldier. Vergil wrote a poem about losing his farm, the *First Eclogue*; his talent was noticed by friends of Octavian, and they restored the farm to him. Antonius' wife Fulvia and his brother Lucius tried to capitalize on Octavian's unpopularity, and the two sides even had a brief war at Perusia, which Octavian won. Fulvia died as Antonius was returning to Italy to fight Octavian; since she had instigated the conflict, the soldiers of the two sides insisted upon peace between the two men. They were reconciled in the Treaty of Brundisium of 40 and redivided the empire between them. Octavian took everything west of the Adriatic Sea, while Antonius took everything east of it. Lepidus retained Africa, while Sextus Pompey controlled Sicily and Sardinia. To cement the pact, Antonius married Octavian's sister, Octavia (the marriage was the inspiration for another poem by Vergil, the famous *Fourth Eclogue*).

Antonius then went to Asia, where he started wearing eastern clothes and engaging in un-Roman practices. He had always been a heavy drinker (once while giving a speech as consul, he was so hung-over that he vomited into his toga), known for consorting with disreputable types. Golden drinking cups were carried before him when he left Rome, as if they were part of a religious procession, and he billeted prostitutes and musicians in the homes of respectable people. Antonius had also taken the modest house of Pompey the Great, and people were angry that Antonius closed the house to generals, magistrates, and ambassadors, and filled it instead with actors, jugglers, and drunken parasites, on whom he squandered vast amounts of money. He started calling himself "the young Dionysus," and insisted that others call him that too. In Athens, the citizens betrothed the goddess Athena to him, and he in turn demanded a huge dowry.

Part of the problem was his new friend, Cleopatra, queen of Egypt. While preparing for the Parthian expedition, Antonius summoned her to face charges that she had aided Cassius. Their meeting at the Cydnus River is famous:

She sailed up the Cydnus river on a barge with a golden stern, which had its purple sails spread wide, with rowers lifting up their silver oars to the sound of a flute, accompanied by a pipe and flute. Cleopatra, reclining beneath a canopy glittering with gold, was made up to look like Venus as seen in paintings, and her slaves, standing next to her, looked like Cupids. Likewise her most beautiful handmaids wore the clothing of Nereids and Graces, and were either at the rudder or the ropes. Marvelous odors from generous amounts of incense spread through the riverbanks. (Plutarch, *Antonius* 26)

Antonius fell under her spell. Cleopatra saw what type of person he was and changed her behavior to please him. She played dice with him, drank with him, hunted and fished with him, and watched him as he exercised with his weapons. He liked also to wander around the city of Alexandria disguised as a slave and to stand outside the homes of ordinary people and make fun of them. So Cleopatra went with him, disguised as a maidservant.

Back in the palace, however, their tastes were not so plebeian. They and their friends called themselves "the ones with the incomparable lifestyles" and gave banquets for each other. When warned of an upcoming banquet, the cook was expected to have the food ready and perfect at precisely the moment that it was called for, whenever that was. Since the guests would not want to wait for the food to finish cooking, or to eat food that had been ready long before and that had been reheated, the cook prepared many different banquets, at different stages of preparation, so that one of them would be ready and perfect when Antonius and Cleopatra and guests were ready.

While Antonius was preparing for the war (squeezing money from the provincials and partying with Cleopatra), his excellent lieutenant Ventidius drove the Parthians from Syria. Antonius finally left Cleopatra and invaded Parthia, but he was immediately deserted by his ally, the king of Armenia. Then, by marching quickly, Antonius allowed his siege-train to become separated from his army, thus giving the Parthians the opportunity to destroy the siege-train. Antonius and his soldiers had to cope with the hostile climate and lack of provisions, as well as the formidable Parthian army. Antonius' expedition against Parthia accomplished little. He returned to Syria after losing twenty thousand soldiers and four thousand cavalry. Eventually he got revenge on the king of Armenia and made his country briefly a province of Rome, but he soon lost it too.

While Antonius was living the life of luxury and decadence with Cleopatra, or failing in his Parthian campaign, Octavian was busy solving the many problems in Italy and Rome. One of the problems was S. Pompey. In 39 Octavian and Antonius reached peace with him by granting him Sicily, Sardinia, and part of Greece; they never intended to live up to the agreement, nor did he. Despite the treaty, he was still engaging in piracy and frequently attacking the Italian shores. With his control of Sicily, he had interrupted the flow of grain into Rome, causing a famine there.

Octavian was consequently forced to fight S. Pompey and his powerful navy. For that he needed ships, so he promised to deliver twenty thousand soldiers to Antonius in exchange for ships; at the same time, the triumvirate was renewed for another five years.

(Octavian received the ships, but never delivered the soldiers to Antonius.) Agrippa, Octavian's admiral and righthand man, needed to train his crews, but S. Pompey's fleet was so powerful that Agrippa could not train them even in the waters off the Italian coast, for S. Pompey's fleet would destroy the new navy during its training. So Agrippa created a huge harbor (the Portus Iulius) by cutting a trench between Lake Avernus and Lake Lucrinus (famous for its oysters) and joining them with the open sea. In that harbor, safe from S. Pompey's fleet, Agrippa was able to train his men. Octavian and Agrippa then defeated S. Pompey in a hard-fought battle in 36. He fled to Asia, where he was caught and put to death, perhaps at Antonius' orders. Octavian also suspected his fellow triumvir Lepidus of collaborating with S. Pompey; when Lepidus was left defenseless by the desertion of his army, Octavian deposed him and banished him to the island Circei.

THE PROPAGANDA WAR

Since Lepidus and S. Pompey had been removed, only Antonius and Octavian remained. Octavian knew that war between them was inevitable; three times before they had been dissuaded from warring on each other, either by their soldiers or by Octavia. In preparation for the coming war, Octavian in 35–34 exercised his army with expeditions against the Dalmatians and Pannonians, tribes in Illyricum. More important were his efforts closer to home, for by them he united most Italians and Romans against Antonius.

Since Antonius was away from Rome, Octavian came to be seen as the source of good government in Italy and the West. The Romans and Italians wanted stability in the state after nearly a century of civil strife, and Octavian provided it. The hatred he had earned for the proscriptions and confiscations waned, and his popularity in the western provinces grew, as peace allowed them to return to prosperity. Octavian's zeal to earn the goodwill of his subjects can be seen in many other acts. For example, he and his friends supported poets whose verses glorified Rome and Italy, and reminded the audience of the good things that Octavian was doing; two of those poets were Vergil and Horace. In 33 Agrippa was aedile and at no cost to the treasury repaired public buildings and streets, and cleaned out and repaired sewers, even sailing through the Cloaca Maxima into the Tiber. Agrippa also distributed free olive oil and salt, charged no admission to the public baths for a year, provided free festivals and free barbers, and distributed coupons to the public, good for cash, clothes, and other useful commodities.

Octavian let the Italians know what Antonius was doing in the East: Antonius had gone to get revenge from Parthia, but had accomplished little in his battles there except for losing money and men; he had fallen in love with Cleopatra and was treating Octavia, his Roman wife and a wonderful woman, badly. When Antonius was short on supplies in Parthia, Octavia, using her own money and help she had begged from her brother, filled ships with clothing, food, and supplies for Antonius and his men, and paid for two thousand soldiers to be Antonius' praetorian guard; Antonius refused even to meet with her, but accepted all that she had bought. Antonius by now had fathered three children by Cleopatra: two sons named Alexander Helios (the Sun) and Ptolemy Philadelphus, and a daughter was named Cleopatra Selene (the Moon). The poses they assumed for statues and paintings portrayed Antonius as Osiris or Dionysus and Cleopatra as Selene or Isis. Meanwhile, back in Rome, Octavia was caring for her and Antonius' children, as well as for his children by his previous wife Fulvia, and was maintaining his house and loyally defending his interests. She inadvertently made Antonius even more detested, for what kind of man would treat such a woman—especially a Roman aristocratic matron—in such a manner? In 32 Antonius sent men to turn Octavia out of his house, a formal declaration of divorce.

Antonius still had many friends and supporters in Rome, but he was not helping himself. News came to Rome of the "Donations of Alexandria":

He filled the exercise area with a crowd of people and, on a silver stage, put up two thrones, one for himself and the other for Cleopatra, and other lower thrones for his children. Then he proclaimed Cleopatra queen of Egypt, Cyprus, Libya, and Coele-Syria, with Caesarion being co-ruler with her; he was thought to be Julius Caesar's son, since she was pregnant when he left her. Then he proclaimed his sons by Cleopatra

king of kings, and he allotted Armenia, Media, and Parthia (once
Antonius had conquered it) to Alexander, and to Ptolemy he allotted
Phoenicia, Syria, and Cilicia. Then he brought his sons forth, Alexander
in Median clothing with a tiara and straight hat, and Ptolemy in Macedonian soldiers' boots, short cloak, and diadem. (Plutarch, *Antonius* LIV)

Some of the Romans merely pitied Antonius, as they thought he
was the victim of some love drug that Cleopatra had given him
to keep him under her control. Cleopatra appeared to be using
Antonius as a pawn in her dream of conquering the Roman empire
and transferring the seat of power to Alexandria; she even swore
oaths with these words: "As surely as I will be giving edicts on the
Capitol, will (such-and-such) happen. . . ."

Finally, from two of Antonius' friends, who had deserted him,
Octavian learned what Antonius had written in his will. Octavian
seized the will, which had been deposited with the Vestal Virgins,
and read it to the Senate. Although horrified at Octavian's actions—
anything concerned with the Vestal Virgins was regarded as sacred,
and Octavian had violated their sanctity—the audience was more
horrified at Antonius' wishes: among other things, he wanted his
body to be buried with Cleopatra in Egypt, *even if he died in Rome.*

The people of Rome and the West, seeing the return of peace,
stable government, and prosperity, probably had little difficulty in
their choice between Octavian and Antonius. Antonius' career
since the death of Caesar must not have inspired confidence.
Octavian too had been brutal during the triumvirate, but he had
restored peace and prosperity. Life under Octavian was good, and
besides Octavian was in control of Italy and the West. When it
became clear that Octavian and Antonius would have a war for the
empire, Italy and the western provinces swore allegiance to
Octavian, a fact he records in his *Res gestae*: "Iuravit in mea verba
tota Italia sponte sua . . . iuraverunt in eadem verba provinciae
Galliae, Hispaniae, Africa, Sicilia, Sardinia" ("All Italy voluntarily
swore allegiance to me . . . the Gallic provinces, the Spanish
provinces, Africa, Sicily, and Sardinia likewise swore allegiance";
Res Gestae 25).

In 32 Antonius collected his forces from the East and transferred
them to Greece; Cleopatra accompanied him. Antonius' associates

told him that bringing Cleopatra was a mistake, for without her Antonius could claim to the Italians that the war was simply a political dispute between him and his former colleague in the triumvirate. Cleopatra's presence, however, changed the war into an invasion of Italy by a foreign power. (Octavian was careful to declare war only on Cleopatra, not on Antonius.) Antonius had no choice but to allow her to accompany him, for she was providing much of the navy.

In 31 B.C. the two forces met in battle at Actium, a promontory on the coast of western Greece that was sacred to Apollo. It was not much of a battle. Antonius' forces, sick and hungry, were deserting him; his fleet quickly fell apart, and Octavian won.

Antonius and Cleopatra fled to Egypt, where they instituted another society of banqueteers (called "those about to die together") and resolved to enjoy the rest of their lives, however long that might be. Cleopatra meanwhile was using her slaves as victims in experiments with different types of poisons, to see which poison brought on the quickest and easiest death.

The next year Octavian arrived in Egypt from Syria, while his generals entered from Libya. Fearing that Cleopatra, in despair, might incinerate the treasury of the Ptolemies, Octavian made various offers to her that would allow her to live. When Antonius' remaining forces deserted him, Cleopatra sent messengers to tell Antonius that she had committed suicide; upon hearing them, he stabbed himself and lived just long enough to be brought to Cleopatra, who was still alive, barricaded within her mausoleum. He died in her arms.

Soon Octavian arrived, and his envoys treated Cleopatra with respect and courtesy, for in addition to the treasury, Octavian also wanted her presence in his triumph. He ordered his men to do everything to keep her alive, and he himself even visited her and tried to reassure her. Despite the precautions, Cleopatra managed to kill herself. In a basket of figs her servants hid a black asp, whose bite was said to confer upon the victim death as well as divinity; by its bite Cleopatra met her end.

Octavian incorporated Egypt into the empire, treating it as his personal property. He killed Caesarion (Caesar's son by Cleopatra) and Antyllus (Antonius' son by Fulvia), and finally found himself without opposition for the rule of the Roman Empire. The poet Horace celebrated Octavian's victory over Cleopatra with his famous "Cleopatra" ode:

Now's the time to drink,
Now's the time to pound the ground with free feet,
my friends, for a long time it's been time to honor the gods with magnificence.
Before now it would have been a crime to break out
the prized Caecuban from ancient wine cellars,
while that queen with her polluted flock of diseased and filthy men was
preparing insane destruction for the Capitol and empire—she, deluded by her
good luck and powerless to hope.
The one ship of hers that barely escaped the fires didn't
humble her at all, but Caesar, with chains ready for the deadly monster, forced
her mind, drunk on Egyptian wine, to face horrible reality,
as she flew from Italy and his rowers in feverish
pursuit, like a falcon diving for tender doves or a quick hunter
in winter pursuing a rabbit in the fields of Haemonia.
Seeking to die honorably,
she had no coward's fear of the sword,
nor did her swift fleet make for hidden shores.
Her face serene, she dared to behold her helpless
palace, brave enough even to clutch deadly snakes
so she could take the black poison into her body.
All the more fierce—she planned her own death—
she deprived Caesar's swift Liburnian ships of her being led in
his proud triumph like a meek woman.
(Horace, *Odes* I.37)

CHAPTER 23

The Roman Empire
The Principate

The Battle of Actium eliminated the danger from Antonius and all other significant opposition to Octavian's rule. Grave problems nonetheless remained for the young Octavian. What form of government would ensure his own political survival, as well as the prosperity of Rome, Italy, and the provinces? He knew that he could not restore the republic of old: Ambitious generals would certainly seize power and in the process provoke a new series of civil wars, which the empire might not survive; the Senate certainly could not be counted on to provide leadership, for it was largely to blame for failing to solve the various problems that destroyed the republic; and the Roman populace itself had degenerated into a mob dependent on the grain dole, placated by "bread and circuses." Nor could Octavian become a monarch: His adopted father's fate, as well as his own conservative republican values, precluded any monarchy. Serious problems, indeed.

But guided by his own conservative outlook (one of his favorite sayings was *festina lente*, "hurry, but slowly"), Octavian slowly and deliberately created a system of government that would bring to Europe and the Mediterranean world the longest period of peace and prosperity that it had ever seen. Once that period ended, such stability did not occur again until after World War II.

Of utmost importance to Octavian was the control of the armies. From 43 to 33 B.C. he had relied upon his triumviral powers for his military might, and from 31 to 23 he was elected to successive consulships. Yet the nobles resented his dominance of the consulship and military; their ancestors, after all, had been consuls, and they felt it their right to reach the highest honor in Roman government. Also, Octavian's own delicate health limited the number and weight of the neverending burdens he could assume in running the empire. Therefore, in 27 B.C., after a serious illness, Octavian offered to restore the republic; the Senate objected, begging him not to desert his country.

The two sides compromised by dividing the empire into two parts, one ruled by Octavian and the other by the Senate. It is not mere coincidence that the provinces ruled by Octavian, called imperial provinces, were those most in need of a large standing army: Gaul, with its armies along the Rhine; Spain, still in the process of pacification; Syria, always threatened by Parthia; and Egypt, which supplied Rome with one-fourth of its yearly supply of grain, a power Octavian could not let fall into the hands of any overly ambitious senator. The senatorial provinces were the peaceful ones: Sicily, Corsica, Sardinia, Greece, Asia, Bithynia, Crete, and Africa. Only two senatorial provinces, Illyricum and Macedonia, had armies—to protect the empire from incursions from across the Danube. After "restoring" the republic in 27 B.C. Octavian was honored with the honorary title *augustus*, which means "holy, sacred, venerable" (*sebastos* in Greek), and the month Sextilis was renamed in his honor. Later, after another serious illness in 23, Augustus was granted *maius imperium* (greater power), by which he could overrule all other magistrates if necessary. He already had *tribunicia potestas* (tribune's power), by which he could veto the undesired actions of any magistrate; by a different law, he was freed from having to obey the laws: "Princeps legibus solutus est." (This caused some problems for the public under later emperors: what were the legal limits to their behavior?)

To all appearances, then, the republic had been restored. Octavian rarely held the consulship after 23, and the powers that he held, if considered separately, were not new or extraordinary. For example, the tribune's power dated to the early days of the republic (see chapter 6). Pompey, who had fought for the republic at Pharsalus, had held *maius imperium* and extraordinary commands. And, of course, individual Romans had always ruled the provinces as governors. Octavian (henceforth called Augustus) chose his legal title very carefully; he called himself *princeps* ("first citizen", from *primus*, "first," and *capio*, "to seize"). This

Augustus, first century A.D. (Courtesy of the Archer M. Huntington Art Gallery, University of Texas at Austin, William J. Battle Collection of Plaster Casts)

was a term with good republican connotations: The *princeps senatus* had simply been the most eminent man in the Senate, and the *principes* had been the leading men in the state. Augustus as *princeps* was nothing new or radical; in his own words, he was simply *primus inter pares*, "first among equals."

The reality of the sharing of power, however, was different, for Augustus controlled the armies and held *maius imperium* and *tribunicia potestas* all at the same time. The consulate, stripped of its military functions—only Augustus, his closest friends, or his relatives led the armies—became solely administrative and ceremonial. When Marcus Crassus, the grandson of the triumvir, killed an enemy king in single combat in 28 B.C., Augustus denied him the *spolia opima*; Augustus had to keep sole control of the military. The Senate's autonomy was greatly diminished, for Augustus ultimately controlled affairs through his various powers and commands; the people's authority too was reduced, for their officials—elected from a list nominated by Augustus—wielded very little real power. Still, Augustus knew that he could not afford to alienate any of the classes and that he could not manage the empire alone; consequently he strove to make them active partners in the new system. So he transformed the Senate into the civil service that the republic had lacked and drew from its educated and experienced members to fill the various posts in the government. The *equites* too were incorporated into the system, as more of them were enrolled in the Senate and given posts in the government. Augustus placated the common people of Rome with generous grants of food and games. Few people opposed the new system, for all enjoyed the benefits of peace; Augustus inaugurated the famous *pax Romana* (the peace of Rome), two centuries of largely unbroken peace and prosperity throughout the Mediterranean world.

Since Augustus himself picked men to become governors, paid their salaries, and scrutinized their performance, he was able to ensure fair and ethical government in the provinces. Governors could be charged with extortion in a court over which Augustus himself presided. He also abolished the horrible tax-farming system (see chapter 15); provincial peoples still paid taxes, but now to a salaried Roman official who was independent of the governor. Communications between Rome and the provinces were improved by the establishment of the *cursus publicus*, a sort of Pony Express for government officials. Consequently, the provinces prospered under the new system: Borders were secure, internal peace prevailed, taxes were fair, roads were built, and piracy was suppressed. Soon a far-flung trade developed across the Mediterranean and all Europe and beyond, from Britain to Egypt, the Crimea, India, Sri Lanka, and even China. Many provinces established cults for the worship of Rome and Augustus, so grateful were they for the prosperity they experienced under the Augustan system.

In foreign policy—over which Augustus, by virtue of his consular power and *maius imperium*, had complete control—Rome won numerous victories. Under Augustus, peace finally came to Spain. He concluded a treaty with Armenia and Parthia, even gaining from the Parthians the standards from Crassus' obliterated army; the loss of the standards had been a source of shame to the Romans. He extended the borders north of Greece as far as the Danube, establishing the provinces of Noricum, Raetia, Pannonia, and Moesia (roughly modern-day Austria, Hungary, Bosnia, Herzegovina, Albania, Yugoslavia, Macedonia, and Bulgaria). He founded twelve new towns in Gaul, and Gaul began to prosper after the horrors of its wars with Julius Caesar. A Roman army penetrated into Ethiopia, in retaliation for the Ethiopians' raid into Egypt. Embassies came to Rome from India and Scythia (modern Ukraine).

Augustus experienced one disaster in foreign policy. Early in his reign he intended to conquer Germany, since Germanic tribes had been attacking Gaul. Marcellus (Augustus' nephew) and Tiberius (the son of Augustus' wife Livia by a previous marriage) were having great success against the Germans, pushing the border between Gaul and Germany beyond the Rhine River, their goal being to establish the Elbe as the frontier. In A.D. 9, however, disaster struck, when the Roman general Varus and his three legions were led into a trap in the Teutoburg Forest and wiped out by the German Arminius. Augustus was devastated by the annihilation of the three legions. He had demobilized and settled one hundred thousand soldiers at the end of the civil wars and had in arms fewer than twenty-five legions; the loss of three was a severe blow. Augustus refused to shave or cut his hair (traditional

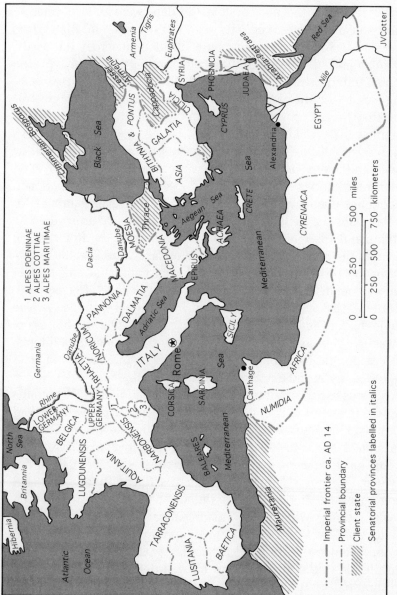

The Roman Empire at the death of Augustus, A.D. 14. (Drawn by John Cotter)

signs of mourning in Rome) and is said to have walked the halls of his palace at night saying, "Quintili Vare, legiones redde!" (Varus, give me back those three legions!). He then decided not to devote any more resources to enlarging the empire, a course followed by his successors.

While Augustus was establishing peace and stability, he was also waging a public relations campaign to solidify his position and to win the support of the Romans and Italians. He had begun the campaign when he assumed the name Caesar and portrayed himself as Caesar's successor and as *divi filius* (son of a god) when Caesar was considered to have become a god. Augustus intensified his efforts to solidify support for himself against Marcus Antonius. Through his righthand man, Agrippa, Augustus worked to improve Rome and Italy. He financed the beautification of Rome, so that he could truthfully say, "I found Rome a city of clay, but left it a city of marble." The Ara Pacis (Altar of Peace) is a good example. The walls surrounding the altar itself are decorated with images in relief. In one of them we see Augustus, wearing a toga (symbolic of peace), in a procession of family members and other Romans who will be making a sacrifice to the gods. The altar kept Augustus' name and achievements before the eyes of the people, and it also beautified Rome. Through Agrippa Augustus repaired and constructed eighty-two temples and aqueducts, repaired sewers (Agrippa sailed up the Cloaca Maxima to inspect it), instituted a fire brigade, and built a new forum, the Forum Augusti. He instituted a type of police force (called *vigiles*) to patrol the countryside and reduce the number of kidnappings and robberies, since innocent travelers on deserted country roads were being abducted and enslaved; the twelve colonies of veterans that he founded in Italy further helped secure the countryside against crime. Augustus also established a special tax to fund the *aerarium militare* (soldiers' treasury), which paid for farms for veteran soldiers upon their retirement from the army. (If the Senate had done that a century earlier, the republic might not have fallen.) Augustus divided the city Rome into 14 *regiones* and 265 *vici* (villages), each *vicus* being administered by a *vicomagister*, to improve the process of taxation and census-taking. The Italian peninsula he divided into eleven regions, for the same purpose. He also established the Praetorian

The Pantheon, whose construction was begun by Agrippa; the Latin inscription reads, "Marcus Agrippa, the son of Lucius, when consul for the third time, made [this]." (Author photograph)

Guard, which consisted of nine cohorts of soldiers, as a permanent military force in Rome. Rome was now the capital of the Western world, and Augustus made the city's appearance match its importance.

Augustus also engaged in literary patronage. He and his friends Maecenas and Messalla gave grants of money and land so promising young poets could devote their energies to their art, and in doing so fostered what is now called the Golden Age of Latin literature. One finds various themes in the poetry: love, of course, but also meditations on ethics and what constitutes a good life, patriotism and appreciation of the peace and stability that Augustus brought, celebration of the joys and beauty of the Italian countryside, and tales from Greek, Roman, and Italian myths. The poetry is of the highest artistry and polish; for example, Vergil

Interior of the Pantheon. (Author photograph)

spent seven years on his *Georgics*, a philosophical poem about farming and the countryside that has only 2,188 lines, and three years on his *Eclogues*, which contains fewer than 1,000 lines. It averages out to less than one line of verse per day.

Vergil's epic poem *The Aeneid* was the greatest literary achievement of the Augustan age and the most famous expression of its outlook. The poem tells the story of Aeneas, a Trojan prince famous for his sense of duty to the gods, his family, and community, who was also a brave and patriotic soldier. He thus epitomized Roman values (see chapter 2). When Troy is destroyed by the Greeks, Aeneas leaves his home and city, carrying his aged and lame father on his shoulders, bearing the *penates* (household gods) in one arm, and leading his young son Ascanius with the other. He leaves in pursuit of some vague destiny; he hears that he is destined to found what will become a great empire. Aeneas does not fully understand his assignment or its importance, yet he toils and

The Pont du Gard aqueduct near Nîmes, France, built by Marcus Agrippa between 20 and 16 B.C. (Courtesy of Alan T. Kohl, Art Images for College Teaching)

sacrifices to fulfill his duty, so others after him can enjoy the fruit of his labors. Vergil had not yet finished the poem when he died, and he commanded that it be burned; fortunately for future generations, his friend Lucius Varius refused to carry out the order. Varius and Plotius Tucca edited the poem, at the order of Augustus himself.

To the Romans, who were searching for answers to the question, "Why an empire, when we cannot rule ourselves?" the travails of Aeneas gave an answer, told to him by Anchises in the Underworld: "Roman, remember to rule countries with power—that is what you do best—habituate them to peace, spare the conquered, and war down the proud" (Vergil, *Aeneid* VI.851–853). *The Aeneid* thus helped to unify Italy, to formulate and express the empire's political reason for being, and to foster the national consciousness.

According to Vergil's *Aeneid*, then, the empire existed because it was in the best interest of the conquered; there is much truth in that statement. In 29 B.C. the Senate formally closed the temple of Janus, thus showing that Rome and its territories were at peace; this had happened only twice before in Roman history, during Numa's reign and in 235 B.C. The temple had to be reopened shortly after, but still most of the empire was at peace, and peace brought prosperity.

Other poets of the times show why the age is rightly called the Golden Age of Latin literature. Maecenas noticed the talent of Horace, the son of a freedman, and gave him a farm in the Sabine hill country. Horace wrote lyric poetry (*Odes* and *Epodes*), satires (*Sermones*, literally, "chats"), and letters in poetic form (*Epistulae*). Another famous poet of the age was Ovid, who wrote epic poetry and elegies. His *magnum opus* is his *Metamorphoses*, an epic poem of tales of transformations, from the beginning of the world to his day; it is the source of such familiar stories as Apollo and Daphne, Narcissus and Echo, Pyramus and Thisbe, Baucis and Philemon, Arachne, Midas and the golden touch, and many more. His other famous surviving works are *Amores*, *Ars amatoria*, *Fasti*, *Heroides*, *Tristia*, and *Epistulae ex Ponto* (the last two written when he was in exile). He was a master of the Latin hexameter (the meter of ancient epic poetry), ranked with Vergil. Like Ovid, Propertius and Tibullus wrote elegies about love. One famous historian of the age deserves mention: Livy, whose history of Rome, *Ab urbe condita* (From the Founding of the City), preserves the stories of Lucretia, Cincinnatus, Horace at the bridge, and others; his history treated of Roman history from the beginning to his day, but only one-quarter of his huge work survives. It is a great loss. (You will probably have noticed that many of the exciting stories of Roman history recounted in this book are drawn from Livy's work.)

Augustus also oversaw something of a revival of ancient Roman religion and morals. Many Romans had rightly sought reasons for the previous century of chaos, and they arrived at this answer: The gods were angry with the Romans for forsaking their ancient religion and the customs of their ancestors. So Augustus revived many religious festivals and games that had been neglected. He also built new temples, which renewed the Romans' belief in the majesty of the gods. Particularly important to Augustus was the cultivation of the worship of Apollo. The Battle of Actium had been fought in an area sacred to Apollo, and his temple looked down upon the scene of battle; furthermore, Augustus' mother, Atia, said his real father had been Apollo.

The literature of Horace and Vergil praised the simple, devout life. Augustus also lived according to his ideals: He lived modestly, while others with his power, influence, and fame would have maintained a palace and regal lifestyle; except on public occasions, he wore clothes made from wool spun by his wife and daughters. One time when he was dining at the home of a noble, one of the nobleman's slaves broke an expensive cup. The owner proceeded to have the slave whipped. Thereupon Augustus called for all the expensive cups to be brought and then broke them, one by one. He instructed the aediles not to allow anyone into the Forum who was not wearing a toga.

August likewise sought to reform the degeneracy of the upper classes. For example, he passed a law concerning adulterers, according to which those guilty of adultery could be banished. When his own daughter Julia engaged in sexual misconduct, he banished her to the island Pandateria, where she was forbidden to see men, drink wine, or enjoy any sort of luxury. The Roman populace eventually began to pity her and begged Augustus to bring her back; bitterly he cursed the crowd, saying they should have daughters like his. He always referred to his daughter and granddaughter as "boils" and "cancers." On his deathbed Augustus ordered that Julia not be buried in the family mausoleum. Similarly, for some breach in morality, in A.D. 8 the poet Ovid was banished to Tomis, a town on the Black Sea. Scholars debate the reasons for his banishment; Ovid wrote only that the reason was *carmen et error*, "a poem and a mistake." Augustus also passed laws encouraging married couples to produce more children, whereby fathers of more than three children would obtain advancement in their careers, while female citizens who had more than three children could gain exemption from the requirement of having a guardian; a freedwoman could gain the exemption by having four. Childless couples, however, would have to forfeit their property to the state upon their deaths.

One problem Augustus had difficulty in solving concerned his successor. He wanted the rule to stay within the family, but those whom he wanted to succeed him died: Marcellus, his nephew; then Agrippa; then Drusus, the son of his wife Livia by a previous marriage. Tiberius, another son of Livia by a previous marriage, was the only one remaining, and Augustus was not overly fond of Tiberius; he nonetheless adopted him and gave him training in the government of the empire. When Augustus died, in A.D. 14, Tiberius was prepared to take over.

Augustus ruled for more than forty-five years. He came to power when Rome most needed a steady ruler, and he provided stability. By the time of his death, Romans had not fought with other Romans since 31 B.C., the borders were secure, and through the *pax Augusta*, the empire was prospering. All these accomplishments and more Augustus recorded in his *Res gestae* (Accomplishments), an account of his life's work, written in his simple and direct style. The Romans had lost some political liberties, but in return they received peace, stability, and responsible government. It is not a gross exaggeration to call his rule the Golden Age of Rome. At his funeral an eagle was released into the air from beneath his funeral pyre, to symbolize the ascent of his spirit into heaven. He was afterward deified.

CHAPTER 24

The Julio-Claudian Emperors

TIBERIUS (A.D. 14–37): "TAMQUAM AMBIGUUS IMPERANDI"

Augustus' successor Tiberius had a hard act to follow. He could do nothing that would measure up to the standard set by Augustus—believed to have become a god—who had "joined monarchy with democracy, and secured freedom for the people, and made the freedom stable and orderly" (Dio LVI.43.4). For Tiberius to do anything less would be considered failure.

It also appears that Tiberius was not happy about becoming emperor. During his career (he was fifty-six when he became emperor), he had already sacrificed plenty for Rome, fighting in long, hard campaigns in Germany, Pannonia, and Illyricum. Augustus had compelled Tiberius to divorce his wife, Vipsania, whom he dearly loved (he missed her so badly that one day, after catching sight of her, he followed her and wept profusely), and to marry Augustus' libertine daughter Julia, obviously before her wild living had become common knowledge. When it became clear to him that Augustus preferred his nephew Marcellus and grandsons Lucius and Gaius as successors, Tiberius withdrew from Rome to the island of Rhodes, so he would not seem to be interfering with their careers; his disgust with Julia may have been an additional reason. Augustus was piqued by Tiberius' withdrawal and would not let him return to Rome until Livia interceded on her son's behalf. Only when all of Augustus' other possible heirs had died did he acknowledge Tiberius as his heir and successor; even then there was a catch, for Tiberius had to adopt his nephew Germanicus (grandson of Livia by a previous marriage) and place him ahead of his own son, Drusus, in line for the succession. It was quite clear to Tiberius that he had been Augustus' last choice for a successor, and Augustus' will even said so: "Since a horrible fate has snatched my sons Gaius and Lucius away from me, let Tiberius Caesar be heir to two-thirds of my estate" (Suetonius, *Tiberius* XXIII). Later gossips said that Augustus had appointed Tiberius as his successor precisely because of his shortcomings, for they would make everybody appreciate Augustus all the more.

Upon Augustus' death, Tiberius feigned hesitation in assuming the power, "as if uncertain about ruling" ("tamquam ambiguus imperandi"; Tacitus, *Annales* I.7). The Senate then begged him to take power. Tiberius offered to split the empire into three parts, and to rule one of the parts while the Senate ruled the other two, but the offer came to nothing. Tiberius' reluctance to take on the responsibility of governing the empire may well have been genuine. He is said to have commented that he was holding a wolf by the ears, and that those urging him to accept the emperor's power would make him a miserable and overworked slave. The last years of his life show some truth to his words.

Immediately after he accepted power, the armies on the Rhine revolted, since they wanted Germanicus, their beloved general, to be emperor, even though he did not want it or at least was willing to wait until Tiberius died. He barely restrained his soldiers from marching on Rome. From the Senate Tiberius could expect little help; many of its members, accustomed to Augustus' domination of politics, had become abject sycophants. "Consuls, senators, and knights made a mad dash into slavery," sneers Tacitus (*Annales* I.7), a bitter critic of Tiberius and the principate. Tiberius appears to have wanted the Senate to take the greater burden of running the empire, but the Senate constantly looked to the *princeps* for leadership and decision-making. One persistent criticism of Tiberius is that he never spoke his mind: "He never strove for the things that he wanted, and the things he said he did not mean; but saying words the entirely opposite of his intentions, he refused what he wanted and strove for what he hated" (Dio LVII.1). Another source mentions that Tiberius simply spoke obscurely. Perhaps Tiberius never spoke his true mind in hopes that the senators, not knowing his real opinion, would be forced to decide for themselves and would thus regain some backbone and independence. Years later Tiberius would mutter in Greek, every time he left the Senate, "Men ready for slavery!" (Tacitus, *Annales* III.65).

Nonetheless, Tiberius' rule began well. He brought all matters to the Senate for discussion. Ambassadors had to discuss affairs with the consuls and Senate, as well as with the emperor. One embassy complained to the consuls that they could make no headway with the emperor, for Tiberius wanted the consuls to conduct business with them. To show his respect, Tiberius also rose from his seat when the consuls entered the Senate. When one senator called him "lord," Tiberius told him not to insult him anymore. He often said, "I am master of my slaves, general of my soldiers, and *princeps* of all the rest" (Dio LVII.8). Another time Tiberius rebuked the Senate for giving him too much work and for not taking enough responsibility.

Other of his actions show his desire to stay out of the limelight and to diminish his stature. Tiberius finished the buildings begun by Augustus, but inscribed only Augustus' name on them. When Pompey's theater was destroyed by fire, and none of Pompey's descendants could restore it, Tiberius restored it, but inscribed only Pompey's name on it. Some cities in Asia Minor asked him for permission to build a temple in his honor and to worship him as a god; Tiberius refused their request. (Tacitus' bias is evident in relating this story, for he criticizes Tiberius for his modesty.) Another senator was accused of treason for melting down a silver statue of the emperor; Tiberius forbade the prosecution. When the Senate proposed renaming the month of November after him, the emperor responded, "And what will you do, if there should be thirteen Caesars?" (Dio LVII.18.2).

Most of his rule was competent and good. The borders were secure, and peace prevailed. Germanicus diverted his rebellious army's attention with an invasion of Germany; they won back the standards lost by Varus' obliterated army and buried their bones. Otherwise, Tiberius followed Augustus' policy of not expanding the empire. The provinces were well governed, as Tiberius oversaw the prosecution of corrupt governors; to one governor, who had suggested raising taxes in the provinces, Tiberius wrote, "A good shepherd shears his sheep; he does not skin them." When a financial crisis threatened the stability of Rome, Tiberius freed up hundreds of millions of his own money to establish fiscal order. He made the countryside safer. His modest way of life echoed that of Augustus: Among the laws he passed were ones that forbade promiscuous kissing in public and forbade men to wear silk. Tiberius was very unpopular with the urban masses, for although the supply of grain was adequate, the frugal Tiberius refused to pay for games, circuses, and wild beast hunts.

Despite the peace and prosperity of Rome and the empire, Tiberius was hated, mostly because of the growth of prosecutions for *maiestas minuta* (diminished majesty), a type of treason. Under Tiberius, charges of *maiestas* included libel against the emperor. One senator, as we saw, was nearly brought to trial for melting down a silver statue of the emperor. Mere gossip and jokes could bring a man to the special tribunal set up for *maiestas* cases. "Little by little," says Suetonius, "the type of trumped-up charges went so far that the following were capital offenses: beating a slave or changing clothes close to a statue of Augustus, or bringing a coin or ring with Augustus' likeness on it into a bathroom or brothel" (Suetonius, *Tiberius* LVIII). Suetonius, however, does not mention any successful prosecutions for those trivial offenses. Since those who had successfully prosecuted someone for *maiestas* received one-fourth of the condemned man's estate, there was no lack of informers to bring charges of *maiestas* against the wealthy or against their personal enemies. The number of *delatores*—the professional spies and prosecutors of *maiestas*—grew, and they became hated by their fellow Romans. Tiberius did not discourage the delatores from carrying out their detestable work.

The hatred felt for Tiberius arose also because of Sejanus, his commander of the Praetorian Guard. Sejanus wormed himself into Tiberius' confidence, until finally Tiberius elevated him to a high position and trust enjoyed by no other. Sejanus aimed at becoming emperor himself and hoped to secure his position by marrying Tiberius' niece Livilla. When Tiberius, ignorant of Sejanus' plans, politely refused his request for his niece's hand in marriage, Sejanus devised another plan. In A.D. 26 he convinced Tiberius to move away from Rome and stirred up his fear of assassination;

once Tiberius was isolated, Sejanus controlled access to the aged
and weary emperor. He used his power over the Praetorian Guard
to rid himself of political enemies, including Tiberius' son Drusus,
and he sent Augustus's granddaughter Agrippina into exile. He
also caused the death of Julius Nero, the oldest son of Agrippina and
Germanicus. (Germanicus had died under suspicious circumstances
shortly after Tiberius' accession to power.) Sejanus appeared to
many to be more powerful than the absent Tiberius.

Tiberius learned of Sejanus' plans in A.D. 31 and formed a plan
to crush him. Having secured the loyalty of the Praetorian Guard
and the connivance of the consuls, he had the consuls convene the
Senate to hear his written instructions. Sejanus attended that day's
meeting, expecting to receive *tribunicia potestas*, a prelude to
becoming emperor. Meanwhile, Tiberius nervously waited on his
island of Capreae (where he spent the last ten years of his life), a
flotilla of the navy at hand to whisk him to safety if Sejanus
somehow proved more powerful.

One of the consuls started reading Tiberius' long and rambling
letter to the Senate. The letter contained no bitter condemnation of
Sejanus, just mild criticism here and there; the criticism increased
in tone and severity, and at this point in the reading of the letter,
Sejanus' friends, sitting next to him in the Senate, slowly moved
away from him, until he found himself sitting alone. The end of the
letter stated that two senators who were among his closest associates were traitors and must be punished. The two were not identi-
fied, but the praetors and tribunes by now surrounded Sejanus, to
prevent his escape. The consul Regulus called for Sejanus to come
forward to jail. "You're calling me?" asked Sejanus, stunned. He
had entered the Senate a short time before as the second most
powerful man in Rome and had expected to rise even higher. He
was taken and executed, his body thrown down the steps of the
Capitol. His family and many of his friends were killed as well.

Tiberius, although he was still emperor, remained on his island
of Capreae, where he directed the Senate and governed the empire
by letters. In those letters he talked of his misery and pain—aged,
virtually a prisoner, unable to trust anybody, spending his days in
drunken debauchery. He became so notorious for his drinking that
some called him "Biberius Caldius Mero," a play on his name,

Tiberius Claudius Nero: Biberius from *bibo*, "to drink"; Caldius from *callidus*, "warm," since the Romans sometimes drank their wine warm; and Mero from *merus*, "pure," since the ancients added water to their wine. Thus, he was a drinker of strong hot wine. His rule of the Roman empire definitely suffered; among other problems left unsolved, he had not arranged for a successor, and no one was trained in the arts of governing.

He became deathly ill in A.D. 37 and was hastened to his end by Macro, the new commander of the Praetorian Guard, who then declared Gaius (Caligula) Tiberius' successor. The Romans are said to have rejoiced when hearing the news of Tiberius' death, shouting, "Tiberium in Tiberim!" (Into the Tiber with Tiberius!). He was not deified. When cheering the death of Tiberius and the accession of Caligula, the Romans little knew that their troubles were just beginning; Tiberius had seen Gaius' true nature when he declared that Gaius would have all of Sulla's vices, but none of his virtues.

CALIGULA (A.D. 37–41): "ODERINT DUM METUANT"

Gaius, the last surviving son of Germanicus, had received the nickname Caligula (Little Boots) from his father's soldiers for wearing military-style boots while a baby. The people had dearly loved Germanicus, and they enthusiastically greeted Caligula as emperor, since he succeeded the dour and unpopular Tiberius. Nor did Caligula disappoint them, at first. He immediately provided circus shows and wild beast hunts, increased the pay of the Praetorian Guard, and repressed the professional prosecutors of *maiestas*. Before long, however, his generosity forced him to increase taxes. Fearing assassination, he ordered the deaths of his co-heir and cousin Tiberius Gemellus (Tiberius' grandson) and of Macro, his commander of the Praetorian Guard, who had helped secure his position as emperor. Others, in fear for their lives, in turn plotted against him, prompting him to kill still more.

After six months in power, Caligula became seriously ill. That illness may have unhinged his mind, for afterward he was a blood-thirsty and insane megalomaniac. Examples of his insanity abound. While Caligula lay ill, one senator, P. Afranius Potitus, offered his life for Caligula's recovery; Caligula heard his vow and forced him to keep it: Afranius was taken and executed. According to another anecdote, Caligula, while at a banquet, suddenly burst into laughter. The consuls asked what he found so amusing. "Oh, nothing, except that both of your throats can be cut right here and now, with just a nod of my head" (Suetonius, *Gaius* XXXII). Another time he said, "I can do anything I want to anybody" (Suetonius, *Gaius* XXIX). As emperor, remember, he had no laws to obey (see chapter 23).

Caligula quickly emptied the treasury of the money that the frugal Tiberius had saved. "In the cost of his extravagance, he surpassed all spendthrifts in sheer creativity. He invented a new type of bath and exceedingly bizarre types of food and drinks; he would bathe in hot or cold oils, or drink highly valued pearls dissolved in vinegar, or serve his dinner guests golden meats and bread, all the while saying that a man must either be frugal or be a Caesar" (Suetonius, *Gaius* XXXVII).

When his beloved sister Drusilla died, Caligula made it a capital offense to laugh, or to dine with one's parents, wife, or children. He also believed that he had become a god. He had the heads removed from the statues of the gods, and replaced them with copies of his own head. He had a temple built for his own worship, and he was co-priest in his own cult (his colleague was his horse Incitatus, which he promised to make consul); the richest citizens vied with each other to become priests in Caligula's cult. He forbade a descendant of Torquatus to wear the customary necklace, and Cincinnatus' descendant was not allowed his curly hair. He forbade the descendants of Pompey to use the nickname Magnus—only Caligula could be great. When he encountered men with beautiful heads of hair, he would have the back of their heads shaved, because he was sensitive about his own baldness; he even made it a capital offense to look down upon his bald head from above. When the consuls forgot to make proclamations about his birthday, he had them removed from office. When his armies were gathered at the shore ready to attack Germany or Britain, Caligula suddenly gave the order for the soldiers to collect seashells, which he called "loot of the sea," and he proudly exhibited this booty when he returned to Rome.

Because of his megalomania and bloodthirstiness, Caligula became hated. When hearing that the people hated him, Caligula quoted his favorite line from the tragedian Accius, "Oderint dum metuant!" (Let them hate, so long as they fear!). He is said to have exclaimed, "If only you Romans had just one neck!" (Suetonius, *Gaius* XXX). The reason for this last outburst was that the crowd at one of the chariot races backed the team that was competing against Caligula's favorite team.

After four long years of rule, Caligula was assassinated and was not deified.

CLAUDIUS (A.D. 41–54): "FUNGUS, DEORUM CIBUS"

Moments after the assassination of Caligula, guards found his uncle, Claudius, hiding behind a curtain in the palace. Recognizing him as the brother of Germanicus, whom they had dearly loved, they proclaimed him emperor and forced the Senate to declare him so, although the senators had briefly discussed restoring the republic. A bonus payment of fifteen thousand sesterces to the members of the Praetorian Guard secured their loyalty, and Claudius became emperor. He was thus the first emperor, though not the last, to buy his position.

Claudius had been an unlikely candidate for emperor. He had been refused the various honors and offices that a young man of the Julio-Claudian family would have expected, as he suffered from an illness that made him perpetually weak and unhealthy. He walked very clumsily because of some paralysis. He had an uncontrollable laugh, a very short attention span, and a runny nose and slobbery mouth. Caligula had not killed him, preferring to make game of him instead. Out of shame, his family had mostly kept him out of the public view; Claudius had spent most of his life in literary pursuits, writing histories of Rome, Carthage, Etruria, and others, under the guidance of his good friend Livy, the great Roman historian. None of Claudius' literary works survives, but copies of his imperial edicts, engraved in bronze, have been found in the provinces.

As emperor, Claudius showed a common sense and devotion that had not been seen in an emperor since Augustus. Among his many accomplishments were the construction of the port at Ostia, which facilitated the transport of grain to Rome; the use of incentives for merchants to increase the amount of grain imported into Rome; completion of the aqueduct begun by Caligula; draining of the Fucine Lake, which frequently flooded nearby farms (before the lake was drained, he staged a mock naval battle on it, to the delight of the Romans); the rebuilding of Pompey's theater, which had been destroyed by fire; and the extension of Roman citizenship to leading men of Gallia Comata, the less Romanized part of Gaul. He took an intense interest in the law courts, presiding over them himself and passing judgment, even though he occasionally fell asleep during the proceedings. When he learned that many slave-owners were abandoning their sick and decrepit slaves at the Temple of Aesculapius, a god of healing and medicine, because it was cheaper than finding doctors for them, he passed edicts freeing those slaves and charging with murder those slaveowners who killed their sick or old slaves instead of abandoning them.

Claudius' best-known achievement was a military one. Whether he was aiming to restore the prestige of Roman arms after Caligula's debacle, to strengthen his own position, or to boost the morale of the army, which had not added territory to the empire since the disaster of Varus, Claudius decided to conquer Britain. In A.D. 43 his general Plautius and four legions plus numerous auxiliary troops landed in Britain. They defeated Caractacus and Togo-dumnus, the sons of Cunobelinus (Shakespeare's Cymbeline), the king of the powerful tribe called the Catuvellauni, who had died in 40. Claudius then sailed to Britain and commanded the armies in a battle at Camulodunum (modern Colchester), the capital of the Catuvellauni. After winning the battle, Claudius returned to Rome to celebrate a triumph; he was awarded the title Britannicus, which he also gave to his son. Plautius—helped by his lieutenant, the future Emperor Vespasian—remained in Britain and carried on hostilities, eventually conquering much of the island.

Britain thus became a Roman province. Owing to the Roman government there, Latin words began seeping into the Celtic language then spoken in Britain. The Latinate and Celtic elements later blended with Germanic elements, upon the Anglo-Saxon invasions of Britain in the fifth century, and later still with Latinate elements from the spread of Christianity and the Norman conquest, eventually evolving into modern English (see chapter 1).

However beneficent Claudius' reign was, it was marred by his falling under the control of his wives and his ex-slaves. His second wife, Messalina, used her position to kill or exile her personal and political enemies; later, while still married to Claudius, she married another man, apparently intending to supplant the emperor with her new husband. She was caught and executed. Claudius then married Agrippina, his niece (she was the daughter of his brother Germanicus); she then forced him to adopt her son Lucius Domitius Ahenobarbus (Nero, after the adoption) who, being three years older than Claudius' own son Britannicus, became the heir to the throne. To satisfy her own personal grudges and to increase her power, she heightened Claudius' fears of conspiracies and implicated her personal enemies in plots, whether real or imagined, for which they were executed or exiled. Claudius' freedmen Callistus, Pallas, and Narcissus became part of the imperial staff and controlled access to the emperor. They exerted a power over the empire that the members of the Senate did not enjoy, and they profited from their power, dying wealthier than Crassus, although they had been born penniless. The last years of his reign saw Claudius slipping in his mental abilities, while his wife and his freedmen ruled the empire. Rome then saw a reign of terror worse than that under Tiberius.

Claudius finally began to reassert himself and to favor his own son Britannicus as his successor, instead of Nero. Agrippina sprang into action. A famous poisoner named Locusta cooked up a strong poison for Agrippina, who then spread it onto mushrooms, Claudius' favorite food. At the banquet Claudius took and ate the choicest, juiciest mushroom, which his loving wife had reserved for him. He died soon after, and Nero, at the age of seventeen, became emperor. After Claudius was deified by the Senate, Nero joked that the food of the gods was mushrooms (fungus, deorum cibus), for by them Claudius became a god.

NERO (54–68 A.D.): "QUALIS ARTIFEX PEREO"

Imagine that before you are old enough to vote you find yourself the master of an empire that encompasses Italy, France, parts of Germany, Spain, northern Africa, Syria, Palestine, Greece, Egypt,

Turkey, Albania, Yugoslavia, Austria, and Hungary. At age seventeen when he became emperor (or, more accurately, when his mother Agrippina took the throne from Claudius for him), Nero found himself possessing the power of life and death over millions of subjects and having the wealth of the empire at his disposal.

Nero was already married to Octavia, Claudius' daughter, but he was a young man and still needed guidance. He had as tutors Burrus, the commander of the Praetorian Guard, and Seneca, the foremost orator and intellectual of the day, known as a philosopher of Stoicism. The person who had the most influence on Nero, however, was his mother Agrippina, who attended meetings of the Senate and conducted the business of the empire, even receiving embassies from foreign countries and kings. Agrippina had long been determined to make Nero emperor. Once, when Nero was quite young, she heard someone predict that one day he would be emperor and kill his mother. She responded, "Let him kill me, so long as he becomes emperor!" Apparently she had known that her control over her son would make her, in effect, empress.

Burrus and Seneca feared Agrippina's power over her son, and both of them tried to make Nero assert himself and show more independence. As part of this policy to diminish Agrippina's influence over him, they allowed Nero to indulge in even more vices than he was already engaged in (which included adulterous affairs with slave girls) and also in socially unacceptable hobbies, such as singing, lyre playing, and chariot racing. Nero did show more independence from his mother; now he allowed Burrus and Seneca to run the empire, while he blithely engaged in his various hobbies, which soon came to include sculpting and painting. Burrus and Seneca governed the empire fairly and justly.

Agrippina sensed that she was losing her power over Nero. She then threatened to supplant him with his younger stepbrother, Britannicus. "I made you emperor!" she said to him, and Nero understood that the woman who had placed him on the throne had the power and influence to replace him. Nero had to do something about Britannicus. He could not think of a good charge to level against him, nor could he simply order his death; perhaps at this point Nero still cared about popular opinion.

Nero therefore sought assistance from the tried and proven Locusta. So powerful was the poison that she concocted on this occasion, however, that Britannicus immediately evacuated it and survived, thinking he had only had a short illness. Nero, desperate, got Locusta to cook up another poison. Tacitus gives a vivid description of Britannicus' death:

They had the custom that the children of the princes would sit with other noble children of the same age while eating their dinner, in the sight of their relatives, but with their own, less lavish table. Britannicus ate his dinners there. Since one of the servants had been chosen to give his foods and drinks the taste test, the following stratagem was invented, so the customary taste test would not be omitted, and so the plot would not be betrayed by the deaths of both.

An exceedingly hot and (so far) harmless drink, which had already been tasted, was given to Britannicus. After he rejected it because it was too hot, cold water containing the poison was poured in, which immediately spread through his body so violently that his breath and voice were immediately and abruptly snatched away.

Among those sitting at the banquet there was agitation and confusion. The foolish ones ran away, while those with a clearer understanding of the situation sat there unmoving, watching Nero. He, lying on his back, nonchalantly said that it was nothing unusual, just epilepsy, which Britannicus had been afflicted with since infancy, and soon his sight and consciousness would return.

But Agrippina's fear and panic, as if pressed onto her face, shone out—it was clear that she and Britannicus' sister [Octavia] had not known. She certainly knew that her last help had been taken away, and that the example of murdering a relation had been set. Octavia too, despite her youthful inexperience, had learned to hide all feelings, like grief or affection. Consequently, after a short silence, the gaiety of the banquet was resumed. (Tacitus, *Annales* XIII.16)

Britannicus was cremated the same night. His funeral had been arranged before his death.

Nero's violence did not end with his family. Disguised as a slave, he would wander the streets of Rome with his friends, stealing from shops and assaulting passers-by. Soon people learned that the emperor was the gang leader, and gangs of pseudo-Neros formed, for only a fool would fight the emperor. Yet one senator, upon being attacked, fought until he recognized his attacker, and then he apologized. He was later forced to commit suicide.

Nero soon turned his violence against his mother. His most recent lover, Poppaea Sabina, whom he had stolen from her husband Otho (he was conveniently made governor of Lusitania, in Spain), also feared Agrippina's power over him. She therefore stirred up his fear of Agrippina and convinced him to kill his mother. Nero could find no acceptable way of murdering his mother until an old friend came forward with a plan. The plan was to build a boat that would collapse and drown its passengers; thus her death would appear an accident, and Nero could appear the dutiful son, by bestowing various honors upon her after her unfortunate death. Nero approved of the plan, and the ship was built. He appeared to be having a reconciliation with his mother and even had dinner with her before she embarked on the ship from Baiae, a fashionable Italian resort on the Bay of Naples.

When the ship had proceeded some distance from shore, the roof fell in, crushing Agrippina's attendant, but only wounding the intended target. Agrippina swam to shore. There she reflected upon the fact that the ship had fallen apart without provocation from wind or waves, and she concluded that her son had tried to murder her. She pretended ignorance; she wrote a letter to Nero, informing him that by divine mercy she had been saved, that she was only slightly wounded, and that he should not trouble himself by visiting her.

Nero, crazed with fear that she might incite the army to revolt against him, sent men to her with orders to kill. When she saw the armed men and understood the purpose of their mission, she ordered them to stab her in the womb. Thus Agrippina died. Nero wrote the Senate a letter, informing its members that a slave of Agrippina had been caught with a sword, about to murder him, and that she had intended to become empress with the slave. Some senators voted to hold thanksgivings in every shrine and to include Agrippina's birthday among the days of ill omen (*dies ater*, like the day of the Allia). Because of the Senate's sycophancy, Nero started thinking that he could do no wrong, even though some Romans secretly draped leather bags around his statues, to remind him of the old punishment for parricides: to be tied in a leather bag with a dog, a monkey, a snake, a scorpion, and a rooster, with the leather bag and its contents then being thrown into the Tiber.

Depressed by the murder of his mother, Nero found ways to lighten his spirits. He started the "Iuvenalia," games to celebrate the first shaving of his beard. In those games he made his musical debut, playing the lyre and singing a song. In the crowd were Nero's five thousand professional clappers, who had been assigned ways of expressing their approval of his genius: the Bees made a loud buzzing noise; the Roof-tiles clapped with hollowed hands; and the Bricks clapped with flat hands. Later, confident after his successful debut, Nero made a tour of Greece, the home of the Muses, where, of course, he always won first place with his poetry and songs. During his performances, however, no spectators were allowed to leave the theater; it is recorded that women gave birth during performances and that some people pretended to be dead so they could be carried out of the theater. After his successful tour of Greece, Nero returned to Rome and enjoyed a triumph, in which he proudly showed off all the trophies and prizes he had won.

Meanwhile, death claimed one of Nero's stabilizing influences, Burrus; Seneca then retired, since his partner's death caused him to have less and less control over Nero, whose new commander of the Praetorian Guard, the evil Tigellinus, was of the same stamp as Nero. Nothing now could restrain Nero: He divorced Octavia, his innocent wife, and when her slaves, despite being interrogated under torture, would not lie and accuse their mistress of infidelity with a slave (one of her slaves, in fact, told Tigellinus that Octavia's private parts were purer than his mouth), he had her banished. Later she too was killed. (A tragedy titled *Octavia* was written after her death; its authorship is attributed by some to Seneca.) Nero then married Poppaea. She gave birth to a baby girl, whom he named Augusta, and in gratitude he dedicated temples to Fertility. The baby died four months later; Nero then declared the dead baby a goddess and dedicated a shrine to it, with a priest.

Perhaps the most famous event of Nero's reign was the great fire of 64 that destroyed half of Rome. It occurred on July 18, the same date the Gauls had sacked Rome. Despite popular myth, Nero probably did not start the fire. Given the people's hatred of him, the story soon spread that while watching the fire he sang a song about the burning of Troy—that is, "Nero fiddled while Rome burned." One source says that goons prevented people from putting out the fires and actually threw torches onto buildings. What increased people's suspicion of Nero was that soon after the fire, Nero started construction of a new palace (the Domus Aurea, or Golden House) in the area cleared by the fire; the complex included huge parks and fields, and was graced by an enormous statue of Nero himself, who may have intended to rename Rome Neropolis. After seeing the palace, Nero said that he could finally start living like a human being. Wanting to avert suspicion of guilt for the fire, Nero found a scapegoat in a recently founded sect called Christians; he had them arrested and killed by being torn apart by dogs, being crucified, or being set afire as human torches. Nero's ruthlessness—which marks the first official persecution of the Christians—further angered the Roman people, who quickly came to pity the Christians, after originally despising them for belonging to what was then seen as a depraved cult (in the words of Tacitus, it was *exitiabilis superstitio*, "a destructive cult"). The apostle Paul, and perhaps Peter as well, was killed during this persecution.

Besides the Christians, Nero had been killing nobles and knights accused of *maiestas*; consequently, he was hated by both groups. In 65 some conspired to assassinate him; one conspiracy, called the Pisonian conspiracy after G. Calpurnius Piso, its instigator, involved senators, knights, officers, women, and poets. The plan was kept a secret until one of the conspirators, at home, complained that his dagger was dull and ordered a slave to sharpen it. Then the senator signed his will, gave a banquet more sumptuous than usual, rewarded his slaves with freedom and presents of money, and ordered bandages to be prepared for wounds. One slave took the dagger and this information to Nero. Nero's action was quick and brutal: Hundreds of nobles were killed, whether innocent or guilty of conspiring against the emperor's life. Among those ordered to commit suicide were the poet Lucan, author of the epic poem *Pharsalia* (much to his discredit, Lucan implicated his own mother in the conspiracy);

Seneca, Nero's former tutor, and author of letters and treatises on the philosophy Stoicism; and later, Petronius, author of the *Satyricon*, the first surviving novel in Latin. Petronius was called *arbiter elegantiae* and apparently served in Nero's court to lend some class and style to Nero's vulgar extravagances. Petronius even died in style: While most of those committing suicide sang abject praise of Nero, Petronius composed erotic poetry while he died, and also recorded and divulged the sordid details of Nero's sexual escapades. Henceforth many Romans knew what type of creature Nero was, and Nero was mystified over how they had learned.

Nero's madness affected only the nobility of Rome. The city and the empire actually prospered during this time. Hostilities in the provinces were infrequent. One rebellion in Britain should be mentioned: Boudicca, wife of the king of the Iceni, a tribe in Britain, was flogged and her daughters raped by Romans and Roman slaves. She then led the Iceni in a revolt, and other British tribes joined them; together they destroyed a small Roman army and are said to have killed seventy thousand Romans and provincials allied to them. The general G. Suetonius Paulinus (no relation to the biographer) then conquered Boudicca. A far more serious matter was a war in Armenia, which actually started at the end of Claudius' reign. When the Roman puppet king of Armenia was deposed, the Parthians took advantage of the turmoil there and invaded. The Romans sent Cn. Domitius Corbulo to drive the Parthians out of Armenia, and he succeeded in doing so. He then concluded a peace with the Parthians that lasted for decades. The Jews in Palestine had also revolted during the reign of Claudius, and General Vespasian was besieging Jerusalem. Otherwise, the empire was at peace.

Nero's lifestyle had caused financial problems and had long before drained the treasury. He never wore the same clothes twice, and he fished with a golden net, strung with purple and scarlet thread. His wife Poppaea had gilded horseshoes put on the mules that drew her carriage and had five hundred asses milked daily so she could bathe in the milk. To earn more money, Nero encouraged convictions of innocent people for *maiestas*, which was very profitable to the emperor.

Running out of money, Nero fell victim to a delusion so absurd it cannot be believed. A Carthaginian man had a dream that on his land were buried the riches of Queen Dido, who had hidden her wealth from her envious neighbors. The man told Nero that these riches were just waiting to be dug up. Nero found warships and manned them with rowers especially selected to convey the gold to Rome quickly. He even started spending his newfound wealth. Not surprisingly, the soldiers hired to dig up the riches found nothing. Nero found consolation in his musical performances and even insisted that he be judged on equal terms with the other musicians; he had a voice coach present at all times, to warn him to refrain from shouting (and hurting his voice) during fits of anger.

Nero's party could not last forever. A bad omen for him occurred when the *ficus Ruminalis*, the fig tree that had sheltered Romulus and Remus, almost died. In addition to his other crimes, Nero had angered the gods by bathing in the source of the Marcian Aqueduct; the gods got their revenge by making him seriously ill. A comet was seen, which seemed to predict a new emperor. After Nero ordered the murder of the excellent general Corbulo, who had regained Armenia for Rome, the governor of Gaul, C. Iulius Vindex, revolted and urged the governor of Spain, Servius Sulpicius Galba, to do the same. The Senate, hearing the news of the revolt, withdrew Nero's bodyguard, prompting Nero to think that if deposed, he could always make a living by singing and playing the lyre. He later committed suicide; among his last words were, "Qualis artifex pereo!" ("What an artist dies in me!"; Suetonius, *Nero* XLIX). He was not deified.

THE YEAR OF THE FOUR EMPERORS

In the year following Nero's suicide, Rome saw as many emperors as it had seen in the preceding eighty-five years. Galba marched to Rome and became emperor. Otho, whom Nero had appointed governor of Lusitania (modern Portugal) so he could take Poppaea Sabina, succeeded in bribing the Praetorian Guard to murder Galba, and Otho became emperor. The armies along the Rhine, however, did not like Otho, and they proclaimed their commander, Vitellius, emperor; the Rhine armies marched on Italy and put Vitellius in the place of Otho, who committed suicide. The armies in the East and along the Danube did not like Vitellius and urged their commander, Vespasian, who was besieging Jerusalem in the Jewish War, to march on Rome. Vespasian's armies marched west and, after a battle near the town of Cremona, conquered the forces of Vitellius, who was quickly murdered. On December 21, A.D. 69, Vespasian entered Rome as emperor.

LATIN LITERATURE OF THE JULIO-CLAUDIAN ERA

Latin writers during and after the reign of Tiberius produced what many scholars call the Silver Age of Latin literature. Since the previous age is called the Golden Age, one can infer that scholars traditionally have thought less of Silver Latin. There are two reasons for this. One is that the Italians and Romans were naturally conservative, preferring to use the tried and proven instead of experimenting with the new and uncertain. What the writers produced seems stale when compared with what their predecessors had created. Another reason is the influence of *rhetoric*: the writers of this period seem to have striven to make every sentence quotable.

The foremost intellectual of the age was Seneca, the Stoic philosopher. He is most famous for his *Epistulae morales*, letters that are really little philosophical essays. He wrote various other essays, such as *De ira*, *De brevitate vitae*, and *De clementia*. The last of these, addressed to Nero, urged him to be merciful in his dealings with his subjects, which incidentally shows how powerless the individual Roman was against the legal authority of the emperor. He also wrote a satire of sorts, *Apocolocyntosis*, generally translated as "The Pumpkinification of Claudius," about the bumbling, drooling emperor's deification. Seneca also wrote tragedies, which were probably never intended to be produced—just read. Seneca the philosopher is not to be confused with his father, called the Elder Seneca, who wrote a history of his times, which has not survived, and some books on rhetoric, parts of which have survived.

The sole surviving work of Pliny the Elder is his enormous *Natural History*, considered a major work in the history of Western science. It contains a wealth of information concerning geography, biology, botany, and zoology.

Lucan's chief work is generally called *Pharsalia*, an epic poem dealing with the civil wars of 49–45 B.C. Lucan, who was the nephew of the philosopher Seneca, is said to have incurred Nero's wrath and jealousy for being a more talented poet than the emperor and for praising Cato, the staunch defender of the republic.

Petronius wrote what is surely the most original piece of literature of the age, a novel of sorts called the *Satyricon*. Only large fragments survive. Written in a literary genre called Menippean satire, which mixes poetry and prose, the *Satyricon* tells the various adventures of two trashy characters in southern Italy. One part of the work has even become common reading for Latin students—the hilarious *Cena Trimalchionis*. Trimalchio is a former slave turned millionaire, and his dinner party gives a portrait of ancient Italy's vulgar nouveaux riches. Since Petronius was describing base characters, he used the common vocabulary and syntax characteristic of everyday Latin, thus leaving for us examples of how common people talked in Latin. Most Latin literature was written by the upper classes, who spoke more educated Latin. Federico Fellini, the great Italian movie director, adapted the fragments of the *Satyricon* to create his movie *Fellini's Satyricon*.

CHAPTER 25

The Flavian Emperors

VESPASIAN (A.D. 69–79): "VAE, PUTO DEUS FIO"

Upon becoming emperor, Vespasian (his full name was Titus Flavius Vespasianus) faced many problems. Various provinces revolted when they heard about Rome's difficulties in keeping an emperor. The Jews in Palestine, who had revolted during Nero's reign, were not yet subdued; Vespasian, who had been sent there by Nero to put down the revolt, left his son Titus to finish the siege of Jerusalem while he went to Rome to become emperor. A Gaul named Civilis incited his countrymen to rise up against Rome; gaining the assistance of the Germans, they quickly overran much of Gaul. The armies in Britain were restless—they had been left out of the emperor-making game. Dacians (in modern Romania) were invading Roman territory, and Oea (site of modern Tripoli) and Lepcis, two cities in the province of Africa, were at war with each other. The treasury at Rome was empty: Whatever had survived Nero's extended party had been distributed to the Praetorian Guard by the emperors Galba, Otho, and Vitellius, to buy their support.

Yet if any person could restore order to the empire, Vespasian was the one. From a peasant background, he had none of the pretensions of the noble Julio-Claudian emperors. For example, while other nobles at Nero's court had applauded his singing, Vespasian had fallen into disfavor with Nero for falling asleep during one of his performances. Vespasian ruled with common sense, and he soon restored order and stability in the provinces, in Rome, and in the treasury.

To put the treasury in the black, he raised taxes, while at the same time showing sympathy for cities and provinces that were already hard pressed. For example, when some cities in Asia Minor suffered an earthquake, Vespasian remitted their taxes for five years. His frugality made him unpopular with some, for he did not spend money on games, as Nero had done. One story of his frugality concerns his tax on the contents of the public bathrooms. Tanners in ancient Rome collected urine from the public bathrooms to cure leather; Vespasian taxed their collection of the urine. When his son Titus complained to him about taxing the urine, Vespasian waved a gold coin under his nose and asked him how it smelled. (*Vespasiano* in modern Italian means "public urinal.") Vespasian established so solid a basis for the treasury that he was able to embark on a building program (see below).

Gone were the days of fear of informers. Immediately after becoming emperor, Vespasian restored citizenship to those who had been convicted of *maiestas*. One source says that the doors of Vespasian's palace stood open all day and that no guard was stationed at them. Vespasian did not subject his visitors to searches, as previous emperors had done, out of fear of assassination. The few people who plotted against Vespasian were forgiven. He committed one political murder, and that was of a diehard republican senator, Helvidius Priscus, who would not stop promoting a revolution. Vespasian regretted the murder. To a Cynic philosopher, who was yelling rude remarks to him, the emperor simply yelled back, "Good dog!" (The word *cynic* comes from a Greek word meaning "dog.") Another source says that Vespasian simply replied, "I do not kill a barking dog."

Vespasian had simple tastes. When one foppish young Roman noble, smelling of perfume, came to thank him for awarding him a prefecture, Vespasian shook his head and in a stern voice said, "I would have preferred that you reek of garlic" (Suetonius, *Vespasian* VIII.3) and canceled the appointment. When some astrologers told Vespasian that he was descended from a friend of Hercules, Vespasian burst out laughing; this is quite a contrast to the pretensions of the Julio-Claudians, who believed that they were descended from Venus and that they became gods themselves after their death. During the restoration of the Capitol, which had burned down

The colosseum, known to the Romans as the Flavian Amphitheater.
(Author photograph)

during the recent civil wars, Vespasian filled up the first basket of
trash and carried it off himself.

After solving the financial crisis, Vespasian embarked on a program to improve Rome, Italy, and the empire. In Rome, he restored
the Capitol and started construction of the Colosseum (which the
ancients called the Amphitheatrum Flavianum) and a new Ara
Pacis; in the provinces he built more roads and bridges. He started
something like public education in Italy by paying for professional
teachers and granting them immunity from taxes. Vespasian
granted Latin rights to all Spain and drafted provincials into the
Senate; because of this, an African became consul in A.D. 80.

The succession was settled; Vespasian's elder son Titus would
become emperor with Domitian, the younger son, as his partner.
Both had been trained in the administration of the empire by
receiving repeated consulships and even censorships. The last

thing Vespasian said before his death in A.D. 79 reveals his common sense and sense of humor; knowing he was about to die, he said, "Vae, puto deus fio" ("Alas, I think I'm becoming a god"; Suetonius, *Vespasian* XXIII). The Senate did, in fact, consider that he had become a god.

TITUS (79–81 A.D.): "AMICI, DIEM PERDIDI"

When Titus first became emperor, people thought he would become another Nero or Caligula, for Titus' youth too had been one of dissipation and decadence. Yet he became immensely popular during his brief reign. He respected private property and provided public entertainment in the form of wild beast hunts and a naval battle on an artificial lake. He seems to have wanted to use his position to make people happy; according to one story, when Titus one day realized that he had done nobody a favor that day, he exclaimed, "Amici, diem perdidi" ("My friends, I have wasted a day"; Suetonius, *Titus* VIII). He repressed the reformers and had some of them either sold into slavery or banished. When two patricians were found to be aiming at the throne, Titus only warned them to stop. Supposedly Domitian too was plotting against him; Titus continued swearing to his brother that he was the successor and begged him to return the affection he felt for him. During the various disasters that afflicted Italy during his reign, one of which was a great fire in Rome in 80, Titus is said to have shown "not just an emperor's concern, but even the love that a parent has for his children" (Suetonius, *Titus* VIII.3).

Another of the disasters was the eruption of Mount Vesuvius in Campania, which buried the cities of Herculaneum and Pompeii. Thousands died, including the writer Pliny the Elder, who was studying the eruption; his nephew, Pliny the Younger, describes the eruption in a few letters to his friend Tacitus, a historian who is one of our main sources for the history of the Julian-Claudian emperors. Archaeologists have excavated the sites of the cities and have unearthed almost a complete ancient Italian town, undisturbed after two thousand years of being buried beneath volcanic lava.

During Titus' reign the British revolted. The rebellion was put down by Gn. Julius Agricola, whom the historian Tacitus memorialized in one of his early works. While stifling the revolt, Agricola's men sailed around Britain, and for the first time Europeans learned that Britain is an island.

Titus died two years into his reign. His last words, "I made one mistake," prompted many people to believe that the one mistake was to trust Domitian and to allow him to live. Titus was deified, and Domitian became emperor.

DOMITIAN (A.D. 81–96): "DOMINUS ET DEUS"

Domitian was very different from his gentle, good-natured, affable father and brother. Shortly after his father became emperor, Domitian used his position as praetor and his authority as the emperor's son for all they were worth and filled many vacancies and positions with people of his choosing. That prompted Vespasian to exclaim that he was suprised that Domitian had not appointed the next emperor, too. He was already known to spend part of his leisure time in his room, stabbing flies with a stylus.

Although an efficient administrator, Domitian knew he was boss and let everybody else know it too. Not content with the personal bodyguard that the emperor had, he had twenty-four lictors precede him, the number that had honored a dictator during the republic. He always dressed in purple, the color of royalty. He assumed the power of *censor perpetuus*, so he could always eject from the Senate any member he did not like, and he used this power so frequently that the senators hated him bitterly. He insisted upon being addressed as "dominus et deus" (lord and god) and required that sacrifices be offered to him, which necessarily brought him into conflict with Jews and Christians. He changed the name of the month October to Domitianus.

Nonetheless, Domitian was an efficient emperor. He strengthened the borders of the empire and raised the soldiers' pay. He had a building program, the most important part of which is the Pantheon. In addition, he rebuilt the Baths of Agrippa and restored the Porticus Octaviae with two libraries, one for Latin works, the other for Greek (he even sent scribes to the library at Alexandria to copy rare manuscripts). He restored the Temple of Vespasian on the Capitoline Hill. He fought some wars with the Germans and Dacians; it appears that his wars were not successful, for a later emperor, Trajan, waged wars with the Dacians to rescue the standards that Domitian had lost. He always gave great and expensive shows, and even a naval combat, in the Colosseum. He gave wild beast hunts and gladiatorial combats fought by women, too. He started a contest every five years in horsemanship, gymnastics, music, poetry, oratory, and lyre playing.

In 88 the governor of Upper Germany, L. Antonius Saturninus, revolted; he was quickly defeated by the governor of Lower Germany, but the revolt had its effect on Domitian and rendered him paranoid and ruthless in hunting out conspiracies. He revived the laws of *maiestas*, and informers were not lacking to accuse someone with loose lips or faulty discretion: "He killed Salvius Cocceianus because he had celebrated the birthday of his uncle, Emperor Otho . . . and his own cousin, Flavius Sabinus, because on the day of the consular elections the herald had mistakenly announced that he was *imperator*, instead of *consul*" (Suetonius, *Domitian* X). Another anecdote says that a woman was executed for undressing in front of a statue of Domitian. He killed another because he had written praises of Helvidius Priscus (executed during Vespasian's reign) and Thrasea Paetus (executed under Nero), both Stoics who longed for a return to the republic.

His popularity with the soldiers could not prevent plots against him. So paranoid was he that he lined the columns where he took his walks with a reflective mineral so he could see every person's every move. In spite of his precautions, he was assassinated in 96; his wife was one of the conspirators. Domitian had kept a sword under his pillow; one conspirator secretly removed its blade, and another stabbed him in the groin. He was killed after putting up a fierce struggle. The Senate, now allowed to choose the next emperor, chose Nerva, a senator respected for his eloquence, sense of justice, and amiable nature. So great was the senators' hatred of Domitian that they voted for *damnatio memoriae* (condemnation of memory) of Domitian: Images of him were destroyed, his name was erased from inscriptions, the many arches erected in his honor were torn down, and his acts were rescinded.

CHAPTER 26

The Culmination of the
Pax Romana

NERVA (A.D. 96–98)

Nerva was chosen emperor by the Senate after the assassination of Domitian. The armies, especially those along the Rhine, had not shared the senators' hatred of Domitian and felt insulted by being excluded from the decision of who would be the next emperor. Clearly, the new emperor could not count on their support. Nor could he count on the Praetorian Guard, for its soldiers demanded the execution of Domitian's assassins. Nerva's power was eroding rapidly; at one point he was even besieged in the palace until the Praetorian Guard killed Domitian's assassins, even though he probably had not taken part in the plot.

Sixty years old and in poor health, Nerva took an unusual step in order to survive as emperor. He named his successor and chose one whom the armies would like: Trajan, the general of the armies on the Rhine (who, people said, was going to be the next emperor anyway, whether named or not). With Trajan adopted as Nerva's son and appointed as his successor, the unrest settled down, and Nerva reigned in peace until his natural death.

Unwittingly, Nerva had started a precedent that would prove beneficial for the empire; his decision to name as his successor a tried and proven man of excellent character inaugurated a century of good rule by four Spanish emperors. In fact, the eighteenth-century historian Edward Gibbon, looking back over the history of the world, described the period from Nerva to Marcus Aurelius as one in which "the condition of the human race was most happy and prosperous" owing to the firmness, wisdom, and virtue of the emperors.

TRAJAN (A.D. 98–117), "OPTIMUS PRINCEPS"

When Trajan became emperor, he is said to have handed the ceremonial sword to his commander of the Praetorian Guard, saying, "Take this sword to use for me, if I rule well, or against me, if I rule badly" (Dio, *Epitome* LXVIII.2). Trajan then swore an oath that he would not shed any citizen's blood, and during Trajan's rule the commander found no reason to turn the sword against the emperor. Once, when many who were jealous of Trajan's wealthy and proud friend Licinius Sura told the emperor that Sura was plotting against him, Trajan, after dismissing his personal bodyguard, went to Sura's house for dinner, called Sura's doctor and had him anoint his eyes, called Sura's barber to shave him, took a bath there, and then had dinner with his friend. The next day he told those who always spoke badly of Sura that if Sura had been plotting to kill him, he would surely have done so the day before.

Trajan's public works enlarged upon those begun by his predecessors. He instituted a building program for Rome, Italy, and the provinces. The projects included baths; the Forum Traiani, which included two libraries (one for Latin books, the other for Greek); and a monument called the Column of Trajan. He repaired the harbor at Ostia, and also the ports of Centumcellae and Ancona, on the Adriatic shore. Trajan built roads extensively throughout the empire, mostly to improve communication of the military.

Trajan, although a native of Spain, believed in the primacy of Italy and Rome, and sought to restore prosperity there. He or Nerva—we do not know for sure which one—started the alimenta system, by which poor children were given an allowance for food and sustenance, paid for by the *fiscus*, the empire's treasury. The purpose of the *alimenta* was more than just philanthropy, for Trajan also wanted to increase the populations of Romans and Italians. To improve agriculture in Italy, he gave cheap loans to farmers and required that senators invest at least one-third of their capital in Italian land.

Trajan is most famous for his military exploits. The first of his two wars resulted in another Roman province and eventually in another Romance language, Romanian. Called Dacia by the Romans, the country had been united by its king, Decebalus, who then attacked his neighbors to the south, the Roman province of Moesia. He also incited Parthia to break its uneasy peace with Rome. Since Decebalus had previously defeated the Romans under Domitian, Trajan wanted to avenge that loss (and to recover the standards that had been lost) as well as to curb the growing strength of Decebalus. Trajan set out in A.D. 101 to invade Dacia.

In the first year of the war, Trajan fought an indecisive battle against the Dacians. When there were not enough bandages for the many wounded, he ripped up his own clothes to make more. The next year the Romans and allies captured the Dacian fortresses and ultimately their king. The Romans reached a treaty with Decebalus that left him his kingdom, but with Roman garrisons, and they recovered the standards that Domitian had lost. Trajan—having now earned the honorary nickname Dacicus—returned to Rome. But Decebalus was not so easily daunted.

Not long afterward Decebalus resumed hostilities. His troops overran the Roman garrisons and attacked Rome's allies. Trajan built a bridge across the Danube in 105 and crossed with a hundred thousand soldiers. The next year, the Romans won a decisive victory over the Dacians. Decebalus committed suicide. Trajan made Dacia a Roman province, settled it with peoples from all over the empire, and took to Rome a large amount of loot, enough for 123 days of games in Rome, with a gladiatorial combat fought by ten thousand Dacian gladiators.

To commemorate the victory over Dacia, there was built in the Forum of Trajan a large column with sculptures in relief that recount the wars with Dacia. The images illustrate the war and its progress, from beginning to end, with scenes of battles, the suicide of Decebalus, and the exile of many Dacians. The reliefs run from the bottom of the column in a spiral up to the top, which shows the end of the war. The Column of Trajan is not reliable for historical accuracy, but its illustrations do give some information about the war, and it is a marvel of ancient art.

Trajan's Column. (Author photograph)

Trajan's other military exploit was not so successful. Parthia had long been a thorn in Rome's side, and when the Parthians deposed Rome's puppet king in Armenia without seeking Rome's approval, Trajan decided to end the problems with Parthia once and for all.

In 113 Trajan left Rome for Parthia. He immediately deposed Parthia's king of Armenia and annexed Armenia. In honor of his victory, the Younger Pliny delivered to the Senate a panegyric in honor of the emperor, declaring him *optimus princeps* (the best emperor). In 115 Trajan crossed the Tigris and captured Ctesiphon, the capital of Parthia, but Osroes, the king, eluded capture. Trajan then became the first Roman emperor ever to see the Persian Gulf, and he commented that if he were still young, he would have crossed over to India, too. He then retired to Babylon. At this point the Roman Empire covered its largest extent, including Armenia and the newly gained provinces of Mesopotamia and Assyria (modern Syria, Iraq, northern Iran, Azerbaijan, and Armenia).

The Parthians quickly revolted and even invaded Armenia. After the ensuing battles, the Romans kept Mesopotamia and Armenia, but did not try to keep Parthia. Trajan had other troubles on his mind: The Jews had revolted again, and he was ill.

In 117, while returning to Syria, Trajan had a stroke. He set out for Italy, but falling into worse condition along the way, named Hadrian as his successor and then died. He was deified by the Senate.

HADRIAN (A.D. 117–138)

If Trajan can be compared to Romulus for his martial character, Hadrian was like Ancus for his peaceful nature. Hadrian concentrated on securing the territory that Rome already held and on improving conditions in the empire. For example, one time as he was traveling, an old lady ran up to him and demanded that he hear her problem. "I don't have time," Hadrian said to the lady. "Then don't be emperor!" she snapped (Dio, *Epitome* LXIX.6.3). Stung by her words, Hadrian stopped his journey and heard her problem.

Hadrian quickly renounced Trajan's gains in Parthia, let Armenia be ruled by its own king, and stopped the Romans' advances in England, for he did not want to overextend the empire's resources and to risk the empire's present security, prosperity, and stability. To improve the defenses of the frontiers, Hadrian toured the empire ceaselessly, himself inspecting the fortifications and improving them. In 120 or 121 he toured Gaul and Germany, and perhaps Raetia and Noricum; the following year he crossed over to England and later to Spain, all the time conducting inspections, sharing in the soldiers' lives, and trying to improve their lot. He boosted the morale of the soldiers by marching alongside them, wearing ordinary soldier's clothing, and visiting sick soldiers in their quarters. In 123–125 he toured Syria, Bithynia, the Aegean Islands, the Bosporus, Pannonia, Macedonia, and Greece. In 127 he toured Italy. In 128 he toured Africa, and also spent six months in Athens. In 129 he traveled to southern Asia Minor and Syria. In 130 and 131 he toured Egypt.

During his stay in Britain he started construction of a massive wall (now called Hadrian's Wall) to keep marauding Scots out of England. The wall was 128 kilometers long, more than 2 meters thick, and more than 4 meters high as it ran from the mouth of the Solway river on the western side of the island to the mouth of the Tyne on the eastern side. Construction of the wall involved moving enormous amounts of rock and soil; eventually a huge ditch was dug on the northern side of the wall. Remains of the wall can still be seen in Britain today.

Hadrian did not neglect the conditions of life in Italy and Rome. He continued to supply free grain for children. "He prohibited masters from killing their slaves, and ordered that they should be condemned by judges if they were deserving. He forbade the sale of a servant or maid to a pimp or gladiator-trainer without a reason offered. . . . He also ruled that not all slaves should be interrogated [that is, under torture] in the house where the master had been killed, but only those who were close enough to have known" (*Scriptores Augustae Historiae* XVIII.7–11). Previously, all slaves in a household would have been executed if their master were murdered. Hadrian did not take any charges for *maiestas*. He also gave the Christians a measure of protection by threatening revenge on whoever hurt them.

Once, while Hadrian was walking along a mountain path, a crazed slave armed with a sword ran to attack the unarmed emperor. Hadrian, himself an excellent swordsman and athlete, managed to subdue the slave and disarm him, and handed him over to his master; he did not order the death of the slave or blame his master for the slave's actions. Another day, while relaxing in the public baths, Hadrian saw an old soldier rubbing his back against a stone wall; learning that the old soldier could not afford a slave to scratch his back, Hadrian presented him with two slaves and their upkeep. Later, two old senators started rubbing their backs against the wall, hoping to get some free slaves; Hadrian told them to scratch each other's back instead. Once when he was giving a banquet, he feared that the caterers were setting excellent dishes before him, but serving everybody else bad food, so he had the caterers bring him dishes from all the tables.

Hadrian also restored many buildings, including Pompey's monument in Egypt, the Forum of Augustus, the Baths of Agrippa, and the Pantheon, and he completed the Olympieum in Athens. Like many other wealthy people of the time, Hadrian built a villa in Tibur (modern Tivoli, outside Rome); it is a popular tourist destination today. His massive mausoleum, now called Castel San Angelo (for it was used as a fortress during the Middle Ages) is still an imposing sight in Rome.

Yet Hadrian was disliked by many people. The persistent rumor circulated that Trajan had never adopted him and that Plotina, Trajan's wife (who was supposedly in love with Hadrian), faked his adoption. Hadrian's boundless energy, unbridled curiosity, and competitive nature also created problems for him. He regarded himself as an expert in astrology and freely criticized poets, orators, and musicians. Since he himself wrote poetry and speeches, and boasted of his ability to play the lyre and sing, no doubt he felt that his performances set the standard, and he resented competition and not being the best. He was skilled in the use of weapons and was an avid hunter—he is said to have killed a monstrous boar with just one blow. It appears that he was an expert at everything he did and that he shared his superior knowledge with all, whether or not they wanted it. Of course, one could hardly argue freely with the man who could just as easily kill as give annoying advice. Without a doubt, that caused some resentment among those who surrounded him.

Hadrian's unpopularity arose also from some executions conducted early in his reign. Shortly after he had become emperor,
and before he returned to Rome, four ex-consuls were executed by
the Senate on the charge of conspiring to kill him. Hadrian
pleaded innocent to their murders, but the cloud of suspicion
remained. Years later, when he was so seriously ill that he named a
successor, he also forced a ninety-year-old man, Servianus, to die
because he thought Servianus was aiming for the throne. While
dying, Servianus cursed Hadrian, calling upon him the punishment of wanting to die but being unable to.

After Lucius Aelius, his first choice for a successor, died in 138,
Hadrian quickly adopted and named as successor T. Aurelius
Antoninus. Hadrian then suffered a hemorrhage and was in such
great pain and misery that he ordered one of his slaves to kill him;
rather than kill the emperor, the slave killed himself, and doctors
refused Hadrian's orders to deliver poison to him. After long suffering, Hadrian died in 138, and Antoninus succeeded him.
Against the wishes of many, Hadrian was deified.

ANTONINUS PIUS (A.D. 138–161), "THE DUTIFUL"

Antoninus is said to have received his nickname Pius for supporting his aged father as he walked up the steps to the Capitol—
or else because he protected those whom Hadrian had ordered to
be killed, or because he refused Hadrian's request for poison when
he wanted to commit suicide, or because he insisted upon Hadrian's
deification when many opposed it, or because he was naturally very
gentle and never committed any violent deeds. Antoninus proved
his *pietas* in many ways during his reign.

Despite being the richest man in Rome (even before he became
emperor), Antoninus had simple tastes: He ate what food came
from his estates, he went fishing and hunting with friends, and as
a farmer "he harvested the grapes with his friends, like any private
citizen" (*Scriptores Augustae Historiae* XI.3). Friends visiting him
might see him dressed in casual clothes, doing his household
chores.

He was generous with his great wealth. He bequeathed his
riches to his daughter, but granted the interest on his fortune to the

Mummy portrait of a woman, second century A.D. (Courtesy of the Kelsey Museum of Archaeology, University of Michigan, Ann Arbor)

Household objects from the town of Karanis, Egypt, fifth century A.D. (Courtesy of the Kelsey Museum or Archaeology, University of Michigan, Ann Arbor)

empire. He made loans to people at the very low rate of 4 percent interest. When wine, oil, and wheat became scarce, Antoninus bought supplies of them with his own money and gave them to the people. "In fact, he ruled over the people under his power with such carefulness that he cared for all things and people as if they were his own," says one source (*Scriptores Augustae Historiae, Antoninus Pius* VII). When earthquakes destroyed towns in Rhodes and Asia, he used his own money to restore them all. He enlarged upon the system of *alimenta* for poor children, and he arranged for help for poor girls in particular, whom he called Faustinians, in honor of his wife Faustina, who had died in the third year of his reign. He enforced fairness in dealings with the provincials: When his tax collectors gathered more than had been called for, they had to explain to him the reason for the excess. Yet his own servants did not like him, for he did not allow them to use their positions to enrich themselves. Like Hadrian, he did not persecute the Christians, and he even showed them some respect.

Front of the Temple of Antoninus Pius and Faustina (his wife). The Latin inscription reads, "For the god M. Antoninus and the goddess Faustina, in accordance with the decree of the Senate." (Author photograph)

Affairs with Parthia were quiet during Antoninus' reign, and he was respected by foreign kings. He used the military sparingly; he was said to have quoted a saying from Scipio, that he would rather save one citizen than kill a thousand enemies. Although no wars were fought during his reign, the armies did see action in Germany, Africa, Dacia, and England. Once a rebellion in England was put down, the Romans moved the frontier farther north into Scotland, where they built another wall, called the Antonine Wall. It was subsequently abandoned, and the frontier reverted to Hadrian's Wall.

Antoninus' last act of munificence to the empire was to name as his successor Annius Verus (known as Marcus Aurelius), who became Rome's bulwark against a rising tide of troubles. When Antoninus died in 161, all praised his dutifulness, clemency, intelligence, and purity; before he died, the Senate voted to rename

September and October Antoninus and Faustina, an honor he characteristically refused. He was deified.

MARCUS AURELIUS (A.D. 161–180), "THE PHILOSOPHER"

According to one source, Marcus Aurelius "surpassed all emperors in the pureness of his life" (*Scriptores Augustae Historiae, Marcus Antoninus* I). He was a follower of the Stoic philosophy, which had long been the philosophy most in tune with Roman mores. He had become a devotee of Stoicism after his twelfth birthday, when he started sleeping on the floor and wearing the clothing characteristic of Greek philosophers. His mother managed to persuade him to sleep instead on a couch spread with skins. After becoming emperor, he asked the Senate to allow his brother Verus to be co-emperor. While Aurelius adhered to the Stoic philosophy, Verus seems to have been more Epicurean in outlook; he was happy to take it easy while Aurelius made sacrifices and suffered for the good of all.

The Romans were interested in Stoicism chiefly for its ethics. The goal of Stoicism is to live in harmony with creation; since creation is the manifestation of god, the Stoic seeks to live in harmony with god, who is just and justly rules creation. Since god is just and perfect, what happens in life is somehow right—god, being perfect, cannot err. People must use reason, the ability to come to an understanding of things, so they can live in harmony with creation, or with the will of god. Wise people do not let themselves be perturbed by life's events, whether good or bad; their duty is to accept and understand what happens and to transcend circumstances: "You will find (if you pay close attention) that what happens is right. I do not mean just that things happen in a regular manner, but that they happen in accordance with justice, as they come from something that distributes things according to what is right," Marcus Aurelius wrote in his journal of inspirational and philosophical thoughts, recorded during his campaigns along the Danube (*Meditations* IV.10). Another key element in Stoic thought is that of the connection among all human beings, and of each person's duty to help others; since everyone is a part of creation, their existence is ordained by god, and Stoics must help them even when they do wrong. "Therefore it is necessary to say at each point, 'This is here from God; this is because of the common lot and the conjoining of destiny and such happenstance and fate. Yet this is from a relative, someone of the same blood, a companion, even though he does not know what is part of his nature. But I know; consequently let me treat him according to the natural law of brotherhood—I'll be kind and fair to him.' At the same time, when things are undecided, I always aim for justice" (*Meditations* III.11).

The Roman Empire was particularly fortunate that Aurelius, the Stoic philosopher-ruler, became emperor, for troubles brewing in the empire demanded selfless devotion and service from the emperor. The least of the troubles was the Tiber flooding, which caused many deaths and led to a famine in Rome. Other troubles included a plague, war in Armenia, and wars with the Germans, who were invading the empire from across the Danube.

First, the Parthian Empire took over Armenia in 161. Verus left for Syria in March 162, but did not arrive until 163, and once he arrived, he lived in luxury while his legates, Statius Priscus and Avidius Cassius, carried on the war. Priscus recovered Armenia, and Cassius invaded Mesopotamia. They advanced into Parthia, destroyed its main city, Ctesiphon, and shattered the Parthian Empire all the way to Iran. The Romans did not want another province, however, and quickly withdrew, after establishing security for their eastern provinces.

The Parthians had their revenge on the Romans, however, for the Roman soldiers brought back a plague. After sweeping through the eastern provinces, it took Rome in 167. The first victims were the soldiers who had picked it up in Parthia; the disease is estimated to have killed one-quarter of the population in Rome.

During the war with Parthia, the Germanic tribe called the Marcomanni had overrun Dacia and had been putting pressure on the troops on the frontiers of Pannonia, where Roman forces had been drawn off for the Parthian War. Crossing the Danube in 166, they swarmed down into northern Italy and even besieged the town of Aquileia; some advanced into Greece as far as Eleusis, which lies a few miles west of Athens.

Aurelius and his brother Verus started out for Pannonia in 168, to drive the Marcomanni out of Roman territory. The Marcomanni departed from Italy at the emperors' advance, but the pressure on the frontiers did not abate, and the armies had been depleted by the plague. Aurelius soon found himself having to face the problems alone, for Verus died two days after they had started the journey. Aurelius returned to Rome briefly to bury his brother, and despite the death also of his six-year-old son, he quickly returned to the front.

Aurelius took extraordinary measures to protect the peoples in the empire. He hired gladiators and auxiliary units of Germans to fight for the empire. To meet their pay, he did not raise taxes, for he did not want to burden the provincials; instead, he sold off the valuables of the palace—clothes, gold goblets, gold statues, paintings, even his wife's silk- and gold-embroidered clothing. The auction of imperial treasures lasted two months and raised more than enough money for the war effort. Aurelius later gave those who had bought the treasures the option to return the goods in exchange for their money, if they wanted their money back.

Aurelius returned to the Danube in 169 and restored order. He returned to the provincial peoples the plunder the Germans had taken from them. Now he realized that the only way to solve the German problem was to complete what others since Augustus had avoided undertaking—the conquest and annexation of Germany.

Aurelius was experiencing great success in this endeavor when more bad news arrived in 175: The governor of Syria, Avidius Cassius, who had led the Romans against Parthia and Armenia, had revolted and wanted to be emperor himself; rumors even said that Aurelius' wife, Faustina, was having an affair with Cassius and had prompted him to rebel. Aurelius had to turn away from the problems in Germany to defeat Cassius; on the journey to the East, he learned that Cassius had been murdered. Then Aurelius is said to have been very sad, for he had hoped to complete his reign without spilling a senator's blood. He traveled in the East to renew the eastern provinces' devotion to Rome and then returned to Rome.

In 178 Aurelius returned to the front to finish the war with the Marcomanni. He was winning the war when he fell ill; naming as successor his nineteen-year-old son Commodus (his one act by which the empire suffered), he died in 180. He left behind him his journal of inspirational thoughts, which shows a noble and humanitarian spirit grappling with life's problems and the purpose of existence. It is easy to understand why his *Meditations* became popular among Christians and was read by rulers of many countries over the centuries for its high principles and ennobling ideals.

LATIN LITERATURE OF THE FLAVIAN AND ANTONINE ERAS

The literature of the time from the death of Nero to that of Marcus Aurelius shows some great talent at work, worthy of any age.

Quintilian (?30–?100) is said to have been the first rhetorician to receive a salary from the empire's treasury, in accordance with Vespasian's program of funding public education. Quintilian's *Institutio oratoria*, a treatise on the education of an orator, is the first book to discuss in detail the education of young people. The tenth book of the *Institutio* contains a critique of Greek and Roman writers.

Martial (40–104) wrote epigrams and short poems on a variety of subjects, usually concerning his own friends and enemies, and the foibles and vices of individuals in Roman society.

Of Juvenal's (?50–?128) work, sixteen satires survive. He attacked the vices of his age—pursuit of wealth, decadence, immorality, love of luxury—in bitter invective. He is the author of the phrase "bread and circuses": "The citizens who once gave their leaders empire, fasces, legions, and all that, now keep to themselves and fervently and nervously wish for just two things, bread and circuses" (*Satires* X. 80).

Tacitus (b. ?56) is arguably ancient Rome's greatest historian, and one of the most distinctive stylists in Latin. His first work, *Dialogus de oratoribus*, written in a Ciceronian style, concerned the decline of oratory in Rome. His *Agricola*, which shows him developing his distinctive style, is a biography of his father-in-law, Gn. Julius Agricola, a general of the empire's army squashing a revolt in Britain. The *Germania* is a description of the German peoples, in which Tacitus contrasts their savage nobility and honor with Rome's decadence and immorality. Tacitus' fame rests, however, on his *Annals* and *Histories*, of which large fragments survive. In the *Annals* we read the brilliant descriptions of the reigns of Tiberius, Claudius, and Nero (some of which have been quoted in earlier chapters of this book); unfortunately, the section on Caligula is lost, along with part of the section on Claudius and Nero's last year. What survives of the *Histories* covers the period of the civil wars following Nero's death through 71. Tacitus hated the principate and especially the despotic Domitian, and his distinctive style—jarring and abrupt—reveals his hatred.

Tacitus' friend Pliny the Younger (61–112) wrote hundreds of letters on various topics. They are not private letters, for he fully intended for them to be published. Among them one finds letters describing the eruption of Mount Vesuvius, the treatment of Christians (as governor of the province Bithynia, Pliny had asked Trajan for official instructions on what to do about them), a cruel father, cruel masters, Roman society, and the tragic death of a friend's twelve-year-old daughter.

Suetonius (b. 69) is a historian, but of a very different stamp from Tacitus. Suetonius was a secretary of sorts in the palace during the reigns of Trajan and Hadrian, and undoubtedly used his access to the palace to search out juicy gossip and dirt about the emperors for his book *De vita Caesarum*. He also wrote *De viris illustribus*, which includes some information on the lives of some Latin writers. (Suetonius, too, has been quoted in this book.)

Apuleius (b. 123) wrote the only Latin novel that has survived intact, *Metamorphoses* (generally translated as *The Golden Ass*). The main character is turned into an ass and goes through many adventures before being restored to human form by the goddess Isis. The novel contains the famous love story of Cupid and Psyche.

Afterword
The Disintegration of the Empire

Commodus (ruled A.D. 180–192), Aurelius's son, failed to complete the annexation of Germany. In a way, Commodus out-Neroed Nero: He had three hundred concubines, one of whom he named after his mother, and he killed his sister. Upon his murder in 192, M. Helvidius Pertinax became emperor (192–193), but was quickly assassinated; how the next emperor gained the position is particularly noteworthy. The practice of buying the support of the Praetorian Guard reached a new level when the soldiers offered the position of emperor to the highest bidder; the buyer was M. Didius Julianus, who was assassinated two months later, on June 1, 193. Septimius Severus (193–211), who was born in Lepcis Magna in Africa, next became emperor and restored order to the empire; his arch still stands in Rome as a monument to his victories over the Parthians. Upon his death in 211, he was succeeded by his sons, M. Aurelius Antoninus (better known by his nickname, Caracalla) and L. Septimius Geta, who hated each other; Caracalla killed his brother in 212 and became sole ruler. That same year he gave citizenship to all free men in the empire. He was murdered in 217.

The empire suffered much during the third century as one man, after becoming emperor, would have to fend off numerous other contenders for the royal power. Hence, there were many emperors during the course of the century. On April 21, 247, during the reign of Philip the Arab (so called because he came from the Saudi peninsula), Rome celebrated its one-thousandth birthday. The failure to solve the problem of the Germans and the Parthians caused a major crisis in the 250s, when the Germans swarmed

Arch of Septimius Severus. (Author photograph)

over the Danube and Rhine Rivers. The Goths also made raids in
the Aegean Sea. In the East the Parthians took over Syria. Emperor
Valerian attacked Parthia, but was conquered and captured in 260;
he died in captivity. In 268 the Germanic tribe the Alamanni
ravaged Italy. Emperor Claudius II Gothicus freed northern Italy
from the Germans, and the provinces were regained.

One of the territories his successor Aurelian (270–275) regained
is particularly noteworthy: the city of Palmyra (today, Tadmur in
Syria). Odaenathus, a nobleman of Palmyra, became king of the
city when Valerian was captured, and he successfully waged war
against the Parthians. He and his son were murdered in 267,
perhaps by his wife, Zenobia, who with her other son Vaballathus
assumed power and expanded Palymra's rule to include Egypt
and much of Asia Minor. Not until she proclaimed Vaballathus
Augustus—that is, emperor—did Aurelian move against her, and
he conquered her in 273.

The reign of Diocletian (284–305) marks a new stage in the government of the empire. Recognizing that the empire and its military demands (created by fronts along the Rhine, Danube, and Tigris and Euphrates) presented too great a task for one man, Diocletian in 293 instituted his famous tetrarchy (rule of four). Bearing the title Augustus, he ruled the eastern part of the empire with the help of his assistant Galerius, who had the title Caesar; the Augustus in the western part of the empire was Maximian, and his Caesar was Constantius Chlorus. To reduce the danger of assassination and usurpations of imperial power, Diocletian also greatly increased the mystique of the emperor and made the principate's power and pomp more like that associated with Persian despots: People addressing the emperor first had to perform *proskynesis*, that is, lie down on the ground before the emperor and kiss the corner of his robe. Even members of the emperor's council and family had to stand in his presence. *Dominus* (lord) became the regular word of address to the emperor, who now wore a diadem and purple gown. The tetrarchy reestablished peace and stability, but the unity of the system suffered when Diocletian retired.

Constantine (324–337), the son of Constantius Chlorus, became sole emperor in 324 and moved the capital of the empire to the Greek city Byzantium, which he later named after himself (Constantinople). His reason for moving the capital was strategic and only sensible, as Italy had for long been declining in the importance of the empire: The constant warfare shifted attention to the Rhine, Danube, and Tigris and Euphrates, far away from central Italy. Constantine, in fact, had been emperor for ten years before he visited Rome for the first time. In the Edict of Milan (313) he granted the Christians full religious freedom, and in 325, at the Council of Nicaea (from which came also Christianity's Nicene Creed), he made Christianity the official religion of the empire. His decision to have the empire embrace Christianity was based on a personal experience: Before the battle at the Milvian bridge (one of the battles that secured his position as emperor), he had seen a cross in the sky with the words, "In hoc signo vinces" (With this as your standard, you will conquer). Officially, Christianity faced no competition from other religions after 391, when the emperor Theodosius (379–395) banned all pagan religions; worship of the pagan gods continued, however, in the villages (*pagus*, hence the English word *pagan*).

Social and political conditions in the empire were changing. As the emperor's power grew increasingly autocratic, the Senate's power decreased; all the provinces, for example, were now imperial, and the Senate exerted no control over them. The Praetorian Guard, however, gained much power at the Senate's expense, including the power to legislate, pass judgment in court, and hear appeals. Citizens were now grouped into two classes, *honestiores* (more honorable) and *humiliores* (more lowly born), and there was separate legal treatment for each: A crime that would cause a member of the *humiliores* to be punished with death, for example, earned one of the *honestiores* only banishment. To support the royal court and constant military expenditure, taxes were so high that many peasants fled to the barbarian lands, rather than be slaves to the empire. To prevent further flight from the empire and the consequent loss of income from taxes, the emperor created a law binding peasants to the soil and allowing the land-lords to chain those who they suspected would flee; this was the legal basis of serfdom in the Middle Ages. Furthermore, sons were bound by law to follow in the occupation of their father.

In 364 the Roman Empire was permanently divided between East and West by the co-emperors Valentinian (364–375) and Valens (364–378). The empire in the East developed into what is now called the Byzantine Empire; it flourished and preserved the Roman Empire in the East until it was sacked in 1453 by Muhammed II, the Ottoman sultan.

The Roman Empire in the West did not fare so happily, for it suffered from more Germanic invasions. Britain was abandoned by the empire after 410, cutting short the Romanization of the island. Most of Gaul, Spain, and northern Africa was taken over by the Germans. In 410 the Visigothic chieftain Alaric sacked the city of Rome. In 475 the general Orestes proclaimed his son, Romulus Augustulus, to be emperor; the death of the empire occurred the next year when Orestes was murdered and his son was deposed by the German Odoacer, the first of the German kings of Italy.

Bibliography

The bibliography includes those works that had a significant influence on the scholarship in this book. Included are the editions of the original Latin and Greek texts that I used for my translations, as well as the English translations of other works to which I also referred.

PRIMARY SOURCES

Aurelius, Marcus. *The Communings with Himself.* Translated by C. R. Haines. New York: G. P. Putnam's Sons, 1930.

Bailey, D. R. Shackleton, ed. *Cicero's Letters to Atticus*, vols. 2 and 3. Cambridge: Cambridge University Press, 1965 and 1968.

Birley, Anthony, trans. *Lives of the Later Caesars.* New York: Viking Penguin, 1976.

Brunt, P. A., and J. M. Moore, eds. *Res gestae divi Augusti.* Oxford: Oxford University Press, 1990.

Caesar, Julius. *The Gallic War.* Cambridge: Harvard University Press, 1979.

Caesar, Julius. *Libri III de bello civili.* Edited by Renatus de Pontet. Oxford: Clarendon Press, 1989.

Cicero, M. Tullius. *Epistulae ad familiares, vol. 1.* Edited by D. R. Shackleton Bailey. New York: Cambridge University Press, 1977.

Cicero, M. Tullius. *Epistulae ad Quintum Fratrem et M. Brutum.* Edited by D. R. Shackleton Bailey. Cambridge: Cambridge University Press.

Cicero, M. Tullius. *Philippics.* Translated and edited by Walter C.A. Ker. New York: G. P. Putnam's Sons, 1926.

Dio Cassius. *Dio's Roman History*, vols. 1–9. Translated by Earnest Cary. Cambridge: Harvard University Press, 1961.

Gellius, Aulus. *Noctes Atticae.* Edited by P. K. Marshall. Oxford: Clarendon Press, 1968.

Livy (Titus Livius). *Ab urbe condita,* vols. 1–4. Edited by Charles Flamstead Walters and Robert Seymour Conway. Oxford: Clarendon Press, 1961.

Livy (Titus Livius). *Ab urbe condita* (Books 43 and 44). Edited by W. Weissenborn and H. J. Mueller. Berlin: Weidmannsche Verlangsbuchhandlung, 1962.

Livy (Titus Livius). *The Early History of Rome.* Translated by Aubrey de Selincourt, edited by Betty Radice. New York: Viking Penguin, 1960.

Livy (Titus Livius). *Rome and Italy.* Translated by Betty Radice. New York: Viking Penguin, 1982.

Livy (Titus Livius). *Rome and the Mediterranean.* Translated by Henry Bettenson, edited by Betty Radice. New York: Viking Penguin, 1976.

Livy (Titus Livius). *The War with Hannibal.* Translated by Aubrey de Selincourt, edited by Betty Radice. New York: Viking Penguin, 1965.

Magie, David, trans. *The Scriptores Augustae Historiae.* New York: G. P. Putnam's Sons, 1922.

Plutarch. *Lives.* Translated and edited by Bernadotte Perrin. New York: G. P. Putnam's Sons, 1922.

Polybius. *The Rise of the Roman Empire.* Translated by Ian Scott-Kilvert, edited by Betty Radice. New York: Viking Penguin, 1979.

Rolfe, J. C., trans. and ed. *Sallust.* Cambridge: Harvard University Press, 1995.

Rolfe, J. C., trans. and ed. *Suetonius,* vols. 1 and 2. Cambridge: Harvard University Press, 1989.

Sallust. *The Conspiracy of Catiline.* Edited by J. B. Greenough and M. G. Daniel. Boston: Atheneum Press, 1901.

Suetonius. *The Lives of the Caesars.* Translated by J. C. Rolfe. Cambridge: Harvard University Press, 1992.

Tacitus, Cornelius. *Annalium libri.* Edited by C. D. Fisher. Oxford: Clarendon Press, 1983.

Tacitus, Cornelius. *The Annals of Imperial Rome.* Translated by Michael Grant, edited by Betty Radice. New York: Viking Penguin, 1989.

Tacitus, Cornelius. *The Histories.* Translated by Kenneth Wellesly, edited by Betty Radice. New York: Viking Penguin, 1986.

Warmington, E. H., trans. and ed. *Remains of Old Latin III: Lucilius, The Twelve Tables.* Cambridge: Harvard University Press, 1938.

White, Horace, trans. *Appian's Roman History*, Vols. 1–4. Cambridge: Harvard University Press, 1958.

Zonaras. *The Epitome of the Histories*. In *Dio's Roman History*, trans. Earnest Cary (Cambridge: Harvard University Press, 1961).

SECONDARY SOURCES

Arlotto, Anthony. *Introduction to Historical Linguistics*. Boston: Houghton Mifflin, 1972.

Baugh, Albert C., and Thomas Cable. *A History of the English Language*. 3rd edition. Englewood Cliffs: Prentice-Hall, 1978.

Botsford, George Willis, and Charles Alexander Robinson Jr. *Hellenic History*. 4th edition. New York: Macmillan, 1956.

Brunt, P. A. *Social Conflicts in the Roman Republic*. New York: W. W. Norton, 1971.

Cary, M. *A History of Rome, Down to the Reign of Constantine*. New York: St. Martin's Press, 1967.

Chadwick, Nora. *The Celts*. New York: Penguin Books, 1970.

Cook, S. A., F. E. Adcock, and M. P. Charlesworth, eds. *The Cambridge Ancient History*, vols. 9–12. New York: Cambridge University Press, 1966.

Copley, Frank O. *Latin Literature from the Beginnings to the Close of the Second Century A.D.* Ann Arbor: University of Michigan Press, 1969.

Cowell, F. R. *Cicero and the Roman Republic*. Baltimore: Penguin Books, 1967.

Gardner, Jane F. *Women in Roman Law and Society*. Bloomington: Indiana University Press, 1991.

Gelzer, Matthias. *Caesar: Politician and Statesman*. Cambridge: Harvard University Press, 1968.

Grant, Michael. *Atlas of Ancient History*. New York: Dorset Press, 1985.

Grant, Michael. *Julius Caesar*. New York: M. Evans, 1992.

Jones, A. H. M. *Augustus*. New York: W. W. Norton, 1970.

Lintott, Andrew. *Imperium Romanum: Politics and Administration*. New York: Routledge, 1993.

Metzger, Bruce M., and Michael D. Coogan, eds. *The Oxford Companion to the Bible*. New York: Oxford University Press, 1993.

Nicolet, Claude. *The World of the Citizen in Republican Rome*. Translated by P. S. Falla. Berkeley: University of California Press, 1988.

Pauly-Wissowa Realencyclopaedie der Classischen Altertumswissen-schaft. Stuttgart: Alfred Druckenmueller Verlag, 1893.

Salmon, E. T. *The Making of Roman Italy.* Ithaca: Cornell University Press, 1982.

Scullard, H. H. *From the Gracchi to Nero.* New York: Routledge, 1991.

Scullard, H. H. *A History of the Roman World 753 to 146 B.C.* New York: Routledge, 1992.

Scullard, H. H. *Roman Britain, Outpost of the Empire.* London: Thames and Hudson, 1991.

Sherwin-White, A. N. "The Roman Citizenship." In *Aufstieg und Niedergang der Römischen Welt.* New York: Walter de Gruyter, 1972.

Syme, Ronald. *The Roman Revolution.* New York: Oxford University Press, 1939.

Tarn, W. W. *Hellenistic Civilisation.* London: Edward Arnold, 1947.

Walbank, F. W. *The Hellenistic World.* Cambridge: Harvard University Press, 1981.

Wolff, Hans Julius. *Roman Law: An Historical Introduction.* Norman: University of Oklahoma Press, 1951.

Index